ND 1314.2 AST 1993

Christ Church

T056180

WITH ROM
CHRIST CHURCH LIBRARY
OXFORD

D1354082

The King's Bedpost is a lavishly illustrated detective story about a painting. *Edward VI and the Pope* is an important visual allegory of the Reformation; but when and why was it painted? Following up a sequence of clues to answer these questions, the author embarks on a fascinating and unusual voyage of historical exploration that takes the reader into book illustration and scriptural iconography, Tudor religion and politics, anti-papal propaganda and iconoclastic manoeuvres.

The discovery of some previously unrecognized pictorial sources conclusively re-dates the painting, and opens a wide-ranging discussion of art and image-making under Edward VI and Elizabeth I which moves between England and the Netherlands, linking the image-breaking movements of the two areas. Iconoclasm, and its effect on artists, is a theme which bears directly on the picture and its sources. A large cast of characters joins the Tudor monarchs as the tale unfolds: Mary, Queen of Scots; the dukes of Norfolk and their repeating tragedy; John Foxe and his 'book of martyrs'; the Dutch humanist Hadrianus Junius; Maarten van Heemskerck, and several artists who migrated to England from the Netherlands. The painting ultimately becomes the key to a series of hitherto locked doors.

THE KING'S BEDPOST

THE KING'S BEDPOST

Reformation and Iconography
in a Tudor Group Portrait

MARGARET ASTON

CAMBRIDGE
UNIVERSITY PRESS

Published by the Press Syndicate of the University of Cambridge
The Pitt Building, Trumpington Street, Cambridge CB2 IRP
40 West 20th Street, New York, NY 10011-4211, USA
10 Stamford Road, Oakleigh, Melbourne 3166, Australia

© Margaret Aston 1993

First published 1993

Printed in Great Britain at the University Press, Cambridge

A catalogue record for this book is available from the British Library

Library of Congress cataloguing in publication data

Aston, Margaret.
The King's Bedpost: Reformation and Iconography in a Tudor
Group Portrait/Margaret Aston.
   p.   cm.
ISBN 0 521 44375 X
1. Edward VI and the Pope: an allegory of the Reformation
(Portrait painting).   2. Edward, VI, King of England, 1537–1553 –
Portraits.   3. Paul III, Pope, 1468–1549 – Portaits.   4. Henry
VIII, King of England, 1491–1547 – Portraits.   5. Portrait painting,
English – Expertizing.   6. Portrait painting – 16th century – England –
Expertizing.   7. Portrait painting, English – Dutch influences.
8. Allegories.   9. Reformation in art.   10. Symbolism in art –
England.   11. Great Britain – History – Tudors, 1485–1603.
I. Title.
ND1314.2.A88   1993
759.2–dc20   92-39660   CIP

ISBN 0 521 44375 X hardback

WITHDRAWN FROM
CHRIST CHURCH LIBRARY
OXFORD

UP

To John Edward Bridges
in memory of his grandfather, my father
Edward Ettingdene Bridges

What was it fetch'd him?
Matthew Mark Luke and John was it? The parables,
the poetry and passion of Christ? Nay 'twas the bloody books
of Jewish war, the story of their Judges and Kings;

Robert Bridges, *The Testament of Beauty*

CONTENTS

PREFACE

It may seem absurd to write a whole book about, or around one picture – and not a particularly great or famous one at that, though *Edward VI and the Pope* has found itself a recognized niche in Tudor iconography. The subject of this story perhaps betrays its character in memory, where the painting seems to become smaller, so that on returning to it one is surprised to find it larger than recollected. But looking closely at anything, however small, may have its own rewards.

The search and discovery that my book is about occurred by accident, not design. Through puzzling over some features of the painting I came across some sources that proved it was something other than it had hitherto been taken for. This in turn provoked other questions and I found myself embarked on a journey of exploration which may not have reached the precise goal I would have chosen, but it took me to some unexpected places and was enjoyable in itself. I would like to think others might enjoy following the same path.

This is not exactly a study of a painting in context. It is rather a search for the circumstances and people involved in assembling the pieces from which a work of art was constructed – perhaps a better word than 'created' for what happened in this case. Trying to make sense of the genesis of this propagandist allegory proves enlightening for our understanding of the forces that bore on image-making in the Tudor period – a time when the arts were under extreme pressure as the church was remodelled according to new spiritual priorities. Images, and the makers of images, themselves became reflectors of the iconoclastic process. It seemed a useful exercise to bring religion, politics and the arts together in an effort to understand this picture. Historians are learning increasingly to look as well as listen, and if nothing else this book's tour shows what the eye can harvest.

Part of the pleasure of working on the book has come from the interest and encouragement of many individuals, friends and others, who have generously given their time to read, listen and answer questions. This has been particularly welcome since I have been trespassing on territory to which I have small claims. Susan Foister, David Freedberg, and Susanna Mitchell all read the first version and made many helpful suggestions and comments, from which I benefited greatly. Elizabeth Ingram read a later version, and her vigilant eye has made me see a number of things differently, besides setting others straight. I am most grateful to them all for all their trouble, and the book is certainly the better for these pains. I owe much to the assistance and encouragement I received at the National Portrait Gallery, from Malcolm Rogers and others, who had the picture examined by infra-red reflectography, and gave invaluable help. Sergiusz Michalski has been unfailingly generous in sending bibliographical information and photographic material. Those who have kindly answered enquiries include Professor Ilja Veldman, Sara Rodger, Tom Freeman and Matthew Alexander. My thanks also to Stanley Baron, Ruth Chavasse, Eamon Duffy, Stuart Dunnan, Kenneth Fincham, Alexander Murray, Molly Frewen Parsons, Colin Richmond and Bob Scribner for their kind assistance. At the Cambridge University Press, William Davies and Mary Richards have shown me the generous and friendly face of publishing. My husband has as always helped in innumerable ways, stylistic, linguistic, and domestic.

In the year which would have been his centenary, I dedicate this book to my father's memory and to one of his descendants who shares his love of pictures.

Michaelmas Day 1992

EDWARD VI AND THE POPE

The painting of *Edward VI and the Pope* or *An Allegory of the Reformation under Edward VI* is one of the more unusual, if not artistically distinguished, pictures in the Tudor collection at the National Portrait Gallery (NPG 4165, colour pl. I). It has none of the qualities of a great work of art, but undistinguished art can make interesting history. Pictures are sometimes like documents, conveying messages about the events or people they delineate and themselves needing to be carefully 'read' by reference to written sources. Looking for clues to explain some of the peculiarities of this painting led me on a tour of exploration which produced some unexpected conclusions, themselves of interest for the history of the times, as well as for art history.

This painting declares itself to be what one might call a 'text-picture' – a painting with a message. In its humble way it is a variant on the theme of *ut pictura poesis*, painting as poetry, on the lines of *ut pictura scriptura*, painting as prose or verbal communication, even as scripture. It carries (or rather it carried or was intended to carry) its own explication, in written captions that were an integral part of the composition. As with a comic strip, or a printed illustration or an engraving in a book, the artist expected his viewers to come to an understanding of his images by means of letters. The inscribed words told the person looking at the painting what to make of it. Its meaning was not completely accessible without these words.

It is therefore unfortunate for us that most of the verbal messages of the painting are lost for ever. However, exploring the background and sources can help to make up for this lack. We can deduce, with some confidence, some of the information that the artist (or commissioner of the picture) wanted to convey about Edward VI. We may even be able to surmise the content of some of the missing captions.

There is a story behind this image which is worth telling, for it is attached to an important element of Tudor history. The story belongs to anti-art, as much as to art. It concerns the iconoclasm that, starting under Henry VIII, and continuing intermittently for a century, destroyed a vast amount of our medieval heritage, changed the face of England's churches with the behaviour of their worshippers, and quite altered the course of English painting. Edward VI, and some of his advisers who are depicted here, were instrumental in accomplishing a very large amount of this destruction.

In what follows I show that the painting has to be dated at least twenty years later than has hitherto been supposed.* It is an Elizabethan, not an Edwardian picture, and has to be placed, not in the religious upheaval of the reign of Henry VIII's short-lived son, but in the ecclesiastical disputes that dogged the reign of his long-lived second daughter. The Dutch sources that point incontrovertibly to this redating, also enable us to see some hard evidence of the links between the art of England and the Low Countries in the later sixteenth century. Setting this piece of visual propaganda in the reign of Elizabeth raises a whole series of new questions about how exactly it should be read – who it was intended for, and the nature of its message. This book is both an anatomy of the content and an exploration of the context of the allegorical painting *Edward VI and the Pope*.

First, some general observations about the picture. It is painted in oil on a panel (measuring 62.2 by 90.8 centimetres, $24\frac{1}{2}$ by $35\frac{3}{4}$ inches) which has been repaired in recent times. The composition falls, rather unhappily from the point of view of its unity, into five parts. The young king, seated on his chair of state to the left of the picture's centre, occupies the focal position. Below him, seemingly pressed down by an open book inscribed 'THE WORDE OF THE LORD ENDURETH FOR EVER', is the collapsing figure of the pope, in company with two evil-visaged religious. Habited in rather indeterminate shades of brown and blackish grey, they appear to be members of the mendicant orders, and each is pulling on a chain that vanishes under the royal dais. Above, on Edward's right, the reclining figure identified as Henry VIII occupies a dominating place in an ornate bed, richly furnished with red curtains, scalloped counterpane, and gilded tasselled pillows. The old king's pointing forefinger directs the viewer's gaze directly towards his son and heir, and beyond him to a standing figure, dark-robed and wearing a collar of the Order of the Garter, on the other side. Linked to this solitary standing knight by the square tablet beneath his hands, is the group

* A first presentation of these findings was given at the 27th Congrès International d'Histoire de l'Art at Strasbourg in 1989, and is to be found in *L'Art et les Révolutions*, Section 4, *Les Iconoclasmes*, ed. S. Michalski (Strasbourg, 1992), pp. 127–38.

of seated figures, occupying the lower right side of the picture-space, which constitutes a fourth section of the composition. Seven clerics and laymen are placed rather awkwardly (showing more hands than the painter could easily cope with), on two sides of a table which is covered with a greyish cloth. Finally, the entire corner above this group is filled with a scene of figures destroying statues in front of a ruined building.

Adding to the lack of unity of these poorly integrated parts, there are five blank spaces, obviously intended for texts. It is worth noticing their nature and positions. They differ in size and kind. The largest, like the scene of iconoclasm, is set inside a frame, and is placed between Henry VIII's bed and the papal party. The one in the top right-hand corner itself forms part of the image-breaking inset, and is painted to look like a kind of paste-down attached to this framed scene, terminating at a point well within the picture's edge. The two empty labels in the centre are so positioned that one seems to belong to the standing figure, the other perhaps to relate him (or the young king) to those seated round the table. The horizontal space at the top, unattached to any single feature, holds the place which one might expect to have held the most generalized text of all.

When the picture was examined by infra-red reflectography (fig. 1), it was revealed that these tablets, or framed spaces for texts, were an integral part of the original composition. They seemed, indeed, to have been the feature that was most important to whoever organized the elements of the composition. Lines were drawn, and in some instances rather liberally or carelessly redrawn or ruled, on the wooden panel on which the picture is painted, to define the places where the texts were to go. They also marked out the position of the dais on which the king's feet rest, and the outlines of the cushion and book.

In several cases there were changes in the size and position of the text-spaces. A whole flurry of lines affected the large tablet nearest Henry VIII, which was enlarged, as well as being moved down from a place in which it would have cut into the royal bed. Likewise the square next Edward's throne was moved to a lower position, preventing collision with the king's hand and chair. The two top tablets both grew larger in the final version. The one between the king and the standing knight, the left side of which exactly marks the picture's centre, stayed in the same position but was extended downwards.

It was unfortunate that this examination revealed no traces at all of

1. *Under-drawing revealed by infra-red examination of the panel.*

any inscriptions, which could either have been erased, or, alternatively, never completed. Nor is there any technique which could answer that all-important question. The five lead white spaces remain uncompromisingly blank. But such findings as there were are of interest for our understanding of the picture. They reveal the centrality of the texts to the original composition, and seem to indicate that the artist did not deem it necessary to outline the other (figural) parts of his picture. There might, as we shall see, have been good reasons for this.

Looking further into the painting we may notice some peculiar features. Prominent among these is the king's bedpost. The corner of the bed on which the pointing king is couched juts conspicuously out through the turned-back bedcover. The sphinx-like appearance of this bedpost (a hooded female bust with scalloped edge) must strike any observer as a most unlikely Tudor bedpost. Could such a bed ever have been found in the royal apartments of Henry VIII at

Whitehall, Hampton Court or Nonsuch? Another oddity is the spatial structure of the picture. The dais on which the king's feet rest on the fat cushion has no visible means of support and is finished along its front edge with a tasselled fringe. It hangs unsatisfactorily in the picture space which, though this does not lack perspective (in the bed and dais), noticeably lacks any floor or ground level.[1] The inset of iconoclasm stands out in being painted virtually in mono-chrome, and it contains a slightly awkward disjunction between the column and its supporting pedestal, suggesting they do not quite belong together. If some of these anomalies seem to point to an artist who was immature or unsure, there may – as will be seen – be other explanations.

In addition to these features, the picture's subject-matter as a whole seems to require explanation. What could be the reason for depicting a pope being downed by Edward VI? It was Henry VIII who dealt the decisive blow to the 'bishop of Rome', and though Paul III had hopes of persuading the emperor Charles V to support Mary's claims against those of Edward in 1547, this was entirely unrealistic and got nowhere.[2] Dynastic legitimism and schism were the order of the day in 1547, and Edward's reign was not marked by any significant developments in Anglo-papal relations. Of course, as the words written around the falling pontiff show, 'POPS' (that is popes) were symbolic representatives of 'IDOLATRY', 'SVPER-STICIO[N]', and all the abuses of 'FEYNED HOLINE[S]' which reformers in England and elsewhere strove to eliminate. If all believers were mortal ('ALL FLESHE IS GRASSE'), the scythe of the living Word had to mow down in the first instance the deadly misbeliefs of soul-destroying popes. But our picture seems to be saying something more specific than this. Though the pope is clearly on the way out, he is exacting his price. His two henchmen are pulling on chains that are attached to the royal dais; he is undoubtedly threatening the stability of the throne. We shall hear more of this later.

5

A PAINTING OF 1548–49?

For the last thirty years, *Edward VI and the Pope*, whose painter remains unknown, has been dated to about 1548–49. The grounds for this dating were given by Sir Roy Strong in an article published in 1960. It rested on two features; the identity of some of the people portrayed, and the scene of image-breaking.[3]

Before we start to look again at this evidence, it is important to be clear about the possible implications of what is obviously a historical painting. Our picture is a portrayal of a particular moment, or the implications of a particular event. The determination of date may therefore be double, not single. We must satisfy ourselves in the first place as to the time and event depicted. The date at which the depiction was made may, or may not, coincide – a self-evident point, but one hitherto not taken into account in consideration of this painting.

Besides Edward VI, Strong identified three of the secondary figures in our group portrait by reference to existing pictures. The figure of the young king presented little difficulty, since there are numerous depictions of Edward, both as Prince of Wales and after his accession, and a number of these show him with the feathered black bonnet and head turned slightly to the left, as in our picture. Among these the version at Petworth was singled out as a dated example (of 1547) of the earliest portrait series of the young king. Another very good portrait, which seems always to have been in the Royal Collection, is that of about 1546 by an unknown artist (fig. 2).[4]

The nobleman who stands on Edward's left was identified as Protector Somerset, on the basis of a miniature painted by Nicholas Hilliard (fig. 3).[5] This shows the duke's face, long-nosed, with drooping moustache and forked beard, seen from exactly the same angle as the tall man placed beside the young king. Hilliard's miniature is dated 1560, by which time the duke had been dead for eight years. Strong suggested that Hilliard (aged thirteen in 1560) worked from a no-longer surviving miniature of the duke, perhaps by Levina Teerlinc. The daughter of a celebrated Flemish illumina-tor, Teerlinc was in royal service for over two decades before her

2. *Prince Edward, painted c. 1546 for Henry VIII by an unknown artist, possibly William Scrots, who came to England in 1545 and succeeded Holbein as court painter. See below, fig. 89, for the painting of Princess Elizabeth which appears to be a companion piece.*

3. Edward Seymour, duke of Somerset, painted in 1560, eight years after his death. A miniature attributed to Nicholas Hilliard (aged thirteen), probably copying an original by Levina Teerlinc, this is the only certain portrait of the duke.

death in 1576, and pleased Queen Elizabeth by presenting her with a whole series of miniatures. Since this court miniaturist was patronized by Catherine Grey, who in 1560 became the wife of Somerset's son and heir, Edward Seymour, earl of Hertford, Hilliard, when working for the latter, might have found in the same circle both the guidance of an experienced limner and the likeness which he copied. Whatever the prototype which Hilliard used, it was presumably in the hands of Edward Seymour. He was about the same age as his cousin, Prince Edward, with whom he was educated, and was knighted at the young king's coronation.[6]

Two places away from Somerset is a seated cleric, wearing clerical cap, white rochet and black tippet. Comparison with the portrait of Thomas Cranmer, painted by Gerlach Flicke in 1545 (fig. 4), pointed to the identification of this figure with the archbishop, who had celebrated his fifty-sixth birthday about two weeks before the completion of this likeness.[7]

The archbishop is seated between two Garter knights. Strong conjectured that the one on his right might be John Dudley (later duke of Northumberland), who was made a knight of the Garter in 1543 and at Edward's accession was created earl of Warwick; two and a half years later it was he who pushed Somerset from power. However, since there appear to be no known portraits of Northumberland, this must remain conjectural. On Cranmer's other side sits a white-bearded figure who might well be the oldest person in the painting. If this is John Lord Russell (created earl of Bedford in 1550), he was about sixty and had a long career in royal service behind him in 1547, having been made a baron and elected to the Garter in 1539. He was Lord Privy Seal from 1542 until his death. A

portrait of the earl at Woburn (fig. 5), which shows him seated with his staff of office, wearing his Garter collar, with the same forked white beard and thick white moustache as the figure in our picture, is certainly similar. This portrait is dated 1555, the year the earl died.

Before moving on to Strong's other reasons for his dating, it is worth noticing that two of the three pictorial sources used to identify these characters in our picture postdate the reign of Edward VI. The portraits of the earl of Bedford and the duke of Somerset date from 1555 and 1560 respectively. That does not mean to say that an earlier likeness may not have existed in either case, but insofar as we still

9

5. *John Russell, first earl of Bedford: by an unknown painter, dated 1555, the year of the earl's death. He served as Lord Privy Seal through three reigns (1542–55), and is shown holding his staff of office.*

possess evidence that could have been available to our painter, it seems right to keep an open mind as to the possibility of a composition date *after* these extant depictions.

We may also observe a detail in the portrayal of Cranmer which differentiates it from the Flicke portrait. The archbishop is wearing a red collar. This, together with the amount of surplice shown between the lines of his black tippet, gives him an appearance rather more like that of Archbishop Parker, whose portrait at Lambeth, attributed to Richard Lyne, was engraved by Remigius Hogenberg in 1572. Parker there wears a rochet with a red fur collar.[8]

Let us now look at the inset scene of image-breaking (colour pl. II), which, combined with the presence of Somerset, was the main reason for attributing the painting to the years 1548 or 1549. Roy Strong called this 'a visual document of great and indeed unique interest, being the only contemporary English representation of image-smashing'. He described the events depicted above the heads of the seated dignitaries.

> Above this group a window opens out on to an open space where two men are hauling down an image of the Virgin and Child and another is busy smashing a statue into pieces. In the distance there lies a heap of smouldering ruins.[9]

Some years later, this observation was altered in Strong's *Tudor and Jacobean Portraits*. The scene of 'two armed men hauling down a statue of the Virgin and Child from a column' against its background of collapsing buildings is now described as 'an inset', not something seen through a window.[10]

In both these accounts the inset is used to narrow the date of the painting. The beginning of Edward VI's reign saw England take its first serious plunge into widespread destruction of church imagery. The articles for the royal visitation in the summer of 1547 authorized the clergy to 'take away, utterly extinct and destroy' all shrines, pictures, paintings and monuments of superstition or idolatry in their churches, and to encourage parishioners to do the same in their own houses. The execution of this order led to considerable differences of opinion, arguments and disputes over the status of images (were they, or were they not, being abused by worship?). This allowed the extreme iconoclasts to take their cue, and in February 1548 orders were issued for the complete removal of all remaining imagery from churches and chapels throughout the land. Strong thought it probable that our picture was painted not long after the issue of this order (which was sent out by Archbishop Cranmer on 24 February 1548), and before the fall of Protector Somerset in October 1549.[11]

But there are some difficulties here. Strong at first regarded the image-breaking as a so to speak 'live' action painting, seen through an open window over the heads of the seated councillors. Rightly, he dropped this idea, and subsequently referred to the scene as an 'inset'. That is clearly what it is. The artist has made this plain by showing (through a fairly common pictorial convention of the time) a wooden frame that encloses the scene on the two inner sides. This effect of a framed inset is increased by the fact, already noticed above, that along the top, inside the frame, is a kind of paste-down for an inscription or caption. It seems indubitable that this is a picture within a picture – again something for which we can find pictorial parallels.[12]

Another difficulty, which originally started me on this investigation, lies in what we see in the inset. Can the figure on the column really be intended for Virgin and Child? It is very hard to discern any infant Jesus – though admittedly the scale and nature of the painting do not make for clarity. More important, it is impossible to think of any medieval English statue of a Virgin and Child on the top of a free-standing column, rising from a classical plinth. This, and the other architectural evidence of the inset – the pile of ruins and the altar by the figure with the axe – seem to point not to any realistic depiction of what was happening in England in 1547–8, but rather to an effort to delineate pagan antiquity. The figures of the iconoclasts themselves may seem contemporary enough – but are they 'hauling' or rather trying to push down the statue? We have here undoubtedly a vivid illustration of iconoclasm, but as a whole it does not look much like Tudor image-breaking. What is the explanation?

Trying to answer this question will take us back to the Old Testament, as well as forward to the Low Countries in the 1560s. Before pursuing it, we must give a little more attention to Edward VI and his councillors.

Looking at the scene in our picture as a whole, it is most naturally interpreted as representing the beginning of Edward VI's reign, which started on 28 January 1547. In the early hours of that day Henry VIII, corpulent, bloated, and immobilized by the painful ulcers that had long affected his legs, finally met his maker. The figure of the recumbent king ('elegant and far from moribund' as G. R. Elton described him[13]) looms benignly over our picture-space from what seems like a painless carefree couch. Indeed he may not seem to have much in common with the regally strident Henry who – thanks mostly to Holbein (fig. 6) – tends to dominate our mental picture. But the head (icon-like with its frontal gaze) in one version of Holbein's *Henry VIII and the Barber-Surgeons* reveals something of the later king (fig. 7).

The departing monarch's pointing finger appears to tell us that those to whom our glance passes, via the head of the new king, are the men on whom now rests responsibility for directing the new régime. Henry took particular pains to provide for the rule of his nine-year-old son, listing in his will the names of sixteen executors whom he wished to form Edward's Privy Council. Things did not, however, take the course prescribed in Henry's will. Edward Seymour speedily exploited his advantage as the king's uncle, and by the middle of March 1547 had established effective control over both king and council as governor of the king's person and protector of the realm.[14]

If we assume that our picture is related to this moment of regnal transition, it is proper to take account of the conciliar records that might elucidate the seated group on the king's left. The painter, we may notice, though lacking skills of characterization and composition (all those hands!), seems to have taken some care over certain features of these sitters. There are the Garter collars (on five out of the eight) for one thing (fig. 10 and colour pl. I). There are also distinctions of age differentiating the archbishop (3) with his left neighbour, and the profiled peer in the corner (6), from the two fresher-faced, not at all greying figures nearest Edward, and the red-bearded man at the picture's edge (5). Also it seems that we should

6. *Henry VIII with Henry VII in Holbein's cartoon of 1536–7 for the wall painting in the Privy Chamber of Whitehall Palace. In the ornate frieze at the top a mermaid and a merman support the initials of H and I for Henry and Jane (Edward VI's mother).*

7. The head of Henry VIII. Detail from the cartoon of Holbein's unfinished group portrait of Henry VIII and the Barber-Surgeons. The painted version, in the possession of the Barbers' Company, commissioned in 1541, was completed after Holbein's death.

take account of the picture's horizontal divide, which separates – to see it at its crudest – good from bad, or godly from unredeemed. The front edge of the king's dais, on which reposes the open book of God's law, acts as a divider between the régime of the young king, above, and the régime of the proscribed pope, below.[15] We may surmise that as well as the two accomplice friars on the left, the three councillors below the table on the right are unworthy allies of the idolatrous pontiff.

Can we get any closer to naming all these people? So far only two, Protector Somerset (1) and Archbishop Cranmer (3), have been identified with certainty. Edward Seymour's position, standing between the young king and the seated councillors, represents the position of dominance he secured within days of Henry VIII's death. The success-story of his career had started in earnest at the young king's birth, and had not been seriously hindered by the death of his sister Queen Jane twelve days after her delivery. He was created earl

of Hertford three days after Edward VI's christening – at which he had carried the four-year-old Princess Elizabeth[16] – and early in 1541 he became a knight of the Garter. He was created duke of Somerset within days of Edward's accession, on 16 February 1547. A half-length portrait of Somerset at Longleat (fig. 8) which (like our painting, but unlike the Hilliard miniature of 1560) shows him wearing his Garter collar, also features the curious vertical trim of hair on his chin, which emphasizes the length of an already determinedly long face.[17] The staff which he holds in his right hand in the group portrait is that of the lord treasurer, an office which, like that of earl marshal taken over by the protector at the same time, had previously been held by Thomas Howard, the duke of Norfolk, who forfeited both offices when he was arrested on 12 December 1546.

Somerset was about forty in 1547, and is appropriately depicted as much younger than Cranmer. The archbishop, who held Henry VIII's hand as he died, was the first of the privy councillors named in the king's will, and, with Somerset, regularly headed the lists of

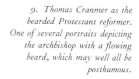

9. Thomas Cranmer as the bearded Protestant reformer. One of several portraits depicting the archbishop with a flowing beard, which may well all be posthumous.

those attending council meetings at the start of the new reign. There is one striking difference between Cranmer's appearance in Flicke's 1545 portrait, and the archbishop (3) in our painting. He is no longer clean shaven; a more than five o'clock shadow has turned into tufts of moustache and beard. This suggests historical accuracy in our artist, for the growth on Cranmer's chin only appeared after the death of Henry VIII, when he started a fashion for clerical beards. According to one account his refusal to shave was a gesture of sorrow for the old king, but there was also a general tendency for reforming clergy to wear their faiths on their heads, and as tonsures grew out, beards grew in. There seems to be no extant portrayal of Cranmer with the nascent beard of our picture, but one of the archbishop's portraits at Lambeth (almost certainly posthumous) shows him in his hirsute post-Reformation appearance – the very stereotype of the reformed pastor (fig. 9).[18]

If we go by the record in seeking names for our remaining six councillors, possible candidates include William Paulet, Lord St John (later earl and marquis), who was Great Master of the king's household and President of the privy council; Thomas Wriothesley, the Lord Chancellor; John, Lord Russell, keeper of the privy seal;

10. The Councillors. Proposed identifications: (1) Edward Seymour, Protector Somerset (2) Thomas Seymour, Lord Sudeley (3) Thomas Cranmer, archbishop of Canterbury (4) John Lord Russell (5) Sir William Paget (6) William Paulet, Lord St John (7) Cuthbert Tunstall, bishop of Durham (8) Thomas Wriothesley, earl of Southampton.

John Dudley, Viscount Lisle; Cuthbert Tunstall, bishop of Durham; and Sir William Paget, one of the two chief secretaries of state. All these men were among the sixteen executors named in Henry VIII's will who duly became privy councillors for his son.[19]

Two or three of these seem reasonably identifiable. Lord Russell (?1486–1555) has already been seen as a likely candidate for the grizzled figure (4) on Cranmer's left (fig. 5). It also seems possible that the younger reddish-bearded man who sits on Lord Russell's left (5) was William Paget (1505–63), whose portrait, painted perhaps about 1549 (fig. 11), shows him with similar colouring and beard, wearing his Lesser George on a chain (he became a knight of the Garter after Edward's accession, on 17 February 1547). The tonsured clerk on the opposite side of the table (7) could well (his age aside) be Tunstall (1474–1559) – of whom no likeness seems to survive – whose conservative views would doubtless have inhibited him from losing his tonsure or gaining a beard. There is no evidence of Tunstall's attendance at council meetings after 23 December 1547. Somerset (very likely owing to the bishop's religious views) seems to have decided he was not of privy council status – and no other cleric took his place.[20]

This gives us names for five of our eight councillors. Suggestions for the remaining three are complicated by the events that took place at Henry VIII's death. The king did not die alone, nor with the last word that he assumed was his to command. Edward Seymour and his friend William Paget, who took control of the execution of Henry's will – and seemingly tampered with it too – managed, amazingly, to suppress the news of the king's death for three days. Things were then arranged very nicely for their own advantage. It was Paget who, armed with the late king's will and direct knowledge of his last expressed wishes, was able to explain what titles and properties Henry had wished to be bestowed. As a result, besides

19

Edward Seymour becoming the duke of Somerset, his brother Thomas Seymour became Lord Seymour of Sudeley, while John Dudley (Viscount Lisle) and Thomas Wriothesley were elevated respectively to the earldoms of Warwick and Southampton. In addition to the bequests they received in Henry VIII's will, all these individuals, together with Lords Russell and St John, were the beneficiaries of substantial grants from the forfeited lands of the imprisoned duke of Norfolk and his recently executed son, the earl of Surrey.[21]

The three remaining figures in our group might therefore be identified as follows. The seated Garter knight (2) on Somerset's left might be not (as Strong conjectured) John Dudley, the new earl of Warwick, but the protector's younger brother, Thomas Seymour (figs. 12–13). He had been individually appointed to the privy council only five days before Henry VIII's death, on 23 January 1547, and appears attending council meetings during the first weeks of Edward's reign. In the middle of February he became a Garter knight and replaced the earl of Warwick as Lord High Admiral, much to the latter's chagrin. Thomas Seymour, Lord Sudeley, gained social precedence over Somerset by marrying (about April 1547) Henry VIII's widow, Queen Catherine Parr.[22] This helped to poison his relations with his brother Edward,[23] but at the time that interests us that rupture still lay in the future, and the two Seymours, possibly here pictured side by side, presented a united front and consolidated ambition in the young king's world.

13. Thomas Seymour by an unknown artist (NPG 4571). The accompanying lines in his praise end: 'yet against nature reason & iust lawes/his bloud wase spilt iustlese w^thout iust cause.' According to Sir John Harington (1561–1612), his father (who served Elizabeth when princess) gave her when queen a picture of the Lord Admiral 'with a pretie verse written on it, and it now hangs in the gallerie at Somerset house'.

On the 'wrong' side of the council table, opposite the Seymour side, the profiled councillor with raised hands (8) may be Thomas Wriothesley (1505–50), who was pushed out of the office of Lord Chancellor, and from his seat on the council in March 1547. He seems suitable for this position by reason both of his age and his role (since the fall of Thomas Cromwell) in the conservative reaction, which would appropriately place him alongside Tunstall and (perhaps) St John (6), whom reformers considered a papist, and who (as marquis of Winchester from 1551) was to remain in office as Lord Treasurer all through Mary's reign, up to 1572.[24]

21

These names would fit the period of transition, ending before the middle of March 1547, that lasted from Henry VIII's death to the establishment of Protector Somerset's dominance. However uncertain some of these identifications, there seems no reason to move beyond 1547 for the scene before us. There was image-breaking enough that year, as the royal visitation went ahead in the summer, to make it unnecessary to move forward to 1548 or 1549. Before leaving these lists of names, it is worth making one final observation about them: several of the individuals who may here be set before us, had been enemies of the Howards, and profited from their fall. Thomas Wriothesley played a leading part in the proceedings against the earl of Surrey and the duke of Norfolk, and the former, on whom Wriothesley (the Lord Chancellor) delivered the sentence for treason, had been in his custody before going to the Tower. A whole group of Edward VI's councillors, headed by the two Seymours (both of whom were among Surrey's judges), benefited from the forfeited Howard estates. This may be relevant to our investigation.

THE MEMORIAL OF LORD DARNLEY:
ANOTHER TEXT-PICTURE

Pictures with texts were not unusual in Tudor England. Our problem is one of reconstruction, given the absence of so many words from what was designed as a wordy pictorial address. It may help this task to consider at the outset another comparable painting, whose genesis is better documented, and whose texts survive in place.

The Memorial of Lord Darnley (colour pl. III) was painted in January 1568 as a call for vengeance of the murder of Mary Queen of Scots' husband, who had died in such incriminating circumstances in the night of 9–10 January 1567. It was commissioned by Darnley's parents, the earl of Lennox and his wife, Lady Margaret Douglas, as part of their determined campaign of denunciation of their daughter-in-law, Mary Queen of Scots, for the 'tragic and lamentable killing' of their son.[25] As soon as Mary found refuge in England, the earl and countess hastened to take their charges to Elizabeth's court, and the earl of Lennox played a leading part in accusing the Scottish queen of conspiring against Darnley's life. The picture (two copies of which survive, at Holyroodhouse and Goodwood House), signed 'Livinus Voghelarius' – Livinus de Vogelaare – was completed in London in January 1568 as part of this campaign, the *operis huius causa*, the reason for the work, being inscribed in the wall tablet under the window on the far right.

The scene – with its elaborate series of texts and carefully contrived iconography – amounted to an advertisement for retribution on behalf of the infant James VI. He is shown kneeling in front of the tomb of his father, between two medallions of the murder (one of Darnley and his servant being dragged from their beds, the other of their corpses in the garden). Behind are the figures of the young king's grandparents and uncle (Charles Stuart) calling on God to avenge the spilling of innocent blood. Framed below, on the left, in a lowland landscape bumpy with hills and flooded with light, the encounter at Carberry Hill on 15 June 1567 takes place between recognizable views of Edinburgh and Arthur's Seat (colour pl. IV). Mary Queen of Scots is surrendering to the insurgent lords, whose forces flourish a banner depicting Darnley's corpse. 'IUDGE AND

14. Drawing of the banner carried at Carberry Hill on 15 June 1567, a month after Mary Queen of Scots married the earl of Bothwell, with a Protestant rite. The infant Prince James kneels beside the corpse of his father, as found after the explosion at Kirk o'Field on 9 February, calling for revenge.

REVENGE MY [CAUSE] O LORD' — words that are echoed in the Latin caption surrounding James's head. Above this inset, dominating the left side of the painting and seemingly the focus of the praying family, is an altar, covered with a rich cloth, on which stands the figure of the risen Christ with the wounds of the crucifixion, holding his cross.

This inset is critical to the reading of the picture, and the painting as a whole may be seen as a monumentalized version of the famous banner carried at Carberry, before which the defiant queen was reported to have quailed. The banner (of which we have a contemporary sketch) also shows the infant king kneeling beside the half-naked corpse of his father, invoking Christ to endorse his call for revenge (fig. 14). But the IHS for the name of Jesus at the centre of the banner is replaced in the painting by the triumphant resurrected Christ on the altar. At this point de Vogelaare's picture, which runs closely parallel to the account of *The Tyrannous Reign of Mary Stewart* given by George Buchanan, parts company most decisively from his avidly reformist viewpoint, and from the iconography of the banner. For Buchanan and others would have seen the figure of Christ on the altar as reflecting the 'filthy' papal idolatry that the Scottish queen and her supporters wished to see restored in England as well as in Scotland.

It would have been understandable for James VI and I to have taken against so explicit an indictment of his mother as murderer of his father. The king did his best to discredit the work of George Buchanan (his tutor), who was so virulent a propagandist against Mary Queen of Scots. It has been plausibly suggested that the defacing of the medallions, and of sections of text traducing the queen as Darnley's murderer, in the Holyroodhouse version of the painting, may be attributed to James.[26]

The Memorial of Lord Darnley presents us therefore with a rather interesting parallel. It is a blatantly propagandist painting, whose explicit meaning was explained in the texts that are set within the picture-space in different ways, both as caption scrolls attached to individual figures, and as framed inscriptions hanging on the walls. As with our picture, some inscribed words (in one version) are missing, but in this case the second copy supplies the lacking portions. Again, there is an inset scene placed in a frame in one corner, which illustrates the central subject-matter. This picture within the picture, integrally related to and extending the central scene, forms something like a source from which the whole has developed.

THE YOUNG JOSIAH

It may seem peculiar now to turn back to a time more than two thousand years before the Tudors, but that would not have seemed in the least odd to Edward VI – not that he would have measured this switch in terms of years. This is a matter of biblical precedent, and the young king was educated to think of himself in terms of the best scriptural patterns. He copied into French for his 'very dear uncle' the duke of Somerset, biblical passages that showed 'how those who do not worship the images are in eternal memory after their death, as Hezekiah and Josiah were and are' (fig. 15).[27] It was natural and appropriate to seek models of royal behaviour in the rulers of the Old Testament; kings read *Kings* and pondered and perhaps acted accordingly. Particular models in the old law were deemed appropriate for particular individuals. Edward's identikit was Josiah.

This was not a new development, but Judaic models were much in vogue in the sixteenth century as patterns for contemporary monarchs. Solomon and David had always been examples to conjure with, and in this age Henry VIII (fig. 16) and Philip II (fig. 17) were happy to lend their features to depictions of King Solomon, while Francis I (fig. 18) did duty for King David.[28] It was, however, the preoccupations of the reformers, with their fierce fidelity to the old law that gave new prominence to certain kings of the Old Testament. The religious renovators of this age, whose battle against the idolatry of Rome made them more ardent than any earlier reformers in their championing of the old law alongside the new, introduced a new familiarity with those kings of the Old Testament who had been faithful to this cause. Church-goers in Protestant England, like citizens of Basel or Geneva, knew what to expect when they heard commendations (as they did in the Elizabethan homilies) of 'the good kings of Juda, Asa, Ezechias, Josaphat, and Josias': they even began using these names for their own children.[29]

Monarchs likewise knew what was in the wind when they were praised or primed with these examples. Henry VIII was looked to as Hezekiah for having dealt with the idolized images of England's monastic shrines just as the brazen serpent had been dealt with, and

> Dieux qui au Seigneur, quil le vou
> loit destruire. 4. Rois .1. D.
>   Voicy comme ceux qui n'a=
> dorent pas les ymages, sont apres
> leur Mort d'Eternelle Memoire,
> comme Ezechias, et Iosias surent
> et sont. 4. Rois. 18. zz. A. C.
>   Aussy Dauid dit au Pre=
> mier Liure de Paralipomenon.
> Tous les Dieux d'Estranges Na=
> tions sont ydoles mais le Seigneur
> Dieu tout puissant a sait Ciel, et la
> Terre. 1 Paralipome. 16. C.

15. A page in Edward VI's copybook hand, from his collection of scriptural passages against idolatry.

his picture collection included in 1542 a painted cloth telling 'the storye of King Aza of the breking and casting downe of the aulters with the idolls'.[30] Edward VI was often invoked as the new Josiah of his age. It seemed a particularly valid and useful prototype.

The story of King Josiah (*c.* 640–609 BC) is told in the books of Kings and Chronicles. He was one of a series of kings of Judah who were celebrated for their fidelity to divine law in eradicating idolatrous Assyrian cults. Josiah, the son of Amon and grandson of the wicked Manasseh, came to the throne aged eight after his father, who had served idols 'and walked not in the way of the Lord', had been assassinated. The young Josiah proved exemplary in doing 'that which was right in the sight of the Lord'. He purged Judah and Jerusalem 'from the high places, and the groves, and the carved images, and the molten images. And they brake down the altars of Baalim in his presence; and the images, that were on high above them, he cut down; and the groves, and the carved images, and the molten images, he brake in pieces, and made dust of them, and strowed it upon the graves of them that had sacrificed unto them'.[31]

The other notable occurrence of Josiah's reign, which in the narrative in 2/4 Kings, 22–23, precedes and inspires his destruction of idolatry, was the discovery of the book of the law. In the course of the king's repairs of the temple in Jerusalem, the high priest found the 'book of the law', which was read before the king. When Josiah heard its words 'he rent his clothes', deeply conscience-smitten and fearful of the wrath of the Lord against those who had been serving

16. Henry VIII in the guise of Solomon receiving the admiration of the Queen of Sheba, whose words (adapted from 1 Kings, 10: 9) are inscribed over his head ('Blessed be the Lord thy God, which delighted in thee, to set thee on his throne ...'). A miniature painting by Holbein, perhaps a New Year's Day gift to the king.

other gods. It was as the result of this event that the destruction of high places and idolatrous priests and images was initiated.

'And the king sent, and they gathered unto him all the elders of Judah and of Jerusalem', and the king went into the temple 'and he read in their ears all the words of the book of the covenant which was found in the house of the Lord'. Josiah 'stood by a pillar, and made a covenant' to keep the Lord's commandments as written in the book of the law. He then ordered the priests to bring out of the temple all the vessels that had been made for Baal 'and he burned them without Jerusalem in the fields of Kidron'. The idolatrous priests who had burnt incense to Baal were themselves put down and

17. Lucas de Heere, Solomon and the Queen of Sheba, *signed and dated 1559. Solomon is portrayed as Philip II, who that year attended a chapter of the Order of the Golden Fleece in the cathedral of St Bavo, Ghent, where the painting still is.*

their bones burnt on their own altars. The idolaters' grove was burned and stamped 'small to powder'; the high places were broken down; the altars were beaten into powder. 'And he brake in pieces the images, and cut down the groves, and filled their places with the bones of men'.[32]

Josiah was a paradigm. 'Like unto him was there no king before him, that turned to the Lord with all his heart, and with all his soul, and with all his might, according to all the law of Moses'. His incomparable achievement rested on his relentless destruction of 'the images, and the idols, and all the abominations' whose elimination was described at such length (2 Kings, 23: 24–25).

Besides the recovery of the book of the law, which could stand for England's new championing of the Bible, the story of Josiah presented a perfect model for the more urgent reformers who returned home from foreign havens after the death of Henry VIII. The Biblical Josiah had come to the throne at nearly the same age as Edward VI, who was nine at his father's death. The completeness of his purges offered a useful argument against the conservative

29

18. *King David, carved with the features of Francis I, in the early sixteenth-century choir stalls of Auch Cathedral.*

objectors who were dragging their feet and maintaining that no further religious change or purification should take place in England until the new king came of age.

From the very beginning of his reign, Edward was looked to as a new Josiah. Even at his coronation, Archbishop Cranmer is reported to have called on him 'to see, with your predecessor Josiah, God truly worshipped, and idolatry destroyed, the tyranny of the bishops of Rome banished from your subjects, and images removed. These acts be signs of a second Josiah . . .' The reign seemed to get off to a good start and some enthusiasts were jubilant. Bartholomew Traheron wrote to the Swiss reformer, Bullinger, at the end of September 1548 celebrating Edward as 'firm, learned, and pious beyond his age. If there has ever existed a Josiah since the first of that name, this is certainly he'.[33]

John Hooper, who was to be a Zwingli for England in Edward's reign, was still in Zurich in 1547, having spent the later years of Henry VIII's reign in exile. He published a book (in English) at Zurich at the start of the new reign, in which he expressed his views of the old and new kings in terms of the Book of Kings. Henry VIII 'of a blessed memory' had delivered England from the papal antichrist, but what had happened after that? King Manasseh had repented his sinful ways and destroyed idolatry, but he died after reigning fifty-five years (Henry VIII was fifty-five at his death), 'before he could conveniently restore the book of the law and the true word of God unto the people'. It was for Edward VI, 'the most godly young prince Josiah' to remove false doctrine and idolatry out of the church, and restore the book of the law.

In the time of Manasses, grandfather unto this virtuous king Josijahu [Josiah], it was no marvel though the people left not their idolatry, because the king, being prevented by death, could not, with the taking away of the vice, plant virtue, as he would have done doubtless. But the merciful Lord vouchsafed to perform this old king's godly intention by the young, virtuous, and holy servant of God that was crowned king in the eighth year of his age; whose example I doubt not but that our most gracious king will follow, having so godly a governor and virtuous councillors . . .[34]

As bishop of Gloucester Hooper helped implement this agenda, but he had reason to become disillusioned about the godliness of some of Edward's councillors. In 1551, when Hooper was imprisoned for a time because of his rigidity about idolatrous ceremonies, the course of reform entered a rough phase. Those models in Kings were still useful, and Calvin addressed words of encouragement to the English king, calling on him to stand firm, whatever the difficulties he was currently encountering with his council, keeping steadily in view the example of the good king Josiah.[35] Given the readiness of contemporaries to type-cast him in this way, it is scarcely surprising if Edward began to view himself as another Josiah.

The invocation of the royal iconoclasts of the Old Testament

19. John Frewen, 'Puritan John', with his Bible open at the passage in the book of Kings telling of Josiah's zeal against idolatry.

continued as long as image-breaking remained a reforming issue; and that was a very long time. Queen Elizabeth's subjects, as well as the queen herself, had every reason to be familiar with the famous victories of Josiah and Hezekiah against abused idols. Two particularly well-known sources saw to that: both the Homilies and Foxe's Book of Martyrs had plenty to say on the subject.

The long tripartite Homily 'against peril of idolatry' occupied a large part of the *Second Tome of Homilies* published in 1563. It adverts more than once to the example of those Old Testament rulers who had acted strenuously against man's proneness to idolatry, showing the modern magistrate the indubitable need for

32

imageless churches. Josiah ('the excellent king Josias') and Hezekiah ('the good king Ezechias, who brake the brazen serpent to pieces, and burned it to ashes') receive special mention. In the Homily 'against disobedience and wilful rebellion' which was first published in 1570 after the northern rebellion of the previous year, reference was made to 'our good Josias, King Edward', whose early death was God's rebuke for the wickedness of the people.[36]

John Foxe's ecclesiastical history, *The Acts and Monuments*, popularly known as the Book of Martyrs, first appeared in its English form in 1563. The next edition, of 1570, much enlarged and altered and widely read, helped to give currency to the role of the Tudor Josiah. Foxe opened his new account of Edward's reign

21. John Frewen's Bible, open at 2 Kings, 23, 'Iosiah his Zeale'.

with the scriptural analogy: 'if I should seek with whom to match this noble Edward, I find not with whom to make my match more aptly, than with good Josias' – comparable in age, and acts and zeal:

for as mild Josias plucked down the hill altars, cut down the groves, and destroyed all monuments of idolatry in the temple, the like corruptions, dross, and deformities of popish idolatry (crept into the church of Christ of long time), this evangelical Josias, king Edward, removed and purged out of the true temple of the Lord.

Edward had purged as Josiah had purged, restoring religion to 'a right sincerity'.

Moreover, in king Josias's days the holy Scripture and book of God's Word was utterly neglected and cast aside, which he most graciously repaired and restored again. And did not king Edward the like, with the selfsame book of God's blessed word, and with other wholesome books of christian doctrine, which before were decayed and extinguished in his father's days, by sharp laws and severe punishments, here in England?[37]

22. *A Bible of the Authorised Version, printed in 1620, open at 2 Kings, Chapter 23.*

The scriptural analogy seemed very exact. Elizabethans, hearers or readers of Homilies and the Book of Martyrs, knew all about their own Young Josiah.

The posthumous reign of the Young Josiah went on for a long time. His was still the regal model for reforming churchmen in the seventeenth century, an emblem of zeal in implementation of the law. Two clerical members of the Frewen family, whose portrait collection survives in the house (Brickwall) they built at Northiam in Sussex early in the seventeenth century, were painted holding Bibles open at the page describing Josiah's destruction of idolatry. John Frewen (1558–1628, fig. 19), who was rector of Northiam from 1583 until his death, did his bit in the battle against papal idolatry, including preaching to his parishioners, some of whom were active opponents, about the patterns to be found in the Book of Kings, Jehu, Hezekiah, and Josiah. He also had a hand in bringing the

35

instructive example of Josiah to the attention of James I in 1603. Rubicund, earnest but not unkindly in his huge black hat, 'Puritan John' – as his descendants came to know him – confronts us with one hand on a skull and the other on a Bible which is open at 2 Kings, chapters 23–24. The rector's long fingers rest on the first verse of chapter 23: 'And the king sent . . .' (fig. 21 and above p. 28). The painter has faithfully reproduced the running-head that tops the page in the Authorized Version, making it impossible to miss the allusion: 'Iosiah his Zeale and . . .' (fig. 22).

Likewise, when John Frewen's eldest son Accepted Frewen (1588–1664, archbishop of York 1660–4) was painted (fig. 20), he too chose to be shown with his hand on this page of scripture. In his case it may seem surprising, given the stained glass windows, organ and altar he had installed in the chapel of Magdalen College, Oxford, during his presidency. But Accepted Frewen like his father, knew the duties of kings to *Kings*. In Madrid in 1623, when Prince Charles was actively pursuing marriage with the infanta, the younger Frewen preached to the heir to the throne on a text from 1 Kings, 18: 21: 'How long halt ye between two opinions? if the Lord be God, follow him: but if Baal, then follow him'.[38]

Edward VI's reforms became indissolubly linked with his biblical prototype. Thoughts about the achievements of his reign, in particular his abolition of papal idolatry and destruction of images, automatically prompted associations with Josiah. Might this have some bearing on our painting? Could there be some relationship between this biblical model and the depiction of Edward VI and the pope? Are there any pictorial sources for the scriptural Josiah which might be relevant to his Tudor follower?

Since *Edward VI and the Pope* makes a central theme of the king's iconoclasm, the royal biblical analogy can scarcely have been forgotten. An obvious way of testing the hypothesis that the young king in the picture was some sort of Josiah-Edward, is by looking at Bible illustrations.[39] The reform of King Josiah, as narrated in 2 (or 4 – see p. 222, n. 31) Kings, chapter 23, was an accepted topic for Bible illustration, and came to take a fairly common format. We can trace the development of this image from incunable woodcuts right up to English Bibles printed in the reign of Elizabeth.

Figures 23 and 24 are from an Italian Bible printed in Venice by Lucantonio di Giunta in 1490 – the *Biblia Vulgare Istoriata* of Niccolò Malermi (d. 1481).[40] These small, well executed woodcuts are placed in Numbers 34 and 4 Kings 23, both of which included divine injunctions to destroy. In the land of Canaan the children of Israel were to drive out all the inhabitants, 'and destroy all their pictures, and destroy all their molten images, and quite pluck down all their high places' – words that in today's Bibles are placed in the preceding chapter (Numbers 33: 52). We may notice the classical plinth with its swag, and the beheaded statue on the altar to the right which – with the figures wielding axes – bear comparison with our inset (fig. 23, cf. colour pl. II). The illustration of Josiah (fig. 24) has three parts. In the centre the bearded king sits enthroned; to his left stands the priest reading the book of the law; on the other side flames engulf an altar, simultaneously consuming idolatrous priest and idol.

Images of Josiah feature in English Reformation Bibles. The Coverdale Bible of 1535 included a small cut illustrating 2 Kings, 23: 'How Josias caused the boke of the covenaunt to be red unto all the

23. *The destruction of 'pictures'*
and 'molten images', as enjoined
in the book of Numbers.
Woodcut in 1490 Italian Bible,
printed in Venice.

24. *King Josiah: a woodcut*
illustrating 2/4 Kings 23, in the
same 1490 Italian Bible.

25. *Josiah and the reading of*
the book of the convenant.
Woodcut by Hans Sebald Beham
used in a Frankfurt Bible of
1534 and in the 1537 Biblicae
historiae. *Note the lack of the*
purifying bonfire.

people, and setteth up the true honoure of God againe'. This woodcut was the work of the Nuremberg engraver, Hans Sebald Beham. It appeared illustrating the same passage both in a Frankfurt Bible of 1534 and in several editions of an illustrated bible history printed by the same Frankfurt publisher from 1533, entitled *Biblicae historiae artificiosissime depictae* in 1537 (fig. 25). 'Josias coram populo legit verba foedereis'; 'Josiah reads the words of the covenant to the people', or as versified by an English owner of this edition (whose annotations included reflections on Charles I and Charles II), 'Josias reads the law, and lets them know / What is the way wherein to go'.[41]

For a great many readers of 2 Kings, 23, however, the 'way to go' included something more than this. For this scene, we should note, is bipartite, not tripartite; it shows the reading of the words of the law and the renewal of the covenant – not the destruction of idols. There is a curious blank wall behind the reader in Beham's cut, and it is not difficult to discover what filled that space elsewhere.

In the 1541 edition of the English Great Bible there is a delineation of Josiah that combines the reading of the book of the law with the destruction of the idols (fig. 26). This small woodcut has been misplaced in the text, and stands at the beginning of chapter 18 of the second book of Kings – being applied to Hezekiah, instead of Josiah. Its true subject is unmistakable. Opposite the figure holding the book of the law who stands on the king's right, flames are licking vigorously up round an altar, consuming three disembodied heads, which might belong either to broken idols or 'put down' priests.[42] The scene is similar to Erhard Schön's woodcut in

39

27. Josiah. Woodcut by Erhard Schön in the Vulgate printed in Lyons in 1520. A copy was owned by Thomas Bilney, who preached against the abuses of images, and wrote beside this chapter 'laus Josie' – 'praise to Josiah'.

the 1520 Lyons Vulgate, a book which Thomas Bilney owned and annotated and in which he recorded his approval of Josiah (fig. 27).[43]

Holbein helped to popularize this image of Josiah. Though it was not until after his own death and that of Henry VIII, that Holbein's Old Testament woodcuts were published for the English market, his contributions to the Coverdale Bible seem to reflect the concern with idolatry that was gaining strength in the 1530s.[44] Holbein's Josiah appears in his *Historiarum Veteris Testamenti Icones ad vivum expressae* (Pictures of Old Testament stories drawn to the life), which was first published at Lyons in 1538. The influence of these images – which was considerable – started before that, for already in 1531 the German Bible published in Zurich by Christopher Froschauer used many of Holbein's drawings, including his Josiah (seen in reverse, fig. 28). An edition with English texts, *The Images of the Old Testament*, was printed at Lyons in 1549. The Josiah of the *Icones* (fig. 29) is the law-enacting idol-burning king with whom we are now becoming familiar, though here the scribe or priest reading the book of law from a lectern occupies the central position. To the left King Josiah is seated on a rounded dais, sceptre in hand. Outside the vaulted room, which seems to be filled by priests and elders, an arched opening on the right shows the bonfire of idols. It is just possible to make out their heads in the flames. The original Latin inscription that accompanied this cut was replaced in 1549 by

28. The first published version of Holbein's drawing of Josiah, in the German Bible printed by Froschauer in Zurich in 1531.

IOSIAS legit Deuteronomium coram po
pulo . Idôla demolitur, & facerdotes Baal
occîdit .

29. Josiah's reform, with bonfire of idols taking place outside, in the edition of Holbein's Icones printed in Lyons in 1547. The same woodcut was used for the 1549 edition which had texts in English and French.

IIII.   REGVM   XXIII.

30. The 1572 Lutheran Bible gave Old Testament reformers the features of heroes of the Lutheran Reformation fifty years earlier. Josiah and his high priest were Frederick the Wise, Elector of Saxony, and Martin Luther.

English and French texts; 'Josias redith the boke of Deuteronomy before the peple. He destroyth Idols, and kyllyth the preysts of Baal'.[45]

Catholics and Lutherans, fearful as they were of image-breaking extremists, preferred to gloss over or omit Josiah's destructive purgings. It was prudent to play safe with scriptural patterns. So Michael Aitsinger's *De Leone Belgico* (dedicated in 1583 to Rudolph II in memory of Philip II), which described and depicted — with a print by Franciscus Hogenberg (below fig. 39) — the fearful iconoclasm in Antwerp in 1566, showed singular restraint when describing the reforms of King Josiah in the appended index of Old Testament events. There is no mention here of the destruction of idols.[46] It is interesting to find that these different viewpoints affected biblical iconography.

As the reforming destruction of church art was followed by counter-reforming reconstruction, the relationship between Old

*31. King Asa, who deposed his
mother on account of her idol,
'and burnt it by the brook
Kidron', giving instructions,
supported by a priest (Martin
Luther), for the removal of 'all
the idols that his fathers had
made' (1 Kings, 15: 12–13).
1572 Wittenberg Bible.*

Testament and modern iconoclasm became more explicit. Even
Lutherans (after Luther's death), could read the Book of Kings in the
light of their own history. In 1572 an edition of Luther's Bible was
printed at Wittenberg with a full set of illustrations by Johann
Teufel. In the woodcut to 2 Kings, 23 the reader sees King Josiah
listening to the reading of the law (fig. 30). The godly king
enthroned at the centre of this arcaded temple is Frederick the Wise
of Saxony, and the high priest who reads the word of God to him has
the unmistakable features of Martin Luther. There is no destruction
depicted here. But the introductory remarks on Josiah's 'admirable
history' left no doubt that the example of his deeds against idolatry
applied to the idolatrous pictures and imagery of the godless papacy.
And readers only had to turn back a few pages to see what royal
piety of this kind entailed. In 1 Kings, 15 King Asa 'did that which
was right in the eyes of the Lord . . . and removed all the idols that
his fathers had made' (fig. 31). Johann Teufel's Asa presides over a
scene in which statuary is being smashed, while a plume of smoke
rises into the sky from the bonfire made for the idol. This too is the
Elector Frederick, with Luther at his right hand.[47]

England's view of the image-breaking young Josiah was still
being presented to Bible readers in image as well as word in the reign
of Elizabeth. The Bishops' Bible in 1568 included in its stylish

43

32. Woodcut of Josiah in the
Bishops' Bible, 1568. The
initial A, centre foreground, has
been identified as the monogram
of Arnold Nicolai of Antwerp,
an engraver and woodcutter who
also dealt in prints and maps.

woodcut series an illustration of the young Josiah, heading chapter 23 of 4 Kings (fig. 32). In this case the iconoclastic reform is clearly visible. This tripartite scene shows the zealous king enthroned on a central dais, sceptre in hand, surrounded by his courtiers – who include reclining female figures. The reading of the law takes place at a lectern on the right, and the idol-burning is seen through a rectangular (frame-line) embrasure on the left. Behind the king's head is an opening from which a curtain is held back, to reveal an outside altar or plinth, on which rest two truncated legs. A lot is conveyed here, legibly, though none too clearly, within a small space. A note in the margin of the text below reads: 'Kyng Josia zelouslie purgeth the temple of God, and destroyeth al the monumentes of idolatrye and superstition'.[48]

The appearance of this woodcut is the more interesting because Archbishop Parker, who was the architect of this Elizabethan church Bible, lifted the main sequence of his illustrations from a woodcut series that had come from Cologne, where they had been used in a Dutch Bible in 1566. This Catholic text did not, however, include the Josiah scene, which was added to the English folio Bible (either being made for this edition, or possibly borrowed from some other source). The cut differs in style from the Vergil Solis designs to which it was attached, and bears the monogram of the Antwerp engraver, Arnold Nicolai. Moreover, when the entire series of woodblocks was shipped back to Cologne to be re-used in Quentel's 1571 *Catholische Bibell*, after an intermediate appearance in a Latin Bible printed in Antwerp in 1570, the Josiah cut was dropped.[49]

But Josiah, as shown to readers of the 1568 Bible, had only a short stay in England. The quarto edition of the Bishops' Bible that came out in 1569 did not contain the illustrations of the 1568 folio. A margin full of notes helps to make up for the lack of any pictorial presentation of Josiah's doings in chapter 23. One of these — which also featured in the Geneva Bible — reads: 'He removed that grove which idolatours for devotion had planted neare to the temple, contrary to the commaundements of the Lord . . . or as some reade, the similitude of a grove which was hanged in the temple'.[50] Archbishop Parker had new illustrations made for the second edition of his folio Bible, which came out in 1572. This fresh set consisted of large composite woodcuts prefacing different scriptural books, and it is an interesting comment on the history of English Bible illustration to find battle scenes from the print prefacing Joshua being used in the 1620s to lend atmosphere to popular ballads.[51]

The Josiah of 1572 repeats, in miniature, the old tripartite formula. The prefatory illustration for the third and fourth books of Kings is divided into twelve scenes, relating to the different chapters that follow. The one for 4 Kings, 23 is in the bottom right-hand corner (fig. 33). It takes us back very much to where we started. Indeed the king on his rounded-stepped dais, and the high priest reading at the lectern, hark back to Holbein (figs. 28–9), but now the image-burning bonfire is placed in the upper register, and seen through a rectangular opening or window.[52]

Who designed the new illustrations for Parker's 1572 Bible? The one artist whose name has been linked, with convincing plausibility, to the 1568 book, is that of Franciscus Hogenberg. To his hand have been attributed the engraved portraits of Queen Elizabeth, Leicester and Burghley, that adorned the first Bishops' Bible, and Franciscus, as well as his younger brother Remigius Hogenberg, was one of the 'drawers and cutters' whom Archbishop Parker reported a few years later as being on his pay-roll. The elder Hogenberg was among those who fled from persecution in the Netherlands, though his stay in England does not seem to have lasted beyond 1568–9, for he was abroad again in 1570 and finally settled in Cologne for the rest of his life. If, as Hind postulated, Franciscus Hogenberg arrived in

45

33. *Illustration prefacing the third book of Kings in the 1572 edition of the Bishops' Bible. The scene of Josiah, enlarged below, clearly borrows from Holbein and bears the initials RB and CT.*

England in time to design the title-pages for Parker's Bible, the duration of his stay coincides so exactly with that of the archbishop's borrowed woodblocks that it seems possible he was the agent who brought and removed them.[53]

Hogenberg, back at work on the continent in 1570, could not have designed the illustrations for the second edition of the Bishops' Bible. The crowded intensity of these scenes (so unlike the clarity of Hogenberg's style) recalls the work of Marcus Gheeraerts the elder, on whom more later, but the initials that appear on some of the cuts point elsewhere. The 'RB' and 'CT' inscribed in the corner of the title cut before 3 Kings have not been identified, though the latter may stand for the Dutchman Christopher Tressell, Treasure, or Tressa. He was referred to in 1582 as 'a carver to the printers', so he might have been the cutter of the block. If this indicates 'RB' as the artist who drew the designs, we are still in the dark as to who this was.[54]

The story of these Bible illustrations exemplifies the iconographic divide that came to separate Catholic from Protestant. The reformation of Josiah was part of the scriptural split in sixteenth-century Europe. Even from this very selective survey it should be obvious that there was an established and readily recognizable iconography for King Josiah. The scheme varied in the disposition of its constituent parts, but the three elements were fairly constant. They were (to sum up): the enthroned king, with his priests and elders; the book of the law, read by the scribe or priest; the burning of the idols, generally placed outside or beyond the main setting.

I suggest that there is a relationship between this scheme and the way Edward VI is presented in our picture. The young king, enthroned in the presence of his councillors, is implementing the book of the law. 'The worde of the Lord endureth for ever'. The words inscribed on the open book come from the last verse of chapter 1 of the first epistle general of Peter; this final verse concludes: 'and this is the word which by the gospel is preached unto you'. Even if all the prepared spaces had texts on them, this one would still occupy a special position. It was the book itself speaking – as the scriptures themselves, printed and circulated in their English form, now spoke directly to all vernacular readers.

Edward's scriptural law is not being read aloud from a lectern, like Josiah's, but the completeness of its fulfilment informs the whole depiction. 'For all fleshe is as grasse, and all the glorie of man, is as the flowre of grasse. The grasse withereth, and the flowre thereof falleth away'.[55] The words inscribed on the chest of the falling pope, whose pomp and power are about to disappear with his tiara and triple cross, come from the same chapter (the penultimate verse) of 1 Peter. The book of the law is central to the composition, and its position was mapped out in the underdrawing on the panel. Immediately below the young king, on the dais by his feet, it is set between him and the collapsing pontiff, linking right-doing king with wrong-doing pope, and providing the scriptural motivation for the entire scene.

But the word 'IDOLATRY' and another important part of the picture tell us that we must seek an Old Testament source in addition to this New Testament one. The scene of image-breaking — the destruction of pagan idols — set over to one side, just as it was in the Bible illustrations, indicates that the king was here acting in the role of his Old Testament prototype. 'Josiah putteth down the idols'. It seems a fair guess that the empty label painted along the top of the inset was intended either for words from 2/4 Kings, 23, or a summary of them.

Having come thus far with possible biblical sources, it seems logical to look at other depictions of King Josiah. There are plenty.

Probably the most common place to find Hezekiah, Manasseh, Josiah and David in late medieval art was in representations of the Tree of Jesse, best known in stained glass windows. The Old Testament kings appear here as shoots on the genealogical tree linking David and his descendants with Mary and the birth of Christ. Examples of Josiah in this scheme are to be seen at Canterbury and York.[56] A late example of this image appears in a book published in Elizabeth's reign, a unique copy of which, beautifully painted, belonged to the queen herself. A Tree of Jesse formed the title-page of both the *Christian Prayers and Meditations* published by John Day in 1569, and *A Booke of Christian Prayers*, the new edition of 1578 for which Day's son was responsible (fig. 34). We see here, perched on the branches that link Jesse at the bottom, with the Virgin and Child enthroned in a rose at the top, the crowned and labelled kings who constituted this biblical lineage. Kings Asa and Manasseh sit either side of the Virgin, and one step below on the right (his name in mirror script) is Hezekiah (ESECHIA). All three had associations for Tudor monarchs, and the frieze below of alternating roses and portcullises brought home the royal compliment.[57]

Doctrinal developments in the sixteenth century added new fame to key figures in this ancient genealogy. The reformers' obsession with idolatry as the cardinal sin, central to the long deterioration of Christ's church, led to a new focus on the scriptural kings who had done most to eliminate idols. Frequent notices of Hezekiah, Josiah and others in doctrinal writings were accompanied by frequent visual depictions. The iconoclastic kings of the Old Testament were effectively launched into a new iconography. The idol-breaking morality that featured so largely in the Book of Kings now came to be applied, in a manner hitherto quite unprecedented in the western Church, to the devotional customs of Rome. The pagan idols of antiquity were equated with the idolized images of modern Christians.

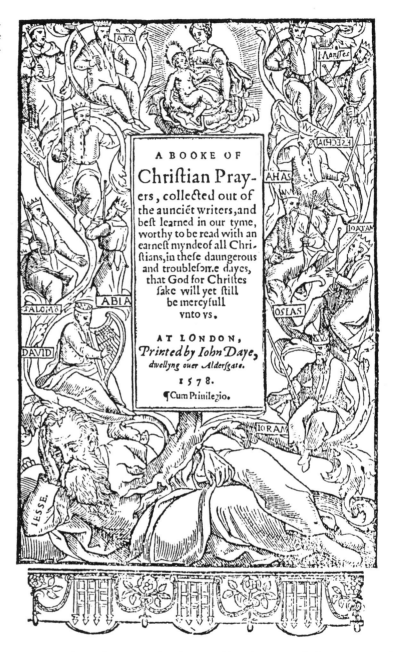

A BOOKE OF

Chriſtian Pray-
ers, collećted out of
the aunciét writers, and
beſt learned in our tyme,
worthy to be read with an
earneſt mynde of all Chri-
ſtians, in theſe daungerous
and troubleſome dayes,
that God for Chriſtes
ſake will yet ſtill
be mercyfull
vnto vs.

AT LONDON,
Printed by Iohn Daye,
dwellyng ouer Alderſgate.
1578.
¶ Cum Priuilegio.

An artist whose work shows this change of direction is the painter–poet of Berne, Nicolaus Manuel Deutsch (1484–1530). He contributed to the contemporary struggle against religious abuses by satirical writings as well as by graphic work, attacking such practices as the sale of indulgences. Deutsch shows us how Reformers exploited Old Testament subjects for their own obsessive concerns. 'Solomon adoring the idols' (as described in 1 Kings, 11: 1–13) – the king who in his old age, failed to keep the covenant, and 'did evil in the sight of the Lord', serving other gods – was painted by Deutsch as a mural on the façade of a Bernese house in 1518. Ten years later, in 1528, Berne – following the example already set by Zwingli in Zurich – publicly swept away this evil. It was accepted that since setting up images to be honoured was 'against God's word of the New and Old Testaments', church images treated in this way should be removed.[58]

In 1527, when Berne was gearing itself for this step, Deutsch made a design (now in Basel) for a glass painting of Josiah commanding the destruction of idols (fig. 35). 'Josia der Küng zü Jerusalem', is portrayed presiding over a scene of breaking and burning that was profoundly topical for contemporary Swiss citizens, including painters like Deutsch and Holbein whose works were endangered or destroyed in the process. Josiah stands by a pillar (above p. 28), sceptre in hand, directing a workman whose raised axe has already shattered the altar of Baal (BALS ALTAR). Next the king stands a bearded man (priest or scribe) clasping a book – the book of the law which is being implemented. To the right flames are consuming the heathen idols, burning them to ashes in obedience to the law, outside Jerusalem in the fields of Kedron. The summary of 4 Kings, 23 identifying the biblical scene is inscribed inside a frame at the top – just as it might have been in Edward VI's picture.[59]

Another continental artist who did much more to extend the currency of Old Testament subjects in the iconoclastic environment that threatened his work, as it threatened that of Nicolaus Manuel Deutsch, was Maarten van Heemskerck. He, no more than Deutsch, does not normally feature in accounts of English painting. But Heemskerck closes the Old Testament circuit we have been following. He brings us back home, to the painting of Edward VI, the centre of this reconnaissance.

Maarten van Heemskerck (1498–1574) was a younger contemporary of Deutsch, and like him – though in a quite different way – was deeply affected by the religious upheaval of his time. He too reflects this in his art. Unlike Deutsch, whom he greatly excelled both as a draughtsman and in the range of his graphic output, Heemskerck came to have a considerable influence, particularly through the prints made from his designs. These included a number of Old Testament

35. King Josiah, sceptre in hand, overseeing the destruction of Baal's altar, and the beating down and burning of idols (given classical attributes). 4 Kings, chapter 23 is inscribed in the cartouche at the top. The glass window made in 1530 from Nicolaus Manuel Deutsch's 1527 design still survives.

subjects,[60] some of which were of special relevance to the reform of images and the iconoclastic movement of the sixteenth century. Such were the *Brazen Serpent*, *The Story of Shadrach, Meschach and Abed-Nego*, and several series of prints, in particular those on *The Ten Commandments*, *The History of Gideon* and *The History of Bel and the Dragon*, as well as sets on the disasters of the Jewish nation, entitled *Clades*, and *The History of King Josiah*. The last (to which we shall return shortly) consists of eight prints, illustrating the account in Kings, from the reading of the book of the law by

Shaphan the scribe (2 Kings, 22: 10–11), to Josiah's solemnizing the Passover (2 Kings, 23: 21–23) after various acts of destruction had eliminated the idolatry of Judah.

Before we go any further it will be as well to consider Heemskerck himself.

MAARTEN VAN HEEMSKERCK

Maarten van Heemskerck was born in the village of Heemskerk near Haarlem in 1498. In the late 1520s he joined the studio of Jan van Scorel (his contemporary), who was then temporarily working in Haarlem. In the next decade Heemskerck followed Scorel's example and went to Italy, where he spent about four years in Rome.[61] They were critical years, which deeply affected his subsequent work and its impact on others. For besides the inspiration he may have derived from Raphael, Michelangelo and (in Mantua) Giulio Romano, Heemskerck was profoundly moved by the grandeur of classical ruins. We know about this in some detail, thanks to the survival of many drawings from his Roman sketchbooks. The close studies Heemskerck made of the buildings, arches, columns and sites of ancient Rome had a marked influence on the work he produced thereafter. Broken vaults and ruined masonry appear repeatedly in his designs (fig. 36). And when years later (in 1553) he painted his self-portrait (now in the Fitzwilliam Museum, Cambridge) Heemskerck placed the image of his younger self alongside the Colosseum, with a figure (presumably the artist) at work sketching (fig. 37).[62]

The bulk of Heemskerck's *oeuvre* consisted of altarpieces, designs for church glass and tapestry and religious topics of a conventional nature, such as the vast altarpiece (which has been at Linköping in Sweden since 1582), painted for the church of St Lawrence in Alkmaar. He died on 1 October 1574, true to the traditional faith, and was buried in the church of St Bavo, Haarlem, where he had been *kerkmeester* (church-master or churchwarden) for twenty-two years.[63] Heemskerck, however, was certainly influenced by the currents of new thought that swept through the Low Countries in his lifetime. His paintings included plenty of classical topics, and his observations of Rome, ancient and modern, contributed not only to these but also to his numerous Biblical prints illustrating both Old and New Testaments. His friends and professional associates included eminent Dutch writers and humanists, and his work (especially his graphic work) touched closely on central controversies of the time – including the role of images in religion.

The prints made from Heemskerck's drawings were an important

part of his work. They extended both the range and availability of his depictions, bringing them into more hands, and — given the hazards that altarpieces, panels and canvases were subject to — increasing their chances of survival. Carel van Mander tells us that Heemskerck did not etch or engrave himself.[64] A series of engravers worked on his designs and made him well-known outside his own country in his own day and long after. In fact it seems to have been this graphic work, rather than his paintings, which spread his fame and which was responsible for his influence on other artists, including Rembrandt, well into the seventeenth century. Sixteenth-century glass painters also made use of these engravings, one example of which, probably dating from the 1570s or 1580s, closely

36. Maarten van Heemskerck, Landscape with ruins and Vulcan's forge *(1538). A drawing executed soon after the artist's Italian visit, making use of his observations of Roman buildings and ruins.*

55

37. Maarten van Heemskerck, Self-portrait with the Colosseum (1553). The painter, looking back on the formative years he spent in Rome in his thirties, and delineating his then self at work on an ink sketch, may intentionally have made himself appear younger than fifty-five.

follows the scene of the destruction of the temple of Bel in Heemskerck's series on *Bel and the Dragon* (fig. 38).[65]

Hieronymus Cock (d. 1570), who had a publishing house in Antwerp, and Dirck Volckertsz. Coornhert of Haarlem (1522–90), were the two most important engravers of Heemskerck's work in the 1550s and 1560s. They were succeeded by Coornhert's pupil, Philip Galle (1537–1612). In 1571 Galle took over Cock's publishing house in Antwerp, but before that he had a print shop in Haarlem and by the late 1550s he was engraving prints after designs by Heemskerck. Coornhert and Galle had other skills besides the art of engraving. They were learned men, and authors in their own right, capable of contributing much more than technology to the designs they saw into print. Philip Galle was a close friend of Hadrianus Junius, the leading Dutch humanist of the time, who wrote verses to accompany some of Heemskerck's designs, for which Galle acted as the link-man. This was an important connection, to which we shall return.

Heemskerck had personal knowledge of papal Rome, as well as experiencing the Calvinist dislocations in his own country. He suffered, with other contemporary painters, from the iconoclasm that destroyed so much of the religious art of the Low Countries, particularly in 1566 (fig. 39). Many of his paintings were destroyed that year, and in 1572 when Haarlem was besieged and he went (then aged seventy-four) to Amsterdam, several of his pictures – as he discovered on his return – were commandeered by the occupying forces and sent to Spain. But Heemskerck's work suggests that his mind was by no means closed to the ideas that were restructuring the Church of his day. He was closely in touch with humanist circles, and quite capable of suggesting the folly of papal grandiosity, as exemplified in the rebuilding of St Peter's, which he had seen for himself.[66] Various of his Old Testament drawings took a sideways look at the painful issue of contemporary image-breaking.

Heemskerck certainly understood the theology, as well as the practice of the reforming iconoclasts who dealt so savagely with the images in the churches of the Low Countries in the summer of 1566. We can regard some of his works as indirect commentaries on this process. He both delineated scenes of idolatry, in the shape of

*39. Iconoclasm in Antwerp on
20 August 1566, engraved by
Franciscus Hogenberg. The
imagery being destroyed includes
painted altarpieces, stained glass
windows, and (the work of a
team of six) a row of statues.*

egregious ancient pagan idolaters (an old theme with novel interest);
and also showed with vivid directness the impact of iconoclasm, as
practised in the Old Testament. A whole series of his prints are
concerned with this issue.

Art historians have been perplexed by Heemskerck's images of
image-breaking. They seem to present a conundrum. Clearly his
artistic production cannot be divorced from the anti-art movement
of his time. A predominantly (and unusually) large proportion of his
graphic output (about 300 out of more than 700 depictions on the
most recent estimate)[67] was of Old Testament subjects, and among
these were many representing biblical iconoclasm. Given the scriptural basis of sixteenth-century image-reform, there must certainly
have been a connection of some kind both in the artist's mind, and in
the minds of readers of his images between these scenes and
contemporary events. But what was the connection?

Whatever their degree of sympathy for criticisms of church
abuses, artists like Heemskerck, whose works were destroyed and
means of livelihood threatened, seem unlikely to have been whole-
hearted supporters of radical iconoclasts. Of course there were artists

who joined the reformers and changed their lifestyle. But it is also important to remember (witness Erasmus who had fled to Freiburg im Breisgau to escape the iconoclastic ravages in Basel) that – even as late as the 1560s – image-reform could still be separated from image-destruction, at least in theory. Also we may notice that it was one of Heemskerck's close associates, Dirck Volckertsz. Coornhert, who in 1566 played a leading and very active role in protecting the churches of Haarlem against attack from the image-breakers.[68]

In 1549 Coornhert and Heemskerck collaborated in the production of a remarkable etching. It depicted 'The adoration of an idol of Isis' (fig. 40). The image of the goddess, fervently adored by a crowd of worshippers, is borne on the back of an ass, with a votive lamp burning in front of it, improbably set on the scrolled pommel of the saddle. The animal has stalled, causing smoke to trail forwards over the heads of the votaries, while a man with a raised whip tries to goad it on. The drawing for this image had been made the previous year by Heemskerck, who borrowed the idea and the accompanying Latin inscription from Andrea Alciati's 1547 *Emblemata*. 'A slow-moving ass bore the image of Isis; he had the venerable mysteries on his curved back. Everyone who encounters him worships the goddess respectfully, and kneels to utter pious prayers. But the ass thought the honour was for him, and was filled with pride until the

driver, curbing him with lashes from his whip, said, "You're no god, ass, you're only carrying a god".'

Besides its allegory of the foolishness of pride in office and position, the print contains satirical comment on contemporary religion. The adoration of images – so many of which had been destroyed, specially in England at this very time, on the grounds of such worship – was a matter of importance on many levels. The papacy, which in 1547 had transferred the Council of Trent to Bologna, thereby effectively stalling its deliberations, had yet to pronounce on this issue. Perhaps Heemskerck hints at Rome's failings in his depiction of the trophies of the goddess's throne and the winged victory in her right hand, as well as the classical ruins and round temple in the background. Coornhert, who executed the etching, was described ten years after his death as one who 'mocked all the religions in these countries, the Popish, Lutheran, Reformed

*42. The aged Solomon,
surrounded by wives, kneels to
worship an idol, conventionally
represented as a pagan figure on
a free-standing column. Woodcut
by Johann Teufel, 1572.*

. . . and issued well-known prints on the subject, very many of which were to be found in people's houses . . .'.[69]

Ten years later Coornhert engraved another drawing by Heemskerck on what we may regard as a related subject. *Solomon's Idolatry* (1559, fig. 41) illustrates a passage in the book of Kings (1 Kings, 11: 1–13), which tells how when Solomon was old his 'outlandish' wives 'turned away his heart' from the Lord, and seduced him into the worship of strange gods. The once wise king provoked God's anger by serving and building high places to Ashtoreth, Milcom, Chemosh and Molech. The print shows half a dozen of Solomon's seven hundred wives successfully engaged in teaching him the worship of their idol. In elaborate oriental garb, their mien and gesture reflect their obeisance to the god before whose statue the humbled king is kneeling.[70]

There were precedents for this depiction. Medieval Bible illustrators had used the scene as an example of women seducing a man

61

43. Achan, 'who transgressed in the thing accursed', being stoned to death with his family, and the burning of the city of Ai which Joshua reduced to 'an heap for ever' (Joshua, 7–8). Engraved by Philip Galle after Heemskerck, Clades series, 1568–9.

44. The destruction of the house and image of Baal by Jehu (2 Kings, 10). The colossal statue may be compared with Nebuchadnezzar's image in Pieter Aertsen's painting, fig. 56, and the man swinging a mallet with the iconoclast in fig. 54. Engraved by Philip Galle after Heemskerck, Clades series, 1568–9.

into false worship, and fifteenth-century 'women's wiles' series also exploited Solomon's fall.[71] But the topic gained new resonance in the Reformation period. Lucas van Leyden has left us three prints of *Solomon's Idolatry*, executed between about 1512 and 1519[72] – just at the time when Deutsch painted his Berne mural. All three show the king kneeling in prayer before a very strange figure sculpture,

45. Gideon's destruction of the altar of Baal (Judges, 6). 1561 drawing by Maarten van Heemskerck, whose head of Laocoon in his Roman sketchbook seems to have been the model for the head in the foreground, as it was later for the statue of Bel (above, fig. 38).

while one of his wives stands enticing or instructing him in this devotion. The sin of the ageing Solomon came forward as a pictorial theme as the case against Christian idols was being ventilated, and Protestant Bibles found it useful to illustrate this folly of the once wise king.

Heemskerck's print is somewhat more ambiguous than the view which Johann Teufel presented to readers of the 1572 Lutheran Bible (fig. 42). Here, instead of the idol standing on top of its column, the form of this alien image is left, above knee level, to the viewer's imagination. That it had a human dimension (like van Leyden's idols) is not in doubt – though its sex is.[73] We may notice also the classical details (including the swag) of the altar, which Heemskerck manipulated to convey an Old Testament setting.

In 1559 iconoclasm had not yet taken its toll in the Low Countries. But the battle against idolatry had long been joined in many parts of northern Europe, and that year England experienced once again, after the interlude of Marian restoration, scenes of destruction like those of 1547–8. Solomon's idolatry showed how even the wisest of the wise might err; age was no protection against the false image. Coornhert's print could not avoid being read in the light of contemporary events.

Heemskerck's prints of the 1560s depict Old Testament icono-clasm in scenes of terminal destruction: statues topple, masonry

63

46. The engraved version of fig. 45 in The History of Gideon. *In the background a bullock is sacrificed on Gideon's new altar with wood from Baal's grove (being felled on the right). The base of the destroyed statue preoccupies the central figure: see above, fig. 32, for a symbolic reference to an altar statue with truncated feet.*

Diruit aram, lucumq, Baal, indeq construit aram Domiho, et holocaustu sacrificat.

crashes to the ground, flames lick up round massive ruins so that we can almost hear the roar of fire and thunder of falling walls. There is no doubt about the apocalyptic scale of these events. But we should also observe their limitations; the destruction portrayed was specific. The idols which, with their altars and settings, were pulled down, broken up, destroyed and burnt, were all of one kind. Whether it was the cataclysmic destruction by fire that accompanied the stoning of the avaricious Achan and his family (fig. 43); Jehu destroying the image and house of Baal (fig. 44); Gideon demolishing the altar of Baal (figs. 45–46); or Daniel's destruction of Bel and his temple (fig. 38): in every case what we see going down are great pieces of monumental figure sculpture. And it is envisaged in a recognizable classical form and setting.

We may justifiably set these biblical scenes alongside Heemskerck's 1552 painting – of which there is an engraving, published by Hieronymus Cock (fig. 47) – of a *Bullfight in an ancient Arena* (Lille, Musée des Beaux Arts). The huge Jupiter statue that dominates this violent scene recalls the colossal statue of Apollo which Pope Sylvester was believed (according to an old legend) to have destroyed as an idol in the fourth century. The foreground scenes of quack doctor (right) and preacher with small group of

AMPHITHEATRVM *sive* ARENA

TAVRILIORVM AD IMITATIONEM ANTIQVORVM ROMANORVM IN THEATRIS EXHIBITORVM GRAPHICA EFFIGIATIO

47. The ruined Colosseum in this print of Heemskerck's ancient arena is dominated by the huge monumental statue of Jupiter. Round it swirls the bullfight 'in imitation of the ancient Romans'. Such events did take place in early sixteenth-century Rome, so possibly Heemskerck saw one. (Fitzwilliam Museum, Cambridge).

listeners (left) place a comment on Christian salvation outside the verdant ruins of the Colosseum.[74]

Heemskerck was a painter. He did not sculpt, nor even – for the most part – engrave.[75] None of the images we see being destroyed in his depictions was of the kind he was himself employed in making – by drawing and painting. In this Old Testament iconoclasm there are no pictures being ripped down and burnt up, as there were in so many parts of sixteenth-century Europe (fig. 39). All Heemskerck's idols were three-dimensional. They represent very exactly (to the letter) the graven images (*sculptile*) of the commandment text that was the iconoclasts' charter.

If pagan statues were idols, painting was a divine art – a divine Christian art. Heemskerck, for whom it was also a livelihood, expressed this himself, by painting St Luke painting the Virgin. Two of his versions of this subject survive, one (Frans Hals Museum,

65

Haarlem) dating from 1532, the other (Musée des Beaux Arts, Rennes) from the early 1550s. They are very different, but both have one thing in common: they show the evangelist at work with his brush in a studied setting of 'antique' carving. St Luke, whether as painter–poet or painter–physician, is practising an art that has divine authority, powerful as the poetic word or the ministry of healing. Behind the saint's back in the later painting is a sculpture gallery whose features are those of the Casa Sassi in Rome, which Heemskerck had visited and drawn (and which Coornhert engraved in 1553). One of the statues in this background is a female figure (perhaps the Erythraean sibyl, associated with the Annunciation) whose pose echoes that of the Madonna, and a sculptor is at work with hammer and chisel — reminders of the paganism on which St Luke has turned his back.[76]

St Luke was the patron of painters, as well as doctors, and those who placed themselves, with their art, under his protection could believe (and such belief was supported by a long iconographic tradition), that their profession had apostolic validation. Book illustrators and graphic artists as well as painters looked to St Luke. Those who were incorporated into the guild of St Luke at Antwerp included engravers like Hieronymus Cock, Arnold Nicolai and Philip Galle, who were all made free of the guild in their time.[77]

In the vast controversial literature spawned by the sixteenth-century image-controversy, St Luke's legendary fame as a painter had a critical place. Nicholas Sander (to cite just one example) published at Louvain in 1567 a treatise on the unlawfulness of breaking images of Christ and the saints, in which he adverted to the 'constant witnesses of many, that St Luke the Evangelist painted both Christes and our Ladies Image'.[78] The long-held belief that the saint had painted the Virgin and Child, and that his work was still in existence, was an important justification for the claim that Christ's features, incarnate in human form, were knowable and could be represented. By painting St Luke in this way — ancient topic though it was — Heemskerck was joining the argument. St Luke's example seemed to legitimate Christian painting as an art that had existed since apostolic times. Sculpture was another matter altogether. Ancient carvings and pagan statues belonged to a rejected world: the world whose dangers had been known since Old Testament times.

EDWARD VI AND HEEMSKERCK

This delving into Biblical iconography yields a positive and rewarding find. It provides sources for *Edward VI and the Pope*. Two portions of the picture, the figure of the king in bed, and the inset of image-breaking, are both derived from Heemskerck. The originals are not in the Josiah series, but in two other Old Testament histories, both of which were drawn by Heemskerck in the 1560s. As I think there can be no doubt that our picture was conceived and executed as a whole on the basis of these pictorial sources, we have to redate it. The panel must be at least twenty years later than 1548. It is not an Edwardian, but an Elizabethan picture.

In 1564 Philip Galle engraved a series of eight drawings that had been made by Maarten van Heemskerck the previous year illustrating *The History of Esther*. Each print was accompanied by a Latin legend, summarizing the biblical story, written by the humanist Hadrianus Junius. We know he was the author since the lines were later to be published in the posthumous book of his verse (*Poematum Liber Primus*), produced over twenty years after Junius's death by his grandson, in 1598.

The sixth print in this series illustrates the moment, described in Esther, chapter 6, at which King Ahasuerus, unable to sleep, has his book of annals read to him (fig. 48). 'On that night could not the king sleep, and he commanded to bring the book of records of the chronicles; and they were read before the king'. English Bibles explained to their readers that the Hebrew word for the king's insomnia, thus described at the beginning of chapter 6, meant literally that 'the king's sleep departed' or 'fled away'. The words which were read out to Ahasuerus told how Mordecai had forestalled the plotting of the king's treacherous chamberlains (Esther, 2: 21–23). This did not help to restore his slumber. For Ahasuerus, learning how his life had been saved, also learned that Mordecai's faithful service had not been rewarded, and ordered the faithless Haman (who was himself plotting Mordecai's downfall) to tell him how this could be put right, and honour properly bestowed on the king's saviour. Junius's caption to the print distils this section of the story. 'Consulting the annals, and recognizing the faithful

Consulit annales, fido præeunte anagnoste,   *Rex, ubi non habitum virtuti discit honorem.*

deed, the king learns about honour from a quarter unfamiliar with virtue'.[79]

The print shows the king lying in a richly upholstered bed. He is propped up against a pile of pillows and bolsters, one hand resting on his knee while the other gestures towards the standing reader with the open book. At the centre, immediately behind the reader of the chronicles, a large square bedside table, covered with a cloth, butts up right against the king's bed. The curtained bed is covered with a patterned counterpane scalloped along its edges, and turned back at the corner to reveal the ornamental bedpost. Two servants approach up steps from the left side of the scene. Just visible behind them, outside, stands the gallows which Haman has prepared for Mordecai, acting on the persuasion of his wife and friends. 'Let a gallows be made . . . and tomorrow speak thou unto the king that Mordecai may be hanged thereon . . . And the thing pleased Haman; and he caused the gallows to be made' (Esther, 5: 14).

If we compare this scene with our painter's delineation of Henry VIII (colour pl. I and fig. 49), there are a number of striking resemblances. The Tudor king has a simpler nightcap, short beard, and his nightgown is fastened with jewelled aglets, unlike the pendant on the breast of the Old Testament monarch.[80] But Henry

leans against his pile of gilded pillows in exactly the same posture as
Ahasuerus, one hand on knee, the other outstretched. In Henry's
case the gesture is no longer a demonstrative open palm, but a
pointing finger. The bed curtain, drawn back in a curving swathe
behind this gesturing hand, is the same in both cases. Heemskerck's
scene has dictated the layout of the entire left side of our picture. The
central perspective of Edward's dais follows exactly the line of the
steps up which Ahaseurus's servants are approaching. The cushion
lies on the floor by Ahasuerus's bed at the same angle as Edward's
foot-cushion. Even the scrolls of the royal chair could have been
suggested by the legs of Ahasuerus's bedside table. Also striking is
the resemblance between the scalloped edge of the bedcover and the
very distinctive detail of the bedpost – the sphinx jutting out
through the turned-back cover.

However, the entire scene is reversed. This does not invalidate the
argument for Galle's print as our painter's source. But as Heemskerck's drawing, from which Galle made his engraving, is still extant
(fig. 50), we can and should consider the possibility that our artist
had seen the original. Heemskerck's drawings for the Ahasuerus

69

*50. Heemskerck's drawing of
King Ahasuerus, signed and
dated 1563.*

series were done in 1563 (the date in this case is inscribed on a step at
the extreme right of the drawing, which also bears the artist's
signature).[81] Careful comparison of drawing and print shows that
Galle was so true to his original that, when it comes to the
borrowings I have just described there is little to choose between
them. We may observe, however, though this does not affect the
appearance of our painting, that the gallows in the distance are much
clearer in the print than they were in the drawing.

I turn now to our picture's inset of iconoclasm. Here the debt to
Heemskerck is even more unmistakable. Given Heemskerck's pen-
chant for portraying collapsing buildings, his taste for 'towns,
towers, and sad ruins',[82] there is a certain appropriateness in finding
him to be the source for the most un-English-looking details in this
part of our painting. The main features of the scene are taken from
The Destruction of the Tower of Babel, one of a collection of
biblical disasters. These were engraved by Philip Galle, first as a

INVENTIONES HEEMSKERKIANÆ   EX VTROQVE TESTAMENTO.

51. Title-print of the second edition of the Clades series, celebrating Heemskerck – alter nostri Saeculi Apelles – and repeating images from his 1553 self-portrait (above, fig. 37). Philip Galle after Heemskerck, 1569?

series of twenty-one *Clades* which may have appeared in 1568, and then probably in 1569 with an added title-print as *Inventiones Heemskerkianae ex utroque testamento* (fig. 51). The new title-print (for which the drawing was made in 1568) repeats the portrait bust and doppelgänger sketching ruins from Heemskerck's 1553 self-portrait (fig. 37). It here became a monument to the seventy-year-old painter, 'Apelles of our age'.[83]

The Destruction of the Tower of Babel (fig. 53), which is the fourth in the *Clades* series, is filled by the dramatic collapse of a great ziggurat tumbling leftwards and away from the spectator. At the top, a huge rounded piece of masonry crashes inwards, while on the left-hand side the jagged hook of a broken arch (one of Heemskerck's characteristic details) hangs suspended. Below, a pedimented door-way lurches forwards; an obelisk lands on its tip, while tiny figures gesticulate helplessly on the diagonal steps. The foreground is dominated by a classical column surmounted by a flaming urn; its base, decorated with a swag, has an entrance doorway with steps leading into it. Among the buildings on the left the largest has classical features, including pilasters. In this case, again, Heemskerck's original drawing (dated 1567) survives (fig. 52), so that we can assess the accuracy of Galle's copy. His fidelity is impressive, though there is one rather conspicuous detail which he omitted. In the drawing a bent figure is just visible disappearing up the steps of the pedestal under the column. In the print the steps are empty.

52. *The Destruction of the Tower of Babel. Heemskerck's drawing, dated 1567 under the lion, with a figure Galle omitted entering the base of the column.*

53. *The Tower of Babel crashes to the ground. Yet the foreground, with its group of departing workmen, remains calm and the tall column is apparently not in danger. Philip Galle after Heemskerck, Clades series.*

54. *Inset from* Edward VI and the Pope.

Comparing the inset in our painting (fig. 54 and colour pl. II) with this print shows some faithful copying. Certain features are carefully reproduced by our painter. The rounded chunk of masonry at the top; the stepped corner of the ziggurat; the jagged half arch on the left; the tilting doorway and falling obelisk are all present in the condensed paintwork of our inset. Also there is the distinctive diagonal line that cuts across behind the upright of the column, as well as a suggestion of the classical building on the left. The column itself attracts attention. Its pedestal is closely copied (and without the figure that appears in Heemskerck's drawing). But the rest differs. In substituting a figure statue for Heemskerck's urn on the column our painter (as noticed above) has failed to attach the replacement convincingly to its pedestal. Although – as has also been observed – the copyist has mainly reproduced the black-and-white tones of his original, he has improved on it by adding touches of smoke and red flames at either side, to indicate the consuming fire which is engulfing the ruins.

If the *Tower of Babel* provides the setting, what about the action? Galle's print has nothing directly to do with iconoclasm – indeed it might seem as if presenting the Tower of Babel in this way was itself a violation of the biblical account. For the story in Genesis (11: 1–9 – Heemskerck wrote the reference on the step of the column in his drawing) tells of an unfinished tower, not a cataclysmically destroyed one. The generations of Noah, united with one language,

En molem ædificant animisque, opibusque parati, Vertice quæ nubes, et vertice tangeret astra.

aspired to build 'a city and a tower, whose top may reach unto heaven' in the plain of Shinar, but the Lord put a stop to this aspiration, confounded the builders with diversity of languages, and scattered them across the face of the earth. So they left off building the city. This city touching the sky, a gigantic tower built (as Genesis says) of brick, was quite commonly depicted. It often features in Bible illustrations, and paintings by Memling (*c.* 1485), by an anonymous sixteenth-century Flemish artist, and two pictures by Pieter Bruegel, are among the examples that show a colossal stepped tower, rising unfinished into the clouds.[84]

However, there was a link from the beginning between Babel and Babylon, between the great staged ziggurat at Babylon, in the land of Shinar, and the place of Babel, where Yahweh introduced confusion of tongues. So it was a natural development to associate the vast incomplete tower-city of Genesis with the mighty city that was thrown down with violence and annihilated in Revelation. 'Babylon the great is fallen, is fallen' (Revelation, 18: 2).

The collapsing mass of masonry copied by our artist was this Babel–Babylon. There are two related prints in the *Clades* series and they make this quite clear. Immediately preceding the destruction of the Tower of Babel is a print (no. 3) which shows the tower as it was, seemingly only moments earlier, in a more nearly complete state (fig. 55). Here we see the gigantic ziggurat rising into the clouds, with countless small figures toiling up the many diagonal staircases on its two visible sides. (The diagonal we have noticed behind the column in our painting represents two of these staircases swept bare of their climbers by the force of the collapse). The erect obelisks rise neatly at the corners. The nonchalantly proud figure of the king, Nimrod, stands defiant with poised spear as he does when disaster overtakes his city in the next picture. But this disaster is already imminent. Flames are gushing out of the rounded top of the tower, and the raging fire and storm send two huge tubes of broken masonry hurtling down on to the populated terraces below. A plume of smoke ('they shall see the smoke of her burning'; Revelation, 18: 9, 18), darkens the sky above the doomed building. The captions to both prints reinforce this interpretation. The words under number 3 paraphrase Genesis, speaking of the massive structure built starwards through the clouds; the text to number 4 takes up the theme of Revelation, and tells of the fall of 'high Babylon' as it shakes the earth and scatters its inhabitants. 'Alta cadit Babylon . . .'[85]

If, by the 1560s, the associations of falling Babylon with papal Rome were unavoidable, it is interesting to find in these two prints of Heemskerck what seems like a pictorial echo of the idolatry theme that so stirred northern Europe. The striking figure of the king, with plumed helmet, enormously long spear and arrogant stance, recalls the gigantic idol of Nebuchadnezzar as depicted about 1560 by Pieter Aertsen (*The Idolatry of Nebuchadnezzar*, in Rotterdam, fig. 56). This parallel is interesting in view of the fact that the legends that grew round the 'mighty hunter' of Genesis 10, not only credited Nimrod with responsibility for the building of the Tower of Babel, but also regarded him as the author of Babylonian idolatry.[86]

Heemskerck was far from being the first to depict the apocalyptic Babel–Babylon. The theme found fresh resonance with Reformation polemic against Rome, and a print of 1547 by Cornelis Anthonisz. – which may itself have been influenced by a woodcut in a Lutheran Bible of 1534 – illustrated the application of this terminal disaster (fig. 57). Angels trumpet divine judgement from the sky, and the masonry of the breaking tower is distinctly reminiscent of the Colosseum.[87] If the stricken Tower of Babel was the falling Babylon, the devastated Babylon stood (in many eyes) for the condemned Rome of the popes.

The theme of the fall of the Tower of Babel was therefore appropriate for a painting concerned with the fall of the pope – even though the modern implications of Heemskerck's print were less

obvious than Anthonisz.'s. And of course, our painter has 'updated' his source by adding the iconoclasts. In our inset scene, the two men toppling the carving from the column and the smaller figure axing a broken statue, take the place of Heemskerck's King Nimrod and the crowd of smaller figures heading away from the collapsing tower-city. Were these additions also borrowed?

This is certainly possible, and there was no shortage of models, in Heemskerck and elsewhere. It is relevant here to consider the techniques used in such destruction. Very high statues (or stained glass, or crosses) presented a problem to iconoclasts, who might decide that idols, when far removed from touch and sight, could be allowed to remain in place. Tall statues could be pulled down, but ropes had first to be secured on which the force of two or more men could be exerted (see fig. 39). The fourth scene in Heemskerck's

57. 'Babylon is fallen, is fallen'. Cornelis Anthonisz., Fall of the Tower of Babel (1547), shows the great tower-city of Babel (Genesis, 11) being struck by trumpeting angels (Revelation, 14) in a scene of general destruction. 'When it was highest | must it not then fall?' (inscription in banderole).

56. Pieter Aertsen, The Idolatry of Nebuchadnezzar. Princes, governors and people worship the colossal golden statue, while in the background Shadrach, Meschach and Abednego walk in the burning fiery furnace (Daniel, 3).

77

58. *Josiah breaks down and defiles the 'high places' Solomon had built for Ashtoreth, Chemosh and Milcom (2 Kings, 23:13–14). Philip Galle after Heemskerck:* History of Josiah.

EXCELSA QVOQVE QVE EDIFICAVERAT SALOMON ASTOROTH IDOLO SIDONIORVM ET CHAMOS OFFENSIONI MOAB/ ET MELCHON ABOMINATIONI FILIORVM AMMON/ POLLVIT, REX ET CONTRIVIT. 4. REG. 23. CAP

59. *Josiah 'took away the horses that the kings of Judah had given to the sun', at the entrance to the temple, 'and burned the chariots of the sun with fire' (2 Kings, 23: 11). Philip Galle after Heemskerck's 1569 drawing:* History of Josiah.

ABSTVLIT REX EQVOS QVOS DEDERNT REGES IVDA SOLI, CVRRVS AVTEM SOLIS COMBVSSIT IGNI. 4. REG. 23. CAP.

60. *Josiah's destruction of the vessels and priests of Baal (2 Kings, 23:4–5). Philip Galle after Heemskerck:* History of Josiah.

61. *Josiah sees Bethel's altar destroyed and defiled by a bonfire of dead men's bones (2 Kings, 23:15–16). Philip Galle after Heemskerck:* History of Josiah.

62. *Baal's image downed with
rope and pikes, and the priest
Mattan slain before his altar in
the thorough destruction that
followed the death of Athaliah
(2 Kings, 11). Herman Muller
after Heemskerck,* History of
Athaliah.

Balicolas sacris operatos maetat & aris   *Excisis populus de marmore signa refringit*   4

Josiah series shows such action, as the Judaic king supervised the
destruction of Solomon's idols to Ashtoreth, Chemosh and Milcom
(2 Kings, 23: 13; fig. 58 and above p. 61).[88] Here, inside a ruined
temple which is clearly based on the Pantheon in Rome, two men
strain on a rope, tight as a hawser, passed round the neck of an
imposing pagan statue.[89] A loose end swings from one pair of hands
as they pit their weight against the huge sculpture.

The stance of the two destroyers is, superficially, like that of the
iconoclasts in our inset (fig. 54), and another posse of rope-pullers
appears in the preceding print in the Josiah series (fig. 59), which
shows the horses 'that the kings of Judah had given to the sun' (2
Kings, 23: 11) being wrenched from their position on the portico to
a temple that is again based on the Pantheon. A painter well-
furnished with Heemskerck prints could have found plenty of
models for iconoclasts at work axing and felling statues, as Baal was
downed in *The History of King Josiah*, and elsewhere (figs. 46,
60–1). Other depictions show a combination of pushing and pulling.
In Luca Signorelli's fresco of St Benedict (colour pl. V and below
p. 92), four monks pull on two looped ropes (note the dangling
rope-end), while a fifth is pushing with a long wooden lance or pole.
Likewise the destruction of Baal's statue in Heemskerck's *History of
Athaliah* (fig. 62), has two men with pikes helping others with ropes.

Looking again at our iconoclasts with these examples in mind, we can see them pushing more clearly than pulling. The hatted man on the right holds a long pike, one end of which rests on the ground (no hanging rope-end here!) as he readies his weapon to thrust at the centre of the carving. His helper *might* have a taut rope attached to the top of the carving, but his stance could also be that of a pikeman ready to push. Perhaps this reading should send us back to the nonchalant Nimrod of the *Clades* (figs. 53, 55), with his spear resting on the ground.

It was Josiah who led us to Heemskerck, but it must remain an open question whether Heemskerck's *Josiah*, drawn in 1569, has any direct bearing on *Edward VI and the Pope*. However, it is now clear that the picture was designed with the benefit of two other Heemskerck prints, and these provide an indisputable terminus for dating. The use made of *Ahasuerus consulting the records*, drawn in 1563 and printed in 1564, and *The Destruction of the Tower of Babel*, drawn in 1567 and perhaps printed in both 1568 and 1569, place this painting in an entirely new context, which is explored in what follows.

These borrowings also help to explain some of the peculiar features noticed above. The disturbingly unlocated position of the king's dais may be accounted for by the fact that it started life as a table. The artist has moved Ahasuerus's bedside table downstage, as it were, to form the platform for the royal throne. Banishing the table legs, he added a row of tassels to disguise the lack of structural support. The cue for the tassels could have come from the bed canopy or tablecloth in *Ahasuerus consulting the records*, or from other depictions in the Ahasuerus series, two of which – *Esther preparing to intercede for the Jews*, and *The Fall of Haman* – show tables with just such fringes.[90] Our painter may not have been very adept, but he or she assembled borrowed images with a purpose.

BEDPOST AND COLUMN

We come now to two details, both of which are in effect clues for investigation. The bedpost of Henry VIII's bed, like the column in the inset remarked on earlier (p. 12), seems surprising in this context, alerting us to something unexpected that calls for explanation. I am not the first to have sensed this.

Twenty years ago a writer in *History Today* suggested that the style of the chair of state on which the young king is seated was anomalous for a picture of 1548. He thought that the 'scroll arms' and 'cabriole legs terminating in volutes' were like mid-Georgian furniture and, noting at the same time that the plinth and column of the inset scene were 'not remotely Gothic in style', concluded that the painting as a whole was a piece of eighteenth-century antiquarianism.[91]

Both observations are just, but there is no need to jump to such a conclusion. In the first place there is nothing unusual about representations in the 1540s of grotesque ornamentation containing classicizing foliage and figures, in settings with arches and columns — witness illustrations in both manuscripts and books. The illuminated initials of letters patent showed both Henry VIII and Edward VI in such renaissance or mannerist frames. In one of these illuminations of July 1547 (fig. 64), Edward VI is seated on a throne surmounted by two putti in front of a renaissance colonnade, while above a larger

63. Edward VI in Council. Detail from title-page of Edward Halle's Chronicle, The Union of the two noble and illustrate famelies of Lancastre and Yorke, printed in 1548 by Grafton and re-used for several other publications up to 1585. Compare with fig. 65 and colour plate 1.

64. *Illumination of Edward VI in letters patent of 1547 relating to a mill in Essex that had belonged to the hospital of St Thomas Acon. On the king's left the last Augustinian master, with his tonsured brethren, is handing over their cartulary. On the other side stand fashionably dressed courtiers, probably including the duke of Somerset.*

65. Henry VIII in Council.
Metal-cut by Jacob Faber after
Holbein, from Edward Halle's
Chronicle (1548). This was re-
used (and better printed) in
Foxe's Book of Martyrs in 1570
and 1576. The female monsters
below are a mixture of sphinx
and mermaid.

God ſaue the Kyng.

cherub dances with wreaths in some accomplished strapwork, to
form the frame for this portrait.[92] Woodcuts of this decade (models
of a kind for our painting) showing Henry in council, and the young
king being presented with a book by John Bale (figs. 65, 67), indicate

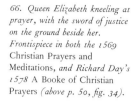

66. Queen Elizabeth kneeling at prayer, with the sword of justice on the ground beside her. Frontispiece in both the 1569 Christian Prayers and Meditations, *and Richard Day's 1578* A Booke of Christian Prayers *(above p. 50, fig. 34).*

that in the artist's eye – whatever the current models of royal thrones – scrolled legs and sphinxes were in fashion.[93]

In the second place, now that we know the picture cannot have been painted before the late 1560s, when decorative strapwork and ornamental grotesque designs were commonplace, there is even less reason for such objections. The opening page of the book known as Queen Elizabeth's Prayer Book (1569, fig. 66 and above fig. 34) is like a carpet-page with strapwork scrolls and feathery volutes on which female figures perch, metamorphosing into branches, while

85

*67. John Bale presenting
Edward VI with a copy of his*
Illustrium maioris Britanniae
scriptorum summarium,
*hopefully dedicated to the king in
1548 at the time of the author's
return from exile. Note the
carved ornament on the throne.*

cherubs adorn the ornate prayer-desk before which the queen kneels on a tasselled cushion.[94]

Nevertheless Henry VIII's bedpost sphinx is an arresting detail. Shiny with gilding, it is placed immediately above the heads of the retreating friars – a peculiar, perhaps deliberate juxtaposition. The sphinx (in its various forms) was part of the repertoire of fantastic grotesque ornament with which print-makers had been experimenting for years, as well as featuring in emblem books. Hadrianus Junius, for example, in his *Emblemata* of 1565 explained the dual nature of the sphinx – simultaneously leonine and virginal, fierce feet and mild face – as a symbol of God, who has to be both loved and feared (fig. 68).[95] Whether or not the irony was intentional, in the picture of Edward VI the golden triple cross of God's broken representative on earth is pointing directly at this emblem. Henry

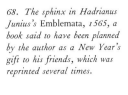

48   EMBLEMA XLII.

Deum & ama & time.

Mysteriis addicta Memphis æde pro sacra
Sphingem biformem dedicauit, symbolum Dei.
Amato numen ceu piis mite, ac placabile:
Rursus time, vt vindex inexorabile impiis.

εἶξας

VIII, whose bed is supported by it, would not have minded the associations for himself. But we must cheat him of that pleasure.

This sphinx, as we now know, started life adorning the couch of an Old Testament king. The painter who copied Heemskerck's view of Ahasuerus, gave quite a close rendering of the heavy ornament at the corner of the bed, with draped head, protruding breasts, and scalloped edge (colour pl. I and figs. 48–9). Only the lion foot,

87

Heemskerck's biblical bedposts and Old Testament grotesques. Details from figs. 71, 48 and 70.

concealed by the friar's head, has to be inferred. Heemskerck made quite a speciality of beds with mythical beasts as corner posts – often using sphinxes. He seems to have felt that this detail lent a note of authentic regal antiquity to historical bedroom scenes – specially biblical ones. A variety of these grotesques with breasts and clawed feet appeared in his drawings of scriptural beds and were engraved between the late 1540s and the 1560s by Coornhert, Muller and Galle (figs. 69–71). Heemskerck's Joseph making his rapid getaway from Potiphar's wife (Genesis 39), left behind as silent witnesses not only his incriminating garment, but also the staring grotesques who peered out from the corners of the furniture, just like Henry VIII's glinting sphinx. Holofernes lost his head (as Heemskerck drew it) in a bed rather like Ahasuerus–Henry's.[96] Henry VIII's bedpost, so striking in the vocabulary of Tudor furniture, so naturalized in Heemskerck's Old Testament domesticity, might on its own have led us to the Dutch source.

88

69. Joseph escaping from Potiphar's wife. Dirck Volckertsz. Coornhert after Heemskerck, in The History of Joseph, *1549. (Fitzwilliam Museum, Cambridge).*

What about the 'Virgin and Child' on the column? What was the model for this? Why did our artist, if he (or she) was content to follow Heemskerck for so many other matters, alter his copy in this respect? As we have seen, this figure was a replacement – and rather a clumsy one at that – of Heemskerck's urn, on the top of a monument which stood erect and apparently unscathed during the fearful final moments of the crumbling Babylon (figs. 52–5). Faithfully copying this classical pedestal, including the torus of the column which itself is now narrower and unsettlingly off-centre, the painter of the inset substituted for the urn a standing female figure. At the same time the

The King's Bedpost

70. Joseph and Potiphar's wife, from The Ten Commandments; *Herman Muller after Heemskerck. (Fitzwilliam Museum, Cambridge).*

71. Judith beheading Holofernes. Philip Galle after Heemskerck, Story of Judith and Holofernes, 1564. (Fitzwilliam Museum, Cambridge).

OBTRVNCAT REGEM. SOMNO TEMETO QVE SEPVLTVM, HINC COMITE ANCILLA, PATRIAM, DISCEDIT AD VRBEM.

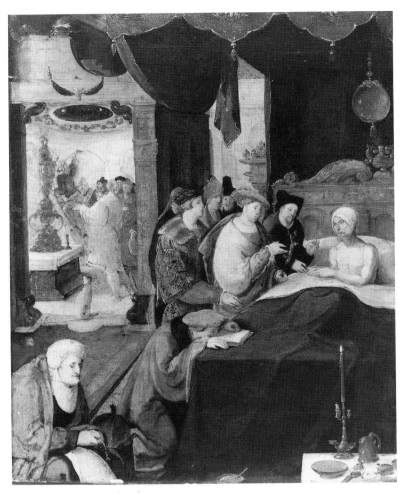

altar against which Nimrod leans in Heemskerck's print, was moved back and its lion replaced with what appears to be a broken relief with figure carvings. On either side of the scene lie two (remarkably similar) fallen statues. All this deliberate alteration was clearly done for a purpose, possibly for a very specific purpose. What might it have been?

The figure on the column (unlike the urn) was a self-proclaimed idol. There is no doubt about this, for it was a well-established iconographic convention to depict idols in this way. There are countless examples in manuscript illuminations, paintings and murals, which show that a figure, human or otherwise, placed on top of pillar or column, represented the illicit face of imaging. The 'idols'

91

73. *Pilgrims surround Erhard
Heydenreich's 1516 statue of the
Virgin and Child at Regensburg.
Part of Michael Ostendorfer's
woodcut of the Schöne Maria
pilgrimage, c. 1520.*

of the later middle ages were made visible in a continuing, if
subverted, pagan tradition.[97] Likewise, the saints who made a stand
against pagan worship are shown contributing to the fall of free-
standing figure statuary of this kind.

In the background of a fresco of St Benedict evangelizing the
inhabitants of Monte Cassino, painted in the 1490s by Luca
Signorelli in the cloister at Monte Oliveto Maggiore in Tuscany
(colour pl. V), a group of monks is shown on the point of toppling a
statue of Apollo: the idol is a free-standing figure on a column,

placed on an altar inside an arcaded temple.[98] Nearer home there is a
painting (of about 1525–30) at Hampton Court, of *St Sebastian and
the priest Polycarp at the sickbed of the Prefect Chromatius* (fig. 72). St
Sebastian (like St George) was celebrated for his stand against pagan
idols, and in this painting too there is an inset scene of an idol being
destroyed. Again it is a free-standing carving on an altar, in this case
an ornate gilded statue placed under a ceiling painted with sun, moon
and stars.[99]

It was rare for Christian saints to be represented in this way, as
free-standing statues, on independent pedestals or bases. But there
are examples. A manuscript illumination suggests that the shrine of
St Edward at Westminster may have included free-standing figure
sculpture, while another illustration shows a Virgin and Child on top
of a column being painted by an artist balanced on a ladder.[100] At
Regensburg, outside the pilgrimage chapel of the Schöne Maria with
its miraculous painting, there stood (from about 1520 until 1544) a
stone carving of the Virgin and Child on a column.[101] (fig. 73) And
in Spain there was the famous Virgin of the Pillar at Saragossa,
devotional likenesses of whom came to include pendant jewels of
Our Lady standing on her column.[102]

The painter of the Edward VI inset, despite the departure from his
or her original, was making a point that Heemskerck would have
understood. The idols proscribed in scripture, which Old Testament
monarchs like Josiah had dealt with so effectively, were three-
dimensional, and to present them in classical forms could be an
oblique way of addressing Roman idolatry, both past and present.
Was the figure on the column Diana? Or was there some more
familiar allusion?

We are left with a number of conundrums. Why would anyone
have wanted to depict Edward VI in this way fifteen years or more
after his death? Who in England might have had such seemingly
intimate knowledge of Maarten van Heemskerck's designs? Is there
anything original in the picture at all – or is it rather a pot-pourri of
copied sources? Might there have been some reason why its texts
have vanished? To answer these questions (or to try to) we shall
have to start another tour of exploration. This one must take us on to
the reign of Elizabeth, to which the painting, as we now know,
belongs.

To begin with we need to consider a rather broad general question. To what extent were Elizabethans bothered about idolatry, and in what terms did they think of it?

The removal or destruction of church images was a continuous feature of the Reformation in England. The issue assumed new dimensions from the moment that Luther's theses of 1517 placed a huge question mark over the charitable validity of the papal rebuilding of St Peter's. Rome could be seen as unchristian in more senses than one. The changing face of antipathy to Rome expresses much of the development of the Church of England. It served its purposes for Henry VIII, and it was a strong force in the time of Queen Elizabeth.

It became commonplace for opponents of church images to view them as the equivalent of pagan idols. The ancients had worshipped Venus and Diana, Hercules and Mercury, seeking particular services from particular deities. Christians, infected by this example, had come to do no better, setting up statues to individual saints and looking to them for assistance and remedies as if they themselves had spiritual power. 'No difference at all between a christian man and gentile in this idolatry, saving only the name', wrote John Hooper in 1548.[103] Thomas Becon made the same point at much greater length early in Elizabeth's reign, producing a catalogue worthy of an iconographer of the various insignia of the many 'puppets' that 'stuffed' the churches of papists, holding in their hands everything imaginable from sword or sceptre to butcher's knife or basket of flowers. 'I think verily, that in the temples of the old pagans there was never found so much vanity and so many childish sights, as there be at this present day in those churches which are under the yoke and tyranny of that bloody bishop of Rome'.[104]

Things moved fast and far from the wit and tolerance of Erasmus. He too saw the analogy between Roman gods and Christian saints, but he did not believe you could break human habits by breaking objects. He was capable of writing with a twinkle in his eye about Saint Roch or Saint Anthony taking the places of Apollo or Aesculapius as helpers in times of sickness, or Saint James and Saint

Margaret receiving prayers once offered to Juno and Lucina for fertility or successful childbirth. Such teasing allusions were altered by the course of events. The many earnest men who concerned themselves with releasing their contemporaries from the deadly sin of idolatry were deeply shocked by Christian uses of images that seemed to them rank paganism, and they acted on their sense of revulsion. They became distanced from Erasmus, who had found no serious objection to converting the superstitious 'coursing around with torches' in memory of Proserpina's abduction, into processing with candles for the Purification of the Virgin.[105] Such an approach became sheer anathema.

When Wycliffe suggested that women worshippers treated sump-tuous gilded statues of the Virgin Mary like the great goddess Diana he was anticipating many sixteenth-century critics.[106] By the acces-sion of Elizabeth there was no doubt, in a great many devout minds, that the practices of the Roman Church amounted to paganism. This is what the 1563 Homily 'against peril of idolatry' had to say about 'the idolatrous opinions of our image-maintainers':

What be such saints, to whom, contrary to the use of the primitive church, temples and churches be builded, and altars erected, but Dii Patroni of the Gentiles' idolaters? Such as were in the Capital, Jupiter; in Paphus temple, Venus; in Ephesus temple, Diana; and such like . . . When you hear of our lady of Walsingham, our lady of Ipswich, our lady of Wilsdon, and such other; what is it but an imitation of the Gentiles' idolaters? Diana Agrotera, Diana Coryphea, Diana Ephesia, &c.[107]

The commonest, most venerated images, were damned by refer-ence to ancient practice. James Calfhill, writing soon after the publication of the *Homilies*, called church roods 'counterfeits of Serapis', comparing them with idols of Egypt, set by east windows to catch the glimmer of the morning sun.[108] No analogy seemed too bad to this generation of image-haters.

Reginald Scot devoted a section of his *Discoverie of Witchcraft* (published in 1584) to comparing the idolatrous gods of the Romans with 'our antichristian gods' *alias* popish idols. It seemed to him that the latter greatly outnumbered the former. These specialized helpers, for every nation, town and village, 'hee idols and shee idols' for men and women, some for beasts and others for birds, rivalled all the gods proscribed in the books of Kings and Chronicles. 'For everie heathen idoll I might produce twentie out of the popish church'.[109].

The fact that popes themselves had had serious reservations about the 'idols of the ancients' made no jot of difference to such northern

95

critics. If there were sixteenth-century Catholics who thought contemporary popes should follow the example of Gregory the Great and destroy such objects, and if the Roman curia itself conceded the dangers of admiring them, that had not prevented an entirely different approach to Christian imagery. The ruling of the Council of Trent proved to Scot that papists had adopted wholesale the 'conceipt of the heathen', by endorsing gross idolatry.[110]

Elizabethans were schooled, therefore, into thinking of erstwhile revered church images – carvings and paintings – as akin to the pagan statues of ancient Rome, and on a par with the idols downed by paragon kings of the Old Testament. They would readily have grasped the implications of our painting's inset scene. But how relevant was the picture's topic – the task of the dutiful Josiah – at the end of the 1560s, or later?

ELIZABETH AND ICONOCLASM

There was nothing remote about Rome, idols and idolatry, when Elizabeth I came to the throne in November 1558. Her sister Mary had seen to that. The reestablishment of papal authority had been accompanied by determined efforts to put imagery back in churches, and if some of the queen's subjects were happy to be able to bring hoarded objects out of their hiding-places, others were indignant at the mushrooming of old idols and the 'cock-sure' reaffirmation of huge new-made roods.[11] The new queen was looked to by a number of influential advisers to undo the work of the previous five years, and to banish, along with the pope, all the imagery that the 'Jezebel' Mary had either restored or helped to keep in place.

Much was achieved during the early months of Elizabeth's reign. Many church images, including the rood carvings on which Mary had concentrated attention, were destroyed and burned in London and elsewhere as the royal visitation, carrying the revival of reform into all parts of the country, took effect in the late summer and early autumn of 1559.

The queen, however, did not see eye to eye with ardent iconoclasts. We have no words of her own on the subject, but plenty flowed from the mouths and pens of others reflecting the reluctance of the Supreme Governor to shoulder this responsibility. Arguments about ecclesiastical imagery were by no means over when the royal visitors finished their work, and the topic became delicate, not to say embarrassing, in view of the queen's personal judgement and some of her own furnishings. She continued to keep a cross or (which was worse) a crucifix in a central position in her royal chapel. To some worthy purists that seemed an intolerable flouting of the law, tantamount indeed to flaunting an idol.

Private chapels, whether aristocratic, collegiate, or royal, were accepted, to some degree, as a law unto themselves, outside the range of normal ecclesiastical controls. But the royal chapel was in a unique and unavoidably public position. Its services were attended by the great and the good, including both visiting dignitaries and domestic courtiers, who observed narrowly and gossiped broadly about what went on there. The ceremonial of the queen's chapel was a kind of diplomatic lighthouse, whose smallest flashes travelled across international waters as signals of England's reforming course. Readings were being taken from the start of the reign and there was plenty to talk about for many years to come, thanks to royal obstinacy over the retention of the cross.

The Venetian ambassador reported to a correspondent in Mantua in May 1559 how England's religion was going to ruin in scenes of crucifix breaking and image defacing. He described how on Ascension Day, as the procession was winding round St Paul's accompanied by a large crowd, a rascally apprentice of some Protestant printer had seized the cross out of the hands of the cross-bearer and struck it several times on the ground, smashing it to pieces. Nobody had tried to intervene. The boy picked up the figurine (presumably the Christ) that had fallen from the cross and showed it to some women bystanders, saying that he was taking away the devil's guts. To the shocked Catholic reporter it was a portent of the disastrous change that the Elizabethan settlement seemed to have endorsed.[112]

On the other hand Catholic observers could derive hope and comfort from the queen's attitude. On 5 October 1559, when one of the queen's ladies was married in the royal chapel, Elizabeth personally directed that a crucifix and candles should be placed on the altar. This reportedly caused so much opposition from her chaplains and the council that the idea was temporarily dropped, though the queen got her way at the evening service on 7 October. According to Bishop de Quadra (envoy of Philip II), who reported these events to the bishop of Arras, the crucifixes and vestments whose use was to be observed in the queen's chapel were more significant for the future than the recent burnings of the same by the royal visitors. 'The fact is', wrote de Quadra, 'that the crucifixes and vestments that were burnt a month ago publicly are now set up again in the royal chapel, as they soon will be all over the kingdom . . .'[113]

Of course the queen was capable of deliberately confusing her public and private faces. Her chapel could be used to damp down some of the more overcharged diplomatic flashes. But it seemed at the time that her retention of the cross reflected some deeper preference. During the early months of 1560 it was driving some of Elizabeth's clergy into a fever of anxiety. How were they to remove this dreadful blot from the reforming landscape? If the queen remained adamant should they show iron resistance in return, even to the point of refusing to stay in office? 'Oh, my father, what can I hope for, when the ministry of Christ is banished from court, while the crucifix is allowed, with lights burning before it?' Thomas Sampson wrote to Peter Martyr in Zurich on 6 January 1560. Altars and images had been removed throughout the kingdom. But at court the crucifix and candles remained. 'And the wretched multitude are not only rejoicing at this, but will imitate it of their own accord'.[114] If the Church's Supreme Governor gave this lead there was no knowing what might follow. How could idolatry be eliminated?

These fears were not confined to church leaders. Towards the end of March 1560 a broadsheet was printed in London in the form of *A Prayer or supplycation made unto God by a yonge man, that he woulde be mercifull to us, and not kepe his worde away from us, but that the truth maie springe*. This prayer, purportedly the words of one John Pyttes, was in effect a plea to Queen Elizabeth to live up to the record of her father and brother in eliminating idolatry.

> Take away Idolatry, O lorde, let that no more upspring
> In this, O lorde, thy poore and symple lande.

Henry VIII of 'moost famous memorie', who abolished the bishop of Rome from England and broke the habit of pilgrimage, had 'plucked down much idolatri'.

> Even as Esechias was unto Judae
> So was Kynge Henry unto Englande
> Unto this Kynge, O lorde, compare we
> Edwarde the syxte whom thou hast in thy hande.

True to God's word, Edward had 'brought doune all' and was 'like to that vertuous kinge Josias' – apart from the lamentable shortness of his reign. The broadsheet expected as much fidelity to scripture in Queen Elizabeth; 'Nowe in her time as before hath bene, / By her godly Father and brother'.[115]

The pattern of Edward/Josiah was still very relevant. This was precisely the message that was conveyed, probably at about this time, in an address prepared for the queen's consumption by members of the ministry. This 'humble petition' renewed a suit already presented on several previous occasions. In gathering together (on the same lines as the 1563 Homily against idolatry) the scriptural case against imagery, it directed Elizabeth's attention to the opposition shown to church images both by contemporary bishops, and her own forebears. The queen was left in no doubt of the godly patterns she should follow in purging the polluted Church.

The entire, remarkably outspoken, case was fenced in, with a modicum of tact, by familial reminders of 'the worthy examples of the godly princes which have gone before'.

> We most humbly beseech your Majesty to consider [they concluded], that besides weighty causes in policy, which we leave to the wisdom of your honourable councillors, the establishing of images by your authority shall not only utterly discredit our ministries, as builders of the things which we have destroyed, but also blemish the fame of your most godly brother, and such notable fathers as have given their lives for the testimony of God's truth, who by public law removed all images.[116]

The pressure was on. The suit of the Young Josiah continued.

By early April 1560 it seemed as if the crisis was over. A committee of bishops met to debate the question of images, and the iconomachs felt they had won it. Edwin Sandys, the bishop of Worcester, was mightily relieved. His vehemence about the matter was such that (he reported) he nearly lost office as well as gaining the queen's displeasure for opposing her view that roods were not unscriptural, and might be beneficial in churches. In a letter to Peter Martyr, Sandys recorded his thankfulness that God had ended the rumpus and 'delivered the church of England from stumbling-blocks of this kind'.[117] He was unduly optimistic.

THE QUEEN'S IDOL

Queen Elizabeth did not make a good Josiah. She failed to see to that total 'cleansing' of church imagery so much desired by those Zeal-of-the-land Busies who were all agog to pull down 'this idolatrous grove of images, this flasket of idols'.[118] She capitulated over the contentious rood imagery, giving orders in 1561 for rood screens (whose images had been destroyed in many parishes in the early months of the reign) to be dismantled, leaving only a 'comely partition' between nave and chancel. But the idolatrous condition of cathedrals, private chapels, and imagery remaining in other churches long continued to vex purists like William Fuller, who addressed the queen on this matter in 1585. In particular Fuller was incensed by the dreadful example set by royal chapels, which still sported images of the Trinity, saints and apostles, and most offensive of all was the placing of 'that foule Idoll the Crosse' on 'the altar of abhomination'.[119]

This sore vexed many before Fuller. The queen's obstinate refusal to allow her purifying subjects to dictate the form of her chapel furnishings became a *cause célèbre*. The cross and candlesticks in the queen's chapel were a point of contention when Elizabeth was at odds with Archbishop Grindal in the 1570s, and the topic was still being harped on in controversial writings in the 1580s.[120] It had provided a number of highly embarrassing, well publicized incidents. The matter refused to lie down, and Elizabeth showed herself impatient of the various attempts to school her. Some of these attempts were quite remarkable.

In 1564 an English exile living in Louvain published at Antwerp a book dedicated to Elizabeth. John Martiall (1534–97), whose adherence to the old faith took him abroad to study divinity, boldly addressed his *Treatyse of the Crosse* to the English queen

knowing youre Maiesty to be . . . so wel affected to the crosse . . . that youre Maiestie have always kept it reverently in youre chappel, notwithstanding many meanes have bene made to the contrary, by the privy suggestions, and open sermons of such, as without order of lawe, or authoritie geven by expresse commaundement from youre Maiestie (as it is thought) have in al churches, chappells, oratories, high wayes, and other places of youre most noble reaulme, throwen downe the signe of the crosse, and image of oure saviour Christ, and in most despiteful manner abused it, and in common assemblies have caulled it an Idol, and kepers of the same idolatours.[121]

This was the prelude to a self-styled 'little treatise' defending the cross and other images by reference to scripture, the fathers, and church councils.

Martiall's work was a red rag to bullish English iconoclasts. There was a predictable reaction and various combatants entered the ring to flourish their defence of England's probity in the matter of church imagery. James Calfhill, Lady Margaret Professor of Divinity at Oxford, published a long reply in 1565. It showed his dogmatic stamina, and gives the appearance of leaving few theological stones unturned. The queen's role was admittedly awkward. Calfhill did not sidestep this boulder, but reprimanded Martiall for misusing the queen's example. 'You have received from your Jove of the Capitol a Pandora's box, to present, (and God will,) to our Prometheus. But she, (God be thanked,) is too wise to credit you'. Elizabeth's favour to the cross was undeniable, but the deductions to be drawn from it were contestable.

As for her private doings, neither are they to be drawn as a precedent for all; nor any ought to creep into the Prince's bosom, of every fact to judge an affection. This can the world well witness with me, that neither her Grace and Wisdom hath such affiance in the Cross as you do fondly teach; neither takes it expedient her subjects should have that which she herself, (she thinketh), may keep without offence. For the multitude is easily, through ignorance, abused: her Majesty too well instructed for her own person to fall into popish error and idolatry.[122]

Many, however, thought otherwise, believing that this dreadful royal example would be a beacon for rekindling idolatry. Some were more tactful (or devious) than others in the methods they chose to admonish the head of the Church. A colleague of Calfhill's, Alexander Nowell (Dean of St Paul's while Calfhill held a prebend there), burnt his fingers badly more than once in flares of regal displeasure. The dean actually tried to preach to the queen about John Martiall's book, on Ash Wednesday (7 March) 1565. What folly! Elizabeth was furious. 'Do not talk about that', she interrupted. Unhearing, the preacher preached on. The queen's rage mounted. 'Leave that; it has nothing to do with your subject, and the matter is now threadbare'.[123] Nowell was barely able to complete his address, and was borne off in dismay to be comforted by Archbishop Parker. It was a sorry scene, but one cannot help thinking that he ought to have known better.

In one way this affair shows that worriers like Calfhill and Nowell were right. For Elizabeth's anger — whether or not revealing in itself — was read as an encouraging sign of her loyalty to the cross. Another Catholic divine who addressed a dedication to the queen this year, took heart from the snub to Dean Nowell. Thomas Harding, in his *Confutation* of Jewel's *Apology*, was thankful for Elizabeth's 'constant bearing and upholding of the banner and enseigne of our redemption (the image I meane of Christ crucified) against the enemies of his crosse'. He was fortified by 'your princely word commaunding a preacher, that opened his lewd mouth against the reverent use of the crosse in your private chappell, to retire from that ungodly digression unto his text of holy scripture'.[124]

Poor queen! The governorship of the English Church was just as burdensome as supreme headship, when there were so many conflicting views about the welfare of souls. And lay people as well as clergy felt it their duty to issue royal reminders. A 'zealous gentleman' of Gloucestershire, Richard Tracy of Toddington, wrote anxiously to William Cecil on 17 April 1565 about the peril the queen was placing herself in. The queen's secretary must know how God commanded his people in scripture 'to destroy all the pyctures' and break all the images, threatening damnation on all who failed in this duty: 'all which terryble thretenynges and horryble curses be easely escaped and avoyded, yff the quenes magestye wyl destroy hyr ymages'. Tracy made clear that God did not except the magistrate from this law, and that it was particularly offensive to place images on an altar and light tapers to them. 'Y am therefor so bolde to put your honour yn rememberance that these holy scryptures threten the ymages and the ymage makers' — as well as the worshippers. Cecil's path was plain. He must 'preserve the quenes hygnes from greate perel, off goddes wrath and dyspleasure'.[125]

Cecil saw the matter rather differently. In 1565 the diplomatic channels with Austria and France were being kept open for the dangling prospects of Elizabeth's marriage alliance. Details of the queen's religious observance, on which so many eyes were glued, had their part to play in the international scene. One can only believe what one sees, remarked the Spanish ambassador, Canon Guzman de Silva, on 26 April 1565. But he was keeping his ears as well as his eyes open. He had reported home to King Philip five days earlier

74. Lead cast of Steven van Herwyck's medal of Elizabeth, inscribed:
ELIZABETH.D.G.AN/GLI/AE.
ET.HIBE/RNIAE.R/EGINA.
Reverse; Faith seated beside a fountain.

how, at the Maundy Thursday ceremony on 19 April the queen had done something that delighted him as much as it grieved others who were watching. After washing the feet of the poor women Elizabeth had deliberately traced out a very large and well-defined cross, and then kissed it.

A miniature attributed to Levina Teerlinc (colour pl. VI) – which may be of this very Maundy – shows the queen just as the ambassador described her, dressed in the customary black, with a head-dress decorated in pearls and precious stones. Accompanied by her courtiers (also wearing black), she is moving towards the line of waiting women, her white apron ready for the foot-washing. Afterwards, the ambassador took the opportunity to congratulate the queen on this demonstration of devotion to the cross. Elizabeth (not slow to use this advantage) replied: 'Many people think we are Turks or Moors here, whereas we only differ from the Catholics in things of small importance'.[126] It was exactly six weeks after Dean Nowell's ill-conceived sermon.

The queen's readiness to demonstrate that not all English believers were cross-breakers, shuddering at the idea of even making the sign of the cross in the air, made headline news in 1565. It was a diplomatic bonus that Cecil himself helped to exploit. He was consulted about the production of a portrait medal that was made this year, designed as a political statement, very likely sponsored by the French ambassador (fig. 74). The obverse shows a half-length profile of Queen Elizabeth, with an inscription that pointedly omits the claim to France that was usual in the royal title of an English monarch. The reverse shows a figure of Faith, seated at the foot of a fountain, with a Greek anagram by Charles Utenhove that reads

75. The figure of Faith, with cross and book, was inscribed below: 'Ob fidem persecutio et crux' – 'Persecution and cross on account of faith'. Dirck Volckertsz. Coornhert after Heemskerck, 1550. (Fitzwilliam Museum, Cambridge).

alternately 'Elizabeth the Queen' and 'divine fountain of the realm'.[127] The sole attribute of the small female Faith is a large cross, which she clasps with both hands. The symbol was conventional (fig. 75), but the context might have lent its own meaning. Catherine de Medici (who soon after this was offering her knobbly-kneed teenage son, Charles IX, as a potential bridegroom for Elizabeth), was to be made aware that the English queen did not share the ruthless aversion displayed by some of her subjects towards the central symbol of the Christian faith. Her Faith was not one in which the Book had become a weapon against the Cross.

This anxious time – anxious for some at least – in the spring of 1565, was several years before the earliest possible date at which our picture could have been painted. But the story of the queen and the cross does not end here. For if Elizabeth showed consistency in her stance, the pain of a troubled conscience continued to embolden her critics. It is a measure of their powerful sense of divine mission, the feeling that God was commanding them against all earthly odds, that some individuals were prepared to take iconoclasm right into the queen's chapel. There could surely be no higher forum for such a demonstration. Who were the Elizabethan Polyeuctes who so bravely undertook to destroy the idols in the royal pantheon?

The first of these occasions was in the summer of 1562, when (as related by Bishop Parkhurst of Norwich) the cross and candlesticks in the royal chapel were broken to pieces and, reportedly, reduced to ashes. Initial delight on the part of the reporter quickly turned to dismay. The offending items were soon back in place, though with the concession that the candles were no longer lighted.[128] Five years later the cross and candlesticks were again attacked, this time in the middle of a service. This latter incident (on 25 October 1567) coincides in date with one of the sources of our painting, and brings us towards the earliest possible date for its composition.

On this occasion the queen thought fit to divert the argument for a time. The items of altar furniture were replaced by a tapestry of the crucifixion — not that such an image, hung over the place of consecration, would have dulled the objections of rigid iconoclasts. (What about that biblical note [above p. 45] on Josiah's removal of the picture of a grove 'which was hanged in the temple'?) In any case, this was only a temporary measure. By 1571 the queen's chapel cross was back in place. Consciences continued to be troubled and the tattling talk went on. Some of those in high places evidently considered that it was useless to look to the archbishop of Canterbury for help in this affair. He was even thought to be on the wrong side — abetting the queen's error. Parker wrote rather sorely to William Cecil on 6 February 1571:

But, sir, as I came yesterday from you I was informed that one nobleman in England should impute it to my doing that the cross is brought into the chapel again, so that I perceive they will load me with envy; but certainly I never knew of it, nor yet in good faith I think it expedient it should be restored. And therefore I think *est modus in rebus*, *&c.*, not too much to exasperate my heart.[129]

The archbishop did not name this nobleman. But one who might be a candidate for his charge is Sir Francis Knollys. Well-known for his reforming convictions, he had spent Mary's reign in exile at Basel and Frankfurt. Knollys's wife (Catherine Carey) was the queen's first cousin; she died at Hampton Court in January 1569, in attendance on the queen. Sir Francis, who was Treasurer of the Chamber at that time, became Treasurer of the Household in 1570 – a post which he held until his death in 1596. In October 1559 Knollys wrote from court (he was then Vice-Chamberlain) to Archbishop Parker, wishing him 'prosperity . . . in your good enterprise against the enormities yet in the Queen's closet retained'. Also, according to the much later reporting of Peter Heylyn, it was Sir Francis who incited the queen's fool, Patch, to the 'desperate service' of breaking the cross in the queen's chapel in 1570. Certainly some years later Knollys put together a series of *Argumentes against the crosse and surplice*, which condemned the cross as 'a monumente of superstition and idolatry', contrary to the queen's injunctions.[130]

Another possible candidate for the derring-do in the royal chapel is the queen's favourite, Robert Dudley earl of Leicester. According to the Spanish ambassador, Guzman de Silva, in 1565, Dudley saw to the removal of an image from the queen's chapel, contrary to her own orders.[131]

The disputes did not stop there. In the next decade, when Archbishop Grindal was in trouble with the queen over his refusal to suppress the prophesyings, the list of 'thinges not merely indifferent', that he regarded as rebutting the adiaphoran argument, was headed by two examples of church crosses. 'Diverse churches of Germanie professing the Gospell and having roodes in their churches'; and 'The crosse and candlestickes in the Q. Chappell'.[132]

These events may seem a far cry from the picture of the young Edward VI. But this digression had a purpose. For it has shown that the anxieties concerning England's unfinished reform that had made Edward into Josiah in 1547 were still acute a generation later. Queen Elizabeth's failure to give the pure iconoclastic example that some looked for, ensured that the pattern of the young Josiah survived as a propagandist device to guide, urge or threaten the governor of the Church. God must 'illuminate the queen's heart', as in times past he had moved the minds of godly rulers for the true reformation of religion, 'whom he inflamed with the zeal of his glory, as Hezekiah, Josias, and other princes'.[133] One magistrate must persuade another.

LONDON'S IDOL

On 19 February 1547, the day before his coronation, Edward VI made a processional entry into the city of London, passing as he did so along Cheapside. The tall Eleanor Cross there had been regilded for the occasion, and the throngs of spectators dressed in their city best, who lined the route and clustered in the windows to watch the young king ride past under his canopy, had plenty to look at as they waited. Among the sights were various tapestries hung on the house-fronts, one of which (appropriately enough) was of St George killing the dragon. Another was of the Annunciation.[134]

There was nothing unusual about this event. Royal entries of this kind were traditional, and it was also traditional for the city authorities to see to the regilding of their major monument as part of their welcome for a new monarch.[135] What is unusual for us about Edward's entry is the fact that we can see it, thanks to an eighteenth-century engraving of a contemporary painting that was destroyed by fire six years after S. H. Grimm made his drawing of it. This engraving (fig. 76), the central section of which shows the king just about to pass Cheapside Cross, enables us to make out something of the three tiers of statues that ornamented what was probably a hexagonal structure. The figures included bishops and kings in niches, with smaller statues projecting on the angles. There was also a standing Virgin, holding the Child in her left arm, in the central section, and at the very top was a cross.

Given its wealth of religious imagery, and its conspicuous place – albeit a wholly secular setting – right at the heart of the city of London, it is a matter of some surprise that Cheapside Cross remained in place until 1643. It was then pulled down with considerable fanfare, and the site was used thereafter for anti-popery bonfires in the capital. Part of the sense of achievement in this event derived from the fact that by the 1640s the monument had been the focus of objections for generations. The protests centred on the imagery of Christ and the Virgin.

The case against the cross in Cheapside seems to have been building up for over seventy years. To begin with (according to John Stow, our main source for these events), some Londoners

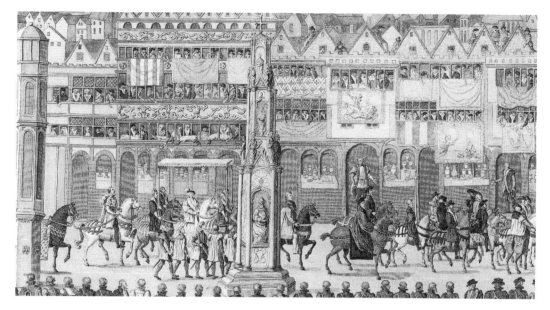

76. Edward VI processing past Cheapside Cross on 19 February 1547, from James Basire's 1787 engraving. The Virgin and Child in the niche of the central tier, and the statue above (? Christ), may be compared with the column statue in fig. 54.

attempted to argue – a line of persuasion that now has an all too familiar ring – that the monument obstructed the traffic. Various juries stated that the cross stood 'in the high way to the let of carriages (as they alleged), but could not have it removed'. Then, in the summer of 1581, some nocturnal iconoclasts seized the initiative.

The 21st of June, in the night, certaine young men, drawing ropes thwart the streete, on both sides the Crosse in Cheape to stop the passage, did then fasten ropes about the lowest Images of the said Crosse, attempting by force to pluck them downe, which when they could not doe, they plucked the picture of Christ out of his mother's lap, whereon he sate, and otherwise defaced her, and the other Images by striking off their armes.[136]

A proclamation was issued offering a reward for information about the offenders, but Londoners kept their counsel, and the image-breakers were not discovered. Stow's description of what happened suggests a scene like some of those illustrated above (figs. 58–59). 'The image of the blessed virgin, at that time robbed of her son, and her armes broken, by which she staid him on her knees; her whole body also was haled with ropes, and left likely to fall ...'

Some repairs were made in 1595, when the Virgin was secured and given a new Christ child – ill-formed, according to Stow, and leaving the other carvings still broken. But on the east side of the cross, beneath the carving of the resurrection, there was erected a tabernacle of grey marble, containing 'an image alabaster of Diana', with Thames water 'prilling from her naked breast'.[137]

What sort of compromise was this between old and new paganism? Many minds — too many for effective action — became focused on the problematical iconography of London's leading monument, and in the last decades of the sixteenth century the main issue came to be the cross at its summit. We can omit that part of the story. What is interesting for us is the prolonged dispute over this Virgin and Child, and the queen's role in protecting the monument.

Elizabeth was certainly not prepared to allow iconoclastically minded Londoners to have their way. In July 1581, when the city authorities were deliberating about the repairs to Cheapside Cross, she intervened and summoned a delegation of aldermen to hear her views. Again in both 1595 and 1600, she issued express directions for restoration, including the cross at the top (which some people wanted to replace with a pyramid), having 'most princely care' for 'the antiquity and continuance of that monument', and 'not approving that weaknes' — as it was put on the latter occasion — 'in any men that will take offence at the historicall and civill use of such an ancyent ensigne of Christianitie'. Such 'weakness' was certainly shared by the city's mayor in 1595, who put the case that in view of the idolatrous worship shown to Cheapside Cross by passers-by, any repairs and redecoration of the monument might give encouragement to seminarians and others engaged in factious enterprises. Popery, faction, and imagery: a familiar triangle of associations, which is relevant to our enquiry.[138]

But action continued to flout instruction. After the queen's insistence, at the end of 1600, the cross was duly repaired and gilded, and the carvings cleaned. Then, twelve nights later, 'the image of our Lady was again defaced, by plucking off her crowne, and almost her head, taking from her her naked child, and stabbing her in the breast, etc'.[139]

Could this long-lasting saga have some bearing on the supposed Virgin and Child in our painting (colour pl. II, fig. 54 and p. 73)? Cheapside Cross certainly presents us with an extremely well-known example of such an image, still standing intact (off and on), as so few Virgins in churches were allowed to be, after the spasms of image-breaking at the start of both Edward's and Elizabeth's reigns. And though not a statue on a column, this Virgin did form part of a free-standing monument with carvings set on attached columns.

We know, too, that purists were voicing hostility to the cross as

early as 1572. For in that year Edward Dering (fig. 77) made an attack on the 'idol' of Cheapside in the preface to a catechism which was to have a wide circulation. He proposed that it would be singularly appropriate to have a bonfire of cheap fiction, the distracting chapbook lives of saints and heroes which took readers into 'the idolatrous superstition of the elder world', in Cheapside, using 'that gorgeous Idoll', the cross, as the 'fyt stake for so good a fire'.[140]

Edward Dering lived up to his name. He dared much in plain speaking. The beneficiaries included both the queen and the duke of Norfolk, the latter of whom he served as chaplain in the late 1560s. One particular sermon, which Dering preached before Elizabeth on 25 February 1570, went several steps too far. Taking as his text words from Psalm 78, 'He chose David ...' Dering proceeded to give the queen a résumé of deficiencies in the Church, specially its ministry, for which she was responsible, praying that the Lord would 'open the Queenes Maiesties eyes'. 'Take heed ... take heed'. The preacher did not believe in diluting divine injunctions on 'the duetie of a Prince' with tact. 'I will not with many words admonish your Maiestie that are wise enough', he declared. But admonish he did. The queen was called in no uncertain terms to be 'zealous as good king David, to worke his will'.[141]

Naturally idolatry featured in this lecture. The godly kings of Judah showed correct ways of implementing God's law. 'It made Asa drive away the Sodomites out of Israel, put downe the Idols ... It made Ieosaphat, Ezechias, Iosias, even in the beginninge of their

111

raigne, to make godly and zealous reformations in Religion, and never consulted further with the hie priest'. The high hopes of events in 1547–8 and 1558–9 had been followed by disillusion. Innuendo compounded insult, and Queen Elizabeth was incensed. Dering's career stopped in its tracks, and he died in 1576 unpreferred (despite his learning and excellent connections), controversial as ever, and well-read by those of puritan sympathies. Elizabeth was unforgiving. Archbishop Parker reported in March 1575 that the 'other day at the court her Majesty disliked Deering's reading'. Edward Dering himself long suffered the penalty of the queen's being 'provoked against mee to high displeasure'.[142]

It is impossible to know whether Edward Dering's words helped to inspire assaults on Cheapside Cross. Certainly, it would not be surprising, given the way events developed, had London's 'gorgeous Idoll' and its provocative Virgin been seen as enjoying the patronage of the Virgin Queen.

ELIZABETH AS HEZEKIAH

In a well-known incident Queen Elizabeth is reported to have said to William Lambarde, 'I am Richard II. Know ye not that?' She might also have said, just as tartly, 'I am Hezekiah. Don't tell me *that*'. In the cast of Old Testament regal prototypes, the queen had her special model, just as her brother had his.

Hezekiah was to Elizabeth what Josiah was to Edward: the pattern of the purifying, iconoclastically purging monarch. To be sure the young queen was also Deborah and Esther (Hester), but she could not escape the mantle of the good king of 2 Kings and 2 Chronicles that had already been cast on her father. 'Good King Ezechias' was a model she soon learnt to be wary of.

Others took comfort from their Old Testament examples.

I think I may affirme that the good king Ezechias had noe greater desire to amende that [that] was amisse in his tyme, nor the noble queene Hester a better harte to overthrowe the mightie enemye to Gode's elect, then our soveraigne Ladye and Mistris hath to doe that that may be iust and acceptable in Gode's sight,

pronounced the Lord Keeper, Sir Nicholas Bacon, addressing Elizabeth's first parliament in January 1559.[143]

In the series of Old Testament kings who were such valuable prompts for Tudor monarchs, expected to implement the purifying code of divine law, Hezekiah seemed as apt a parallel for Elizabeth as Josiah had been for Edward. This model also becomes particularly interesting in the developing controversy over the use of the cross. For Hezekiah's history was closely linked with the typology and symbolism of the cross, which sixteenth-century reformers twisted into a new interpretation.

Hezekiah started his long reign at the age of twenty-five, succeeding a wicked predecessor.[144] The parallel with Queen Elizabeth was exact. 'Calculate her maiesties yeares when shee began her blessed raigne, and ye shall finde her thereabouts and not much under'. William Leigh (1550–1639) preached these words at the end of Elizabeth's rule, but his three sermons matching the queen with the great kings of Judah (David, Joshua and Hezekiah) were not published until long after the accession of James I. Leigh concentrated on the record of 'princely pietie'.

Ezechia at the very first tooke away the high places, and defaced the images, and cut downe the groaves, hee brake in peeces the brasen serpent, that Moses had made (for unto those daies the children of Israel did burne incense to it) and called it in contempt of that their idolatry no more a serpent, but Nehushtan, a peece of brasse.

Queen Elizabeth had purged England in just the same way.

What were your altars of stone but high places? And what were your roode loftes, celles, and shrines of saints, but groaves of superstition? What was all your imagerie, with lights, lampes, pax, and palmes, but grosse idolatrie? And whereunto England burned incense to the Queene of heaven till Elizabeth came, but then even at the first downe they went: and broke they were by her princely power, and warrantie, the carcasses whereof lye at this day, monumentes of popish idolatry, and of her maiesties blessed reformation with this disdaine, what are they now but stick and stone, and worse then Nehushtan, brused brasse?[145]

Elizabeth did not always seem like such a saviour. There were plenty of moments during her reign when it was necessary to remind her of this royal scriptural mantle. One such moment was that occasion in 1560 (above pp. 99–100) when members of the ministry drew the queen's attention to the zeal of 'good king Ezechias, who brake the brazen serpent and burnt it to ashes'.[146] Since the healing image of the brazen serpent prefigured crucifix and crucifixion, Hezekiah's destruction of Nehushtan assumed an alarming relevance.

The serpent of brass was made by Moses at the Lord's command (as recounted in Numbers, 21). The fiery serpent, set up on a pole, helped to cure the children of Israel of the poisonous snake-bites that were killing them, and all who looked at it were healed and survived. Christ's own words established this image as the Old Testament analogy of the crucifixion. 'And as Moses lifted up the serpent in the wilderness, even so must the Son of man be lifted up: That whosoever believeth in him should not perish, but have eternal life' (John, 3: 14–15). The brass snake, twisted round (or hanging from) the *tau* shaped pole, agent of bodily healing, prefigured the body of Christ hanging on the cross, source of spiritual salvation. Perhaps also the analogy came to extend to the benefits of *looking* – respectively at the image of serpent or saviour.

In Wolf Huber's *Allegory of Redemption* – or *Allegory of the*

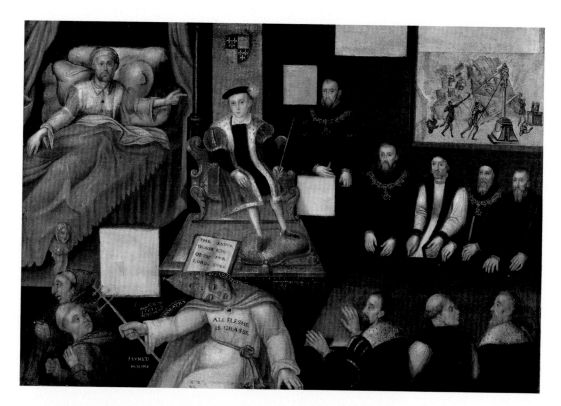

Plate I Edward VI and the Pope: An Allegory of the Reformation. *NPG 4165.*

Plate II Inset of image-breaking from *NPG 4165.*

Plate III The Memorial of
Lord Darnley, painted in 1568
by Livinus de Vogelaare (fl.
?1551–68), was carefully
designed to advertise the Lennox
cause. James VI (who had been
crowned, thirteen months old, on
29 July 1567) kneels in a
chapel surrounded by reminders
of his father's murder and texts
accusing his mother of
complicity, while his
grandparents – who
commissioned the picture – and
his uncle clamour for revenge.

Plate IV Inset of Mary Queen
of Scots' surrender at Carberry
Hill, showing the insurgent lords
holding their banner before the
queen, and the stages of the earl
of Bothwell's flight.

Plate V Iconoclasm accompanies conversion in this fresco of St Benedict by Luca Signorelli (1441–1523). While the saint preaches the gospel, seven monks (four pulling, one pushing) are busy destroying the pagan idol.

Plate VI Originally square or rectangular, and perhaps one of the artist's New Year's gifts to Elizabeth, Levina Teerlinc's miniature of the Royal Maundy (c. 1565), shows the queen with her ladies, wearing white aprons, in front of the lines of women whose feet she washed. At the back stand the choristers and gentlemen of the Chapel Royal.

Plate *VII* The Allegory of the
Tudor Succession, *celebrating
the peace and plenty of
Elizabeth's regime, was presented
by the queen to Francis
Walsingham about 1572 (dating
helped by her dress). Lucas de
Heere (1534–84), to whom the
painting has been attributed, fled
to England from Ghent c. 1566
and during his ten-year stay was
associated with those who
promoted the Protestant cause.*

Cross – of *c.* 1550 (Vienna, Kunsthistorisches Museum, fig. 78), Christ on the cross dominates the foreground while in the background Moses' serpent hangs limp on its cross-bar. The inscription below cites the words in Acts on Christ's saving power, which enabled Peter and John to cure a congenitally lame man (shown at the entrance to the Temple of Jerusalem, centre), 'And Peter, fastening his eyes upon him with John, said, Look on us . . . In the name of Jesus Christ of Nazareth rise up and walk'.[147]

Was there not also healing power in the images of the cross and of Christ crucified? 'As earthly water dropping downe is the lif of greene trees, so spiritual water doth flowe into the signe of the crosse, which is knowen to be the salvation off faithfull soules'. John Martiall quoted Cassiodorus at his English readers (Queen Elizabeth

79. Moses (centre) with the brazen serpent, surrounded by Peter, John, Jeremiah and Isaiah, all holding scrolls with biblical texts proclaiming the Passion. Central medallion of the 'Bury St Edmunds' cross. (The Metropolitan Museum of Art, The Cloisters Collection, 1963. [63.12].)

included) in 1564, to show how the sign of the cross had power, by faith in the merits of Christ's passion, to expel devils, destroy witchcraft, and cure diseases.[148]

Life-saving serpent and life-giving saviour both hung on a tree, and both were associated with the tree of life. The image of snake and tree (female and male) was an ancient fertility symbol. The symbolic wood of the 'asherah' belonged to the worship of Astarte or Ashtoreth, the goddess served by Solomon and put down by Josiah (above p. 61, figs. 41–2, 58). And the tree of life 'which is in the midst of the Paradise of God' (Revelation, 2: 7), was linked with the tree of knowledge that was agent of both Fall and Redemption, yielding in turn forbidden fruit and wood for the cross. A twelfth-century English ivory cross brings these associations together (fig. 79). At its centre, occupying a position which would have made it like a halo behind the head of the (missing) figure of Christ, is a medallion carved with the scene of Moses and the brazen serpent.

ISRAEL rebellis ſerpentibus ignitis percuſ
titur. Serpentem æneum pro ſigno erigit
Moyſes: quem cum percuſſi aſpiciunt ſaſ
nantur.

NVMERI XXI.

The four arms of the cross are themselves partly tree – a tree of life that looks more like thorn than palm.[149]

There are many illustrations (including woodcuts in Bibles) that show the life-giving power of looking at the brazen serpent. One such is in Holbein's *Icones*, the popular picture book which we have already encountered (above p. 40, and fig. 29).[150] The topic was deemed appropriate for a fireback, an example of which is to be seen in Queen Anne's bedroom at Hampton Court. More suitably, it adorned the front cover of a miniature girdle prayer-book traditionally believed to have belonged to Queen Elizabeth, that was made in the 1540s (fig. 81). The embossed and gilded scene of the brazen serpent is paired up with the Judgement of Solomon which appears on the back cover.[151]

There seems good reason to suppose that Elizabeth's view of the brazen serpent was traditional. Some of her subjects, however, no longer liked this association with the life-giving power of the cross. As far as they were concerned the brazen serpent was the prototype of the image which became an idol, and had accordingly had to be destroyed. They could not read Numbers, 21 without turning on to Kings and Chronicles, where the story of Hezekiah showed the proper destiny for an image abused by false worship. If the brazen serpent paralleled the cross, that likewise was an image which was

117

81. Enamel and gold embossed front cover of miniature girdle book (c. 1540, with text of Numbers, 21:8 as in the Great Bible of 1539 and 1540). There is no proof that this belonged to Queen Elizabeth, but c. 1575–80 the original contents were replaced by more Protestant printed devotions, including the only known example of a 1574 set of prayers.

idolized and therefore, in just the same way, ought to be broken to pieces.

For sixteenth-century iconoclastic reformers, the brazen serpent called to mind not so much Moses, as Hezekiah – the Hezekiah who restored the religion of Judah by his destruction of idols. In the Geneva Bible verses 8–9 of Numbers, 21 (describing Moses erecting the healing serpent, at the Lord's command) were cross-referenced to 2 Kings, 18: 4 and John, 3: 14. Turning to the former we find the passage on the destruction of the brazen serpent, with an interesting marginal note.

Hezekiah 'did that which was right in the sight of the Lord'. His record in destroying idolatry was admirable. 'He removed the high places, and brake the images, and cut down the groves'. He also saw to the destruction of the image which, though once divinely sanctioned, had fallen into abuse. He 'brake in pieces the brasen serpent that Moses had made: for unto those days the children of

118

Israel did burn incense to it: and he called it Nehushtan'.[152] The accompanying note on 'Nehushtan' reads:

That is, a piece of brasse: thus he calleth the serpent by contempt, which notwithstanding [it] was set up by the worde of God, and miracles were wroght by it: yet when it was abused to idolatrie, this good King destroyed it, not thinking it worthie to be called a serpent, but a piece of brasse.[153]

With the like fidelity to divine command (as they saw it), sixteenth-century reformers reversed reverence for the cross and crucifix. Miracles had been claimed for this image, but it had become irredeemably abused by false worship. Far from being the 'true cross', it deserved no better name than a stock or a lump of wood. It had to be destroyed on account of this idolatry, and Hezekiah's elimination of the brazen serpent was the model for what should be done. In the repertoire of Old Testament examples the brazen serpent's patterning of the true cross was overlaid by the pattern of the properly destroyed idol. Worship of the cross, Theodore Beza assured Bishop Grindal in 1566, was a horrible superstition, no more to be numbered among 'things indifferent' than the brazen serpent, whose destruction by Hezekiah was a most potent example for Christian monarchs to imitate, by overthrowing the idols of cross and crucifix.[154]

The example of the purifying king assumed new importance once Christian images came to be seen as idols. Hezekiah featured among the patterns of virtuous rulers chosen – it was said – by Beatus Rhenanus to inspire the councillors of the city of Basel as they deliberated in their new council chamber. Holbein, engaged on this work from the 1520s, might indeed have had mixed feelings as he planned the scene of *Hezekiah ordering the idols to be broken in pieces*.[155] Half a century later it was with similar moral intention that Sir Thomas Smith included scenes from the life of King Hezekiah in the murals that adorned his new house at Hill Hall in Essex.[156]

The Hill Hall paintings can be related to Bible woodcuts, and it is in Bible illustrations that we can see the development of the Protestant image of Hezekiah and the brazen serpent. The emphasis falls on idolatrous abuse, instead of the healing power of a divinely sanctioned image. A new iconography emerged, portraying the felling of the raised serpent – the prototype of the image turned idol – sometimes even showing the king himself at work breaking images. Such a woodcut appeared in a German Bible printed at

82. King Hezekiah seeing to the destruction of the brazen serpent. 1532 Strasbourg Bible: the king himself at work.

Strasbourg in 1532 (fig. 82), in which a left-handed King Hezekiah is busily at work in a scene of solitary devastation, giving the *coup de grâce* to the serpent on its altar, while other broken idols lie strewn on the ground beside him. More often the king is depicted directing the elimination of the serpent on its cross-bar, as in the woodcut by Jost Amman of 1571 and the etching by Matthäus Merian of 1630 (figs. 83, 85). This is also the case with Johann Teufel's cut in the 1572 Lutheran Bible, which – like the Josiah we looked at above – gives Hezekiah the features of Frederick the Wise (fig. 84, cf. fig. 30).[157]

Given this background, it is hard not to read religious motivation into the performance of Nicholas Udall's English scriptural play *Ezechias*, which was put on for Queen Elizabeth when she visited Cambridge in August 1564. It was a surprising choice, given that it was by a deceased author of the other university, written many years before, and it was the only English play put on during this visit for the queen's benefit – being performed in King's College Chapel, by

IIII. Regum XVIII.

Hiskia war ein König fein
Er ghorchet Gott dem HERREN sein/
Jn Juda stieß er nider bhend
Die Abgötter an allem end/

Den waren Gottesdienst fürwar
Richtet er auff frey offenbar/
Sennacherib mit Kriegs gewalt
Hiskiam vberzog gar bald.
S   IIII. Regum

83. Jost Amman's wood engraving of Hezekiah in Newe Biblische Figuren *(1579), with explanatory verses by Heinrich Peter Rebenstock. The illustration had already been used in a 1571 Frankfurt Bible.*

members of the college. The text, dating from the high period of Henry VIII's reform (probably written some time before 1540), was doubtless revised. Udall was then headmaster of Eton, a post which he left under a cloud in 1541, though he managed successfully to reconstruct his career, and died in 1556 as headmaster of Westminster School.

Nicholas Udall worked for Thomas Cromwell, and we know from his own words, written in 1549 to preface his translation of Erasmus's Paraphrase of St Luke's Gospel, his view of the Henrician Hezekiah:

84. Hezekiah in the 1572 Wittenberg Bible: note the fires prepared for other idols in the background.

his hyghnesse beyng our Ezechias, by the providence of God deputed and sent to be the destroier not onely of al counterfait relygious (who swarmed among us like disguised maskers ... and were mainteners of al supersticion, idolatry and rebellion) but also to roote up al Idolatry doen to dead images of stone and tymber as unto God ... And in this blindnes had England still continued, had not God of his infinite goodnes and bottomles mercy raised up unto us a new Ezechias to confound al idols ...¹⁵⁸

Udall's play does not survive. But we know a little about the production that Elizabeth attended on 8 August 1564. Abraham Hartwell (fellow of King's) described this occasion in ponderous Latin verse, and makes quite clear what theme was portrayed. The play opened with Hezekiah's destruction of the altars and shrines of the idolaters. The brazen serpent, abused by those who had strayed so far from Moses' law, was struck down; false religion was abolished and true observance set up in its place. The incensed heathen worshippers thereupon rebelled and overthrew (apparently on stage) the altars of Jehovah.

The drama delineated the opposing parties of the unenlightened priests, old women, old men and the rustic crowd, who supported old ways, who 'hate simple worship and unadorned prayers, where there is no noise and no procession', and those, younger and better educated, who had a wiser understanding of God. In the conflict that followed, the play continued in some form to follow the biblical narrative of 2 Kings, chapters 18 and 19, which tells of the threat to Hezekiah and Jerusalem posed by Sennacherib and the Assyrians – dramatic punishment for heathen rebellion.[159] Hezekiah was in deep affliction, mortally sick, and 'turned his face to the wall' (2 Kings, 20: 2). But his prayer was answered, the Lord delivered him and his city and added to the length of his days – a note of cheer and hope that the Cambridge players appear to have ended on.[160]

If it is right to set this revived production in the context of the controversy over the cross in the royal chapel, one can hardly suppose that Elizabeth would have felt complimented. The following evening, 9 August, King's College students were to have played for her a Latin version of a Sophocles tragedy, called *Ajax Flagellifer*. The queen went to bed. Was she tired? Or had she had enough? She had certainly been given her fill of learned allusions to reforming monarchs of the Old Testament, 'Ezechias' et al., and her programme that afternoon had consisted of a wearisome round of theological disputations on the authority of scripture and the civil magistrate in the affairs of the church.[161] Being preached at is not enjoyable, however skilful (or jovial) the presentation. Moreover, Hezekiah's history carried in it a dire warning. He had reached the brink of disaster.

Elizabeth knew all about this threat. It had already been spelt out plainly in various places. The dedicatory Epistle to the Geneva Bible of 1560 instructed the queen in her regnal duties, acknowledging the dangers involved. Royal zeal was called for, like that of the 'noble Josias', to 'roote oute, cut downe and destroy these wedes and impedimentes' that not only 'deface your building' but 'threaten the ruine thereof'. The marvellous diligence and zeal of Jehoshaphat, Josiah, and Hezekiah were examples to all godly rulers to reform their countries and establish the work of God with all speed, 'lest the wrath of the Lord fall upon them for the neglecting thereof'.[162] There was a clear 'you have been warned' notice at the top of the iconoclasts' cliff-face.

In the Bishops' Bible a few years later, a marginal note in 2 Kings, 18 held a special message for royal readers. This chapter was headed 'Hezekia king of Juda putteth downe the brasen serpent, and destroyeth the idols, and prospereth', and in the margin next verse 4 are the words 'It parteyneth to a good Prince to purge the churche of God'. Verse 4 contained the passage already discussed on Hezekiah's breaking of the brazen serpent. 'He put away the high places, and brake the images, and cut downe the groves, and all to brake the brasen serpent that Moyses had made.'[163] The first edition of this Bible, which was promoted as the official Bible of the Elizabethan Church (to take the place of the earlier Great Bible), appeared in 1568 – making it coterminous with the Heemskerck prints used by our painter.

The need to clear England's churches of their polluting images was a cause that continued to be preached throughout Elizabeth's reign. The queen's subjects were often addressed on this topic, sometimes in terms that included instruction in the duties of their church magistrate. Believers had obligations – and so had the Church's Supreme Governor. The third part of the 1563 Homily against peril of idolatry included some plain speaking on the lessons to be drawn from the examples of Hezekiah and Josiah.

The good king Ezechias did know well enough, that the brazen serpent was but a dead image, and therefore he took no hurt himself thereby through idolatry to it. Did he therefore let it stand, because himself took no hurt thereof? No, not so: but being a good king, and therefore regarding the health of his silly subjects, deceived by that image, and committing idolatry thereto, he did not only take it down, but also brake it to pieces,

even though this was an image set up by God's commandment, prefiguring Christ, in the presence of which miracles had been effected, and despite its great antiquity and preservation by many earlier kings.[164]

'I am Hezekiah. Know ye not that?' The godliest of magistrates would not risk keeping for his own use an image that might be idolized by his subjects. For Good King Ezechias read Good Queen Elizabeth, and the passage itself verges on the brazen. (QED: no cross for the queen.)

We read on. 'How, think you, would that godly prince (if he were now living) handle our idols, set up against God's commandment directly, and being figures of nothing but folly, and for fools to gaze on ...?' And what about the 'excellent king Josias', who had completely removed all such 'stumbling-blocks'? The state of the idols was abominable, infinitely dangerous to English souls, damning in the eyes of God. England's images were one with the 'idols of the Gentiles' prohibited in scripture. 'Wherefore God's horrible wrath, and our most dreadful danger cannot be avoided, without the destruction and utter abolishing of all such images and idols out of the church and temple of God, which to accomplish, God put in the minds of all Christian princes'.[165] Some of the devout, hearing or reading these words, prayed for action by the Tudor Hezekiah. Others tried more direct methods.

In this age of protest, being a protector and patron of the Church entailed knocking down in order to put up. The role of the royal destroyer was expounded in the most public and official places, including the first defence of Elizabeth's Church. John Jewel's *Apology of the Church of England* (which appeared in English in 1564, two years after its Latin birth) did not fail to draw on the examples of Hezekiah, Josiah and others, who had taken to heart God's earnest command to the king 'to cut down the groves, to break down the images and altars of idols'.[166] One of the prices one paid for being a monarch was this endless lecture by analogy. Jewel hammered on long after the first appearance of the *Apology*, which itself provoked extensive controversy. He prefaced a defence of his book (replying to an attack on it by Thomas Harding), with an address to the queen.

God evermore enflame, and directe your Maiestie with his Holy Sprite, that the Zele of his House maie thorowly devoure your Graceous harte: that you maie safely walke in the waies of your Father David: that you maie utterly abandon al Groaves, and Hille Aultars: that you maie live an Olde Mother in Israel.[167]

Some messages were more oblique than others. One would have had to be much less subtle than Queen Elizabeth to miss the cue. There seem to have been plenty of prompters, and the royal role remained the same – imperfectly enacted.

Clearly Josiah did not die with Edward VI in 1553. He remained in the wings with Asa, Hezekiah, Jehoshaphat, and returned to the boards when called for. One such occasion was in 1590, when a book was published with the following title: *The Reformation of Religion by Josiah, a commendable example for all Princes professinge the GOSPELL to followe. With a warninge to all faithfull and true-hearted Subiectes, to encourage theire Princes in so happie a course.* It was the old tale continued – a less than serpentine message to the godly prince, with a sting in its tail. Perhaps Elizabeth, now aged fifty-seven and with the wonders of 1588 so fresh in memory, was beyond wincing. But had she seen the book she might well have been more than annoyed at the outspokenness of its address. This was not the work of a man of tact, but a man of passionate conviction – the sort that made and metalled iconoclasts. Its prayer for the queen was a prayer that she keep her covenant with God, and act as the Christian Josiah by duly destroying idolatry and idolaters.

'Kings and Princes, Rulers and Gouvernors need to bestirre themselves' to deal with the rank idolatries and superstitions and abominations still remaining in England, like the 'filth' that had polluted Judah and Jerusalem: copes, surplices, rochets and tippets, the images standing in high streets, and the pictures in church windows. Remembering and reading how such wickedness pro-voked the anger of God 'may humble our Queen', as well as her nobles and subjects. The ways of the Lord were inscrutable. 'Who knoweth whether ... our gracious Soveraigne may not bee sud-dainly taken awaye in token of Gods whoote [hot] inkindled wrath against his people ...?' The cause of reform concerned everyone, both Houses of Parliament, the 'Fathers of the Countrie', the common people, but the pointing finger did not waver.

Shall we complaine of the great hinderers of this work that are informers and advisers in the Senate, or shall the faulte be all layde on Queene

Elizabeth, whom God hath set up in Josiahs place, as one not so willing and ready to this worke as Josiah was?[168]

One should start with self-accusation, but what could faithful subjects do but turn to prayer? Only God could move the hearts of princes, only he could see a maiden queen effect the estimable reformation of Josiah.

Forty years and more after Edward VI's reform, England's pagan idols continued to cause resentment. The admonitions of 1560 were still being preached at Queen Elizabeth a generation later. We may again seem to have moved a long way from Heemskerck and the painting of Edward–Josiah. But it must now be plain that even in the later years of Elizabeth's reign there were plenty of purifiers who would have accepted our reading of the picture − whether or not they were helped by an inscribed text from 2 Kings. Henry VIII/ Hezekiah (or Manasseh/Henry) points towards the young Edward/ Josiah and through him towards the falling Babylon and the breaking-down of idols. Josiah 'did that which was right in the sight of the Lord'; his 'exceeding zealous reforming of Religion'[169] in purging the land of idols was still a necessary spur. *Kings* still spoke to kings.

TUDOR GROUP PORTRAITS

Since Elizabeth was so often invoked to play a Judaic role, whether as Hezekiah to the young king's Josiah, or herself as another Josiah, could *Edward VI and the Pope* be a pictorial version of these many addresses? Was this too an oblique religious admonition calling for decisive action against England's remaining idols? In the years after 1568, to which the painting belongs, there were – as we have seen – plenty of anxious individuals who worried about the dangers of religious images given protection or house room by the queen.

But, it might well be asked, if this was a pictorial address to Queen Elizabeth, why does she not feature in it? Would not the suggestion have been more persuasive, as well as clearer, had the Supreme Governor herself been shown in the reforming context? To approach that question, it may help to look at some other Tudor group portraits. There are two examples of such family groups that are analogous to our picture in that they may be seen as delineating the Protestant succession of the Church of England. Both were painted in Elizabeth's reign, and both, unlike our scene, include the queen.

The *Allegory of the Tudor Succession* (at Sudeley Castle, colour pl. VII) attributed to Lucas de Heere (1534–84), and probably painted after the 1572 Treaty of Blois between England and France, was presented by the queen to her ambassador in Paris, Sir Francis Walsingham, who had played a leading part in these negotiations. 'THE QVENE TO WALSINGHAM THIS TABLET SENTE / MARKE OF HER PEOPLES AND HER OWNE CONTENTE', is inscribed along the bottom. The picture shows Henry VIII enthroned in the company of his successors; Edward VI kneels to receive the sword of justice from his father, while beside him Elizabeth enters commandingly, hand-in-hand with Peace (trampling on the instruments of war) and closely followed by Plenty. She dominates the right side of the scene. On the other side stand Mary and Philip, pursued by the threatening figure of Mars.

If this allegory appropriately celebrates the recently concluded treaty, it also expresses a religious message. The picture space is divided between the fatally warlike associations of the Catholic

Now Prudent Edward dyinge in tender youth,
Queen Mary then the Royall Scepter swayd
With foraine blood she mateht and put down truth,
Which Englands glory suddanly decayd.
Who brought in warr & discord by that deed,
Which did in comon wealth great sorow breed.

Beholde the figure of A Royall Kinge,
One whom sweet victory euer did attende:
From euery parte wher he his power did bringe,
He homewarde brought y Conquest in y end.
And when y fates his vitall thred had spunne,
He gaue his glory to A Vertuous Sunne.

But Sorow care & ciuill broyles lykewise.
This Sacred Queene ELIZABETH exylde:
Falshood did fall before her Gratious eyes.
And perticulation turnd to mercy mylde.
Plenty and peace throughout hir dayes are seene.
And all the world admyrs this mayden Queene.

Mary and her Habsburg husband, and the prosperous conditions accompanying the Protestant régimes of Edward and Elizabeth, towards whom Henry is turning. Yet this allegorical divide is not to be read as a rigid polarization of opposing states. That is made clear by the words of an explanatory verse inscribed on the frame.

A FACE OF MVCHE NOBILLITYE LOE IN A LITLE ROOME.
FOWR STATES WITH THEYR CONDITIONS HEARE SHADOWED IN A SHOWE
A FATHER MORE THEN VALYANT. A RARE AND VERTVOVS SOON.
A ZEALVS DAVGHTER IN HER KYND WHAT ELS THE WORLD DOTH KNOWE
AND LAST OF ALL A VYRGIN QVEEN TO ENGLANDS IOY WE SEE
SVCCESSYVELY TO HOLD THE RIGHT, AND VERTVES OF THE THREE.

Henry VIII was valiant; Edward VI was virtuous; but Mary also had her qualities — her own characteristic zeal. And the Virgin Queen who could now claim to be England's joy did not disown the state of her married Catholic sister, any more than those of her father and brother. She embodied and continued the best features of all three

86. *William Rogers' engraving, made some twenty years later, brought the* Allegory of the Tudor Succession *(colour plate VII) up to date both in the costume of 'This Sacred Queene' Eliʒabeth, and in the condemnation of Mary's Spanish marriage, the cause of 'warr and discord'.*

129

87. Tudor family group: Henry VIII, Edward VI and Elizabeth I, as 'defenders of the true Catholic faith' in 1597.

predecessors. That was the gist of this family portrait. Given Walsingham's decided sympathy for militant puritanism, should we read into the queen's allusion to her people's content some defence of the virtues of a broad-based religion?[170]

The subject was still topical at the end of Elizabeth's reign, when an engraved version of the painting was made (fig. 86). William Rogers' print of the *Tudor Succession* allegory was updated in several respects to suit the 1590s, including some new verses to take the place of the original inscription, with a much more explicit condemnation of Mary. The engraving was dedicated to the archbishop of Canterbury – John Whitgift.[171] The same decade also produced another Tudor group portrait, dated 1597 (fig. 87). This time Mary is absent, and the family circle presents, weakly, the three reforming monarchs of de Heere's painting. Clearly this is a depiction of the acceptable Protestant lineage of the English Church, prepared by or for someone whose view of Marian catholicism was unlike that of Queen Elizabeth. Her management of England's religion had to be rejected, excluded. The inscription declares as much. 'PROFESSORS. AND. DEFENDORS. OF. THE. TRVE. CATHOLICKE. FAYTHE.' We see Henry VIII, Edward VI, and Elizabeth, arranged in a descending line.[172] There was no room for Rome in this little room.[173]

Edward VI and the Pope is also a Tudor group — reduced still further, to the two male monarchs who held supremacy over the Church. But here we have a historical painting of a different kind, which allegorizes a particular scene or moment, instead of setting the generations together with a deliberate disregard for chronological time. Is Elizabeth, in whose reign this group was likewise painted, perhaps present by implication, as the contemporary holder of that supreme responsibility of ensuring the enduring life of the Word?

All these group pictures were Elizabethan — and all in some sense religious pictures. In their differing ways each justifies (or defends) the character of the English Church through the quality of its rulers. But they spoke with different voices: one with the queen's own voice; another with the Church of England voice that claimed to be catholic without Rome; and the last with the voice that so often preached to the queen. That in itself might explain her absence.

Was the group portrait of *Edward VI and the Pope* made for the queen's own eyes, to be read as a letter (or lecture) to herself, comparable to that address of the ministers sent to her early in her reign? Perhaps Elizabeth was not represented because she was present as recipient, the reader who was being transported back in time, on this occasion through images not words, to that moment when (above p. 34) the 'evangelical Josias, king Edward . . . purged . . . the true temple of the Lord'.

Reminding the queen about her princely duties as head of the Church was a hazardous business, as brave speakers like Alexander Nowell and Edward Dering discovered. Hence (other reasons apart) the value of biblical analogues. The hazards that applied to the pictorial address were perhaps even greater, given the queen's sensitivity about representations of her person, and the controls she placed on them. There was everything to be said for indirect approaches. And surely there could be no misreading of the evangelical Edward.

Nor was the queen the only person to be sensitive about royal portraiture. If Elizabeth was concerned about safeguarding the form of her depictions, others were worried about the context — specially

THE

New Testament of our Sauiour
Iesus Christ,

Faithfully translated out of the Greeke, with
the Notes and expositions of the darke
places therein.

Matthew. 13.
The pearle which Christ commaunded to be bought,
Is here to be found, not else to be sought.

EDVARDVS SEXTVS DEI GRACIA ANGLIE, FRANCIE, ET HIBERNIE REX. ET C. ÆTATIS SVÆ. XV.

Imprinted by the Deputy of Christopher Barker
Printer to the Queenes most excellent Maiestie.

as loyalties towards the Virgin Queen began to seem comparable to the worship of the Virgin Mary herself. The hazards of that cult may still have been in the future when in 1570, in the face of the papal threat, Elizabeth's subjects began to celebrate her accession day, but even so there were purists who deemed it inappropriate for any

*89. Princess Elizabeth,
attributed to William Scrots,
c. 1546–7. Possibly the picture
of his sister that was painted at
the request of Edward VI about
the time of his accession.*

living mortal – even the Supreme Governor of the Church – to be
represented in the book of God's word. In 1568 Queen Elizabeth had
occupied a place of honour in the title-page of Archbishop Parker's
new Bible (the so-called Bishops' Bible). But by the mid-seventies
the royal features had been driven from this place of scriptural
honour, and they did not return. Yet throughout Elizabeth's reign,
the woodcut bust of Edward VI (fig. 88) was to be found gracing the
title-page of the New Testament as it had done during his lifetime.

133

Was this an accident of survival, or did the role of evangelical Josiah help to sanction this privilege?[174]

In any event, whatever reminders his features were supposed to bring, Elizabeth was fond of Edward. Brother and sister (four years apart in age) had shared a mutual affection. It was in response to the young king's request, probably a few months after his accession, that Elizabeth sent Edward her newly painted portrait, wishing she was 'oftener in your presence' (fig. 89). She was nineteen when he died, and treasured his memory. Twelve years later, when in September 1565 she stood as godmother to the infant son of Princess Cecilia of Sweden (the Marchioness of Baden), Queen Elizabeth chose the name 'Edwardus Fortunatus'.[175] Elizabeth also owned a jewel which had specific associations with Edward. A tiny girdle-book with gold inlaid covers, which passed as an heirloom into the family of the queen's cousin, Lord Hunsdon, contained in manuscript the last prayer of the young king, made three hours before he died of tuberculosis on 6 July 1553.

These final words, reportedly muttered to himself by the dying king, bring home how closely his fate was linked to England's anti-papalism. 'O my Lord God defend this realme from papistrie, and mainteine thy true religion, that I and my people maie praise thy holie name'.[176] Wearing these words next her person Elizabeth endorsed a tradition that was under threat when Edward breathed his last in the summer of 1553.

THE FALLING POPE

The anti-papal theme may help to throw more light on the composition of our painting. The search for pictorial sources is by no means finished by the finding of the Heemskerck prints.

Part of the picture we have not yet considered is the lower central section showing the pope collapsing at the king's feet under the pressure of the 'WORDE OF THE LORD'. The pontiff, whose discomfiture is expressed in his down-turned mouth and hooded death-like eyes, still bears what Henry Bullinger called the 'fatall badges' of his office: his triple cross and triple crown – signifying his unique claim to triple lordship, as king, prince and emperor with spiritual power over earth, heaven, and purgatory.[177] There is no doubt that he, and all the trappings of his office, are on the way to exile. Two freshly tonsured religious (one fat-faced, the other beak-nosed), possibly representing the Franciscans (grey friars) and Dominicans (black friars) whose dependence on the holy see made them specially vulnerable to condemnation as papal agents, are heading off the scene in the corner, anxious to make their getaway. They are pulling on chains, which join beside the label marked 'POPS' (popes), and then disappear behind the papal tiara under the royal dais. Clearly this effort to topple the young king is destined to fail.

The reasons for the pope's fall are inscribed around him. The words 'IDOLATRY' and 'SVPERSTICIO[N]', inscribed on the lappets of the tiara, encircle the pontiff's head and shoulders; 'FEYNED HOLINE[S]' appears below his right hand, and 'ALL FLESHE IS GRASSE' stands prominently on his chest. Immediately above is the open book that holds so critical a position in the composition. It rests at an angle (pictorially rather unconvincing), partly propped up on the king's cushion, pressing against the pope's head over the edge of the dais, as if its very weight was pushing him down.

The concept of the word of God as weight was in fact current at the time. Foxe's Book of Martyrs included in the 1576 edition (the third) an illustration showing Justice (blindfold) weighing the word of God (fig. 90). *Verbum Dei* is on one side of a pair of scales, attended by Christ and his disciples. On the other side are the papal decretals, with pope, cardinal, bishop, friars and others (including a

90. *The weight of the Word.*
Verbum Dei *proving itself
against the Decretals in Foxe's*
Acts and Monuments, *1576.*

clinging devil) vainly trying to correct the balance by throwing a
miscellany of crosses, rosaries and other 'vanities' in with their light-
weight law. This is headed: 'A lively picture describyng the weight
and substaunce of Gods most blessed word, agaynst the doctrines
and vanities of mans traditions'.[178]

The power and weight of the Gospel drives the empty chaff of
papal claims down and out of the reformed kingdom. The word
endures; flesh withers. The two adjacent texts come from the same
biblical sources. 'The worde of the Lord endureth for ever' – *verbum
autem Domini manet in aeternum* – Isaiah's words, quoted by St
Peter, were a central motto of reformers. We find them inscribed on
coins and medals in reformed German cities, starting with an issue of
1522 by Luther's protector, Frederick the Wise of Saxony (fig. 91).

The new life of purified souls, born again by the everlasting word
of God, stands contrasted with the transitoriness of the body.

1 Peter, 1: 24 For all flesh is as grass, and all the glory of man as the flower
of grass. The grass withereth, and the flower thereof falleth
away:

25 But the word of the Lord endureth for ever. And this is the
word which by the gospel is preached unto you.[179]

We can link this part of the picture with two themes that were
familiar (even commonplace) in Tudor iconography: propaganda

against the pope, and the monarch's divine role as dispenser of the word (on which more shortly).

Henry VIII fostered anti-papal imagery in various art forms. A new year's present to Catherine Howard in 1540 was a tablet of gold, one side of which showed 'a feyer ballas and the pycture of the busshopp of Rome ronnying away lamentyng, and divers persones one settyng his fote upon the busshop overthrowen'.[180] The king's picture collection included a number of anti-papal items, from which little survives – thanks at least in part to the Catholic loyalty of his daughter Mary, for whom imagery of the destruction of Rome itself needed to be destroyed. Delineation of her father 'standing upon a miter with iii Crownes having a serpent with vii hedds going owte of it, having a sworde in his hand wherein is written Verbum Dei' would not have appealed to this loyal restorer of the papal allegiance. It is on record that the 'physiognomy' of Henry VIII at Westminster Palace, 'painted in a table, like an antique', was broken 'because it was the destruction of the Bishop of Rome'.[181]

One item from this early Tudor propaganda art which still remains in the royal collection shows an old theme being turned to new use. The stoning of the blasphemer (a topic with a long pictorial history illustrating Leviticus, 24) was turned into the stoning of the pope by the evangelists. The 'table of the busshopp of Rome and of the foure Evangelists casting stones upon him' that hung in the long gallery at Hampton Court in 1547, hangs in this palace today, now identified as a work of Girolamo da Treviso, an Italian painter who was in Henry VIII's service between 1538 and 1544 (fig. 92). The pope, surrounded by the menacing figures of the four evangelists, is shown falling forwards, landing heavily on a mixed collection of Roman insignia. Hypocrisy and Avarice (YPOCRYSIS and AVARA,

*92. The allegory of the four
evangelists stoning the pope,
painted for Henry VIII by
Girolamo da Treviso, and
inventoried in 1547. If the
steady flame of the candle over
the city (? Rome) represents the
light of the gospel, the
overturned candle under the
cauldron in the foreground stands
for the extinguishing of false
doctrine.*

labels like those in *Edward VI and the Pope*, on what seem to be collapsed bodies of monk and nun) fall with him. Clearly this picture, as Roy Strong long ago suggested, is thematically connected with our painting.[182] The connection may go no further than that.

Imagery of this kind was also to be found under Edward VI. The pope and cardinals featured in disparaging roles in court revels at the beginning of the reign (in which the king himself had a long gown for his attire as a priest).[183] Walter Lynne's *The beginning and endynge of all popery, or popishe kyngedome*, a translation from the German of prophecies of Joachim of Fiore, appeared about 1548. The book (which was reprinted in 1588) included, besides a derivative series of fairly crude anti-papal woodcuts, a more accomplished title-page showing the pope smitten by the spirit of the Lord (fig. 93). This scene of the stricken pontiff, crashing to the ground from his caparisoned mule, still grasping his cross while losing his tiara, is a reminder of the ongoing tradition of Reformation iconography to which *Edward VI and the Pope* belongs. Another comparable depiction is Hans Sebald Beham's woodcut of *The Fall of the Papacy* of about 1525 (fig. 94). This pope too is toppled by the divine word, which strikes as arrows of biblical text, targeting cardinals, bishops and all the papal clergy. And here, as in

And then shall that wicked be vtte=
red whom the lord shal consume with
the spirite of his mouth, and shal de=
stroy him with appearaunce of his cō=
mynge euen him whose comminge is
after the workinge of Sathan.

93. *The pope, with attendant
cardinal, bishops and friars,
struck by the spirit of God's
mouth – a dove descending like
lightning from the celestial
tetragrammaton. Title-page of*
The beginning and endynge of
all popery, *c. 1548.*

our painting, are figures pulling on ropes attached to a throne, but in
this case clergy and princes (perhaps Charles V and his brother
Ferdinand) are trying to sustain the papal throne.[184]

Walter Lynne's dedicatory epistle, addressed to Edward VI and
the duke of Somerset, enlarged on the false claims of the bishop of
Rome, expressing the hope that the young king would continue to
build on his father's godly work. Perhaps this helped to inspire the
'little treatise' against the primacy of the pope which Edward
composed in French, and presented to the duke in August 1549.[185]

Of course there was plenty to say on anti-papal themes. But in
1548–9 (unlike 1538, when the pope's excommunication of Henry
VIII led to an invasion scare) England's reforming government did
not seem threatened from abroad. The difficulty, which we have
noticed above, that the downing of papal authority was not of
serious moment at the start of Edward's reign, evaporates with our
new dating. For the years 1569–70 marked a critical turning-point in

139

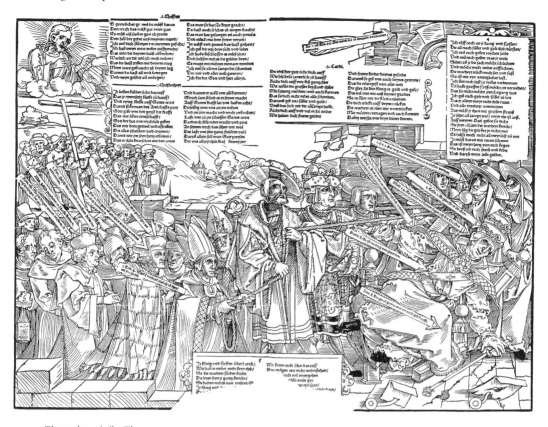

94. *The word as missile. The pope falls under a shower of scriptural arrows, his throne supported by princes and prelates. H. S. Beham*, The Fall of the Papacy, *c. 1525.*

England's relations with the holy see. It was now that Elizabeth's Protestant régime was advertised to the world (as Henry VIII's had been thirty years earlier) by official severance from Rome. On 25 February 1570 Pope Pius V sealed the bull *Regnans in excelsis*, which excommunicated the English queen and released her subjects from their allegiance. If *Edward VI and the Pope* was some kind of *pièce d'occasion* ten years after Elizabeth's accession, that occasion is most likely to have been timed by this bull.

The 'mad and beastly bull', as the chronicler Richard Grafton called it – 'stuffed full of most horrible treason' – certainly brought the pope and anti-papal feelings to the forefront of English consciousness in the summer of 1570. Since England lacked the Lutheran tradition of virulent visual propaganda, Pius V was not lambasted (as he was, for different reasons, at this time in Germany) in popular imagery (fig. 95).[186] But there were other means of publicizing hatred of the pontiff.

Ein jeder fromm er Chriſt ſol leſen/
Was vrſach Diſes Bilds geweſen.

Widerlegung vnd Antwort auff das falſch gedeutet vnd vnbewerte Bild vnd Gedicht
F. Johan. Naſs Minoriten (wider der Augſpurgiſchen Confeſsion verſpanten) newlich ausgangen/Daraus ein jeder frommer Chriſt leicht zuſehen/
wie die Pebſtiſchen den Namen Chriſti vnd ſeiner Kirchen nur zum ſchanddeckel brauchen/In dieſen letzten zeiten ſehr nützlich zuwiſſen.

Autore Vuolff. Meyerpeck Pictore.
1 5 6 9.

95. *Caricature of the Papacy, by Wolfgang Meyerbeck, 1569. The Devil (playing Bruder Nass like a bagpipe) ridicules the pope (with ears of ass-fool, and parody of his arms pinned to the tree). Behind, Babylon is falling as angels cast the millstone into the sea (Revelation, 18), to the consternation of Roman clergy.*

On 8 August John Felton, who in mid-May had posted the text of the bull on the bishop of London's gate, was hung on a specially erected gallows next the place of his crime, in St Paul's churchyard. The lesson of his story was published the same year, in both prose and popular verse, and it was not long before a refutation of the bull was in print. This was written by the Swiss reformer, Henry Bullinger, a father-figure for English reformers, who had already made a substantial contribution to England's protestantism. The long text he now produced, justifying that régime and demonstrating the nullity of the papal bull, was printed by John Day, first in Latin in 1571, and then in English early the following year.[187]

Bullinger addressed his *Confutation of the Popes Bull* to three of the English prelates with whom (as his voluminous correspondence shows) he was closely in touch. Edmund Grindal (translated to York from London in May 1570), together with Bishops Cox (Ely) and Jewel (Salisbury) had been keeping the sage of Zurich informed of

141

the unfolding pattern of events in England, as Mary Queen of Scots' flight to England was followed by the northern rising in the summer of 1569, and then the next year by the 'senseless' bull declaring Elizabeth was not the lawful queen of England.

Jewel, who sent a copy of the bull to Bullinger (who had not seen it) at the time of Felton's conviction, believed that there was a connection between this offensive document (said to have been circulating secretly for some time) and the rebellion in Durham and Yorkshire in November and December 1569. This was in fact not the case, since Pius's action came several months too late to have influenced the northerners' stand for the old faith, but this was no obstacle to the belief (which Bullinger's translator helped to foster) that all recent treason and disorder were to be laid at the pope's door.[188] It was a belief that seems to have become enshrined in popular memory (doubtless retrospectively reinforced by the events of the Armada year). A seventeenth-century print of a series of *Popish Plots and Treasons* from the beginning of Queen Elizabeth's reign, starts with the northern rising (fig. 96), showing how:

> The *Pope* aloft on Armed Shoulders Rides,
> And in vain Hopes the English spoils divides;
> His *Leaden Bull* 'gainst good *Eliza* roares,
> And scatters dire Rebellion round our Shoars.[189]

The revolt of the northerners against 'new found religion and heresie' revived the issue of imagery. The rebels not only destroyed instruments of the new faith (tearing English Bibles and Prayer Books and overthrowing the communion table at Durham), but also returned old images to prominence. They bore the banner of the five wounds of Christ, a symbol of the 'trewe and catholicke religion' that had taken earlier Tudor rebels to execution, and followed a processional cross. Pure consciences of the reformed variety were greatly affronted – witness a letter sent to Bullinger by the merchant Richard Hilles, reporting the 'feigned piety' of this trust in crosses and patron saints. As Foxe put it, preaching under protest (vainly pleading ill-health and fatigue from his literary labours) at Paul's Cross on Good Friday 1570, papists 'make much adoe about the Crosse of Christ, and have fought these 500 yeares for his Crosse; and yet they know not hys Crosse'.[190] This offence was publicly chastized in the new Homily that was issued as a result of the rebellion.

The long, six-part Homily 'against disobedience and wilful rebellion' brought home to all hearers the infamous role of the bishop of Rome in 'the unnatural stirring up of the subjects unto rebellion against their princes'. This was an old game of the popes in England. Innocent III's cursing of King John had called subjects to rebel against their natural lord, and in more recent times rebellions in the north and western counties under Henry VIII and Edward VI were the work of Rome. Had not foolish subjects recently been led into 'the deep ditch of horrible rebellion' by disguised mass-priests 'whispering in the ears of certain northern borderers'?[191]

Yoked with this dreadful offence was the sacrilege of papal heresy. The pope was the father of ignorance, whose withholding of scripture caused radical disobedience, and with disobedience went idolatry and false belief. It was the bishop of Rome who had removed the second commandment from public knowledge, so that the wretched people could not know God's word against images. The rebels of 1569 had shown themselves maintainers of 'false superstition and wicked idolatry', ready to kill all who spoke against it. Had they not brandished the image of Christ in defiance of the word of Christ?

And though some rebels bear the picture of the five wounds painted, against those who put their only hope of salvation in the wounds of Christ; not those wounds which are painted in a clout by some lewd painter, but in those wounds which Christ himself bare in his precious body: though

143

they, little knowing what the cross of Christ meaneth, which neither carver nor painter can make, do bear the image of the cross painted in a rag, against those that have the cross of Christ painted in their hearts.[192]

The standard-bearers of rebellion bore a false standard – a painted cross.

The homilist took his hearers, as Bullinger took his readers, back to the reign of Edward VI, the young Josiah who had set England in the path of God's law. Bullinger's demolition of Pope Pius V's bull as nothing but 'a very flimflaw and a filme of a nutshell', of no validity against the English queen's godly régime, was at pains to show Elizabeth's fidelity to her brother's example. Henry VIII had turned the English Church away from many foul Romish superstitions, but it was the young Josiah who had set the true pattern. Bullinger keeps coming back to Edward VI as the model for Elizabeth's just headship of the English Church. One section of his book was headed, 'That the Queene of England hath not chosen mens opinions for herself, and hir realme to follow, but Gods pure word, heretofore sought out, and receyved by King Edward the sixth . . .' He then goes on to explain the order followed by Edward VI in reforming the Church of England. 'That godly prince of blessed memorie and woorthy of immortall glorie King Edward the sixth, folowing the examples of Josias, and Constantine the great, two of the excellentest princes that ever were in the world, began the reformation of the English church.'

Just as Josiah had called a parliament or council of his nobles, priests and commons, and caused the law of God to be read openly before them, just as Constantine had summoned a general council and set the books of gospels, epistles and ancient prophets before it, so Edward had convoked nobility, bishops and learned men to parliament in London, commanded them to show by holy scripture what should be done, and then reformed his realm accordingly. Likewise, after the interlude of Queen Mary, Elizabeth had restored the rule of scripture.

And therefore nothing els hath she received and delivered to be kept of hir whole Realme, then that hir brother of blessed memorie King Edward, heertofore most godlily and wisely thought meet to be received and beleved of himself, and to be conveighed over to his subiectes, out of the lively woord of God . . .

The Edwardian pattern to which Queen Elizabeth had so faithfully bound her kingdom embraced those holy Old Testament

*97. 1587 Dutch medal
presenting Queen Elizabeth in an
anti-papal role as defender of the
northern provinces of the
Netherlands.*

destroyers of groves and altars of idols – Hezekiah and Josiah.
Brother and sister alike had displayed their true mettle by making
England into a haven for opponents of Rome's idolatry. Elizabeth
like Edward had dutifully followed scripture 'and taken away the
Idols and Idolatrie of Baal', including Baal's chapels, temples and
chaplains, and 'all Popish abhominations'.[193]

Bullinger ended his book with a piece of polemical anti-papal
history. He cantered through more than four hundred years between
Popes Gregory VII and Paul IV in order to signpost the casualties
inflicted by 'the Bishop of Rome'. This brief tendentious survey,
with its focus on kings who had been deposed, imprisoned or
humiliated at the hands of the pope, naturally put the spotlight on
the emperors Henry IV and Frederick Barbarossa.[194] Anti-papal
propaganda was clearly very much the order of the day in 1569–70.
And it brought Elizabeth close to the young Josiah–Edward.

Elizabeth, however, unlike her father, does not seem to have
promoted anti-papal visual propaganda. Images of this kind did
appear, depicting the queen as the defender of true religion against
papal superstition and error, as the maintainer of the faith against the
monstrous hydra of the Roman Antichrist. A medal of 1587 (fig. 97)
shows Queen Elizabeth enthroned, with the vanquished beast of the
Apocalypse beneath her feet. On her right the earl of Leicester holds
the queen's mantle in a protective stance, while five kneeling putti
support shields of northern provinces of the Netherlands. On the
reverse the pope with an assortment of Roman clergy and their
'idols' (monstrance, chalice, eucharistic host) are falling into the
abyss, blown downwards by the spirit of the Lord, represented by
the tetragrammaton in the clouds. The medal was an expression of

Dutch Calvinists' hopes of the English queen's continuing support in the struggle against Rome, at a time when worries were growing about the planned Spanish Armada.[195]

A similar image that appeared two years before this, took up the same theme in the same cause. Pieter van der Heyden's satirical engraving shows Elizabeth as Diana, judging the pope in the guise of Callisto, whose pregnancy is mercilessly revealed by Time and Truth (fig. 98). The queen is supported by four Netherlands provinces (Holland, Guelderland, Zeeland and Friesland), bearing their shields as they do in the medal. A nest of poisonous eggs is hatching under the pope, including one 'full of venom' from which emerges a cockatrice with a friar's head, named 'inquisition'. This print, issued between the murder of the Prince of Orange in July 1584 and the death of Pope Gregory XIII in April 1585, was another call to the English queen to play her part against the Roman Antichrist.[196]

These were blatant anti-papal images. Produced as prompts for a godly Deborah, whose throne was itself an anti-papal eminence, they displayed a propagandist militancy that was alien to English depictions of Elizabeth. Only years after the queen's death did it

146

*99. Queen Elizabeth, about a
generation after her death, as the
triumphant St George, releasing
Truth and ready to slay a
hydra. Engraved by Thomas
Cecil.*

become possible to delineate the Virgin Queen in this manner in
England. An allegorical print by Thomas Cecil (fig. 99) presents
Queen Elizabeth on horseback as defender of realm and faith.
Wearing helmet and cuirass and bearing sword and shield, this royal
St George is trampling on a seven-headed hydra with its implications
of Rome, while receiving a lance from the rescued virgin, Truth. In
the background we see the crescent of the Armada fleet and massed
blocks of English troops at Tilbury. But this print did not appear
until about 1625, and its tone is unlike that of the imagery of the
queen's reign.[197]

Elizabeth controlled the appearance of her own images, and
censored offensive portraits. If such extreme propagandist themes
were absent during her reign, this could well have been deliberate
policy — for the image-makers certainly knew they had to take
account of the royal mind. Even after 1570 care was needed in
depicting the royal governor's defence of the faith against papal
idolatry. Delicate issues were involved in both contests — the war
against the papal hydra and the war against idols — and it was a
matter of common knowledge that even courtiers had run into

147

100. Woodcut initial C used in the Book of Martyrs from 1563. A decorative surround with cornucopia above and pope below encloses the queen: beside her John Day the printer, and John Foxe the author (centre, cf. fig. 125).

trouble broaching such matters. True, there were instances of these topics being delineated. A well-known example, directly related to our theme, is the initial letter C (for Constantine or Christ) that appeared in editions of Foxe from 1563, at the opening of the author's dedication to the queen (fig. 100). This shows Queen Elizabeth enthroned with orb of sovereignty and sword of justice, on a dais beneath which we see the pope and writhing serpents. The broken metal of the papal keys, held by a pontiff who is seemingly as naked as the lively putto over his head, is the moribund equivalent of the flourishing rose and cornucopia above. There is no doubt about this allusion, but it takes the tactful form of a piece of ornamental decoration, in which the papal figure is half-screened by the strapwork. This scrolled pope belongs to quite a different world from the three men who stand respectfully beside and below the queen.[198]

Foxe's book did (as we shall see) represent the falling pope in a more direct manner, but he fell before Henry VIII, not before Elizabeth. Likewise in our painting, although its collapsing pontiff belongs to the time when Pius V excommunicated Elizabeth, the Tudor monarch presiding over this failing 'pope-holiness' was Edward, not the queen. One monarch could stand in for another. Elizabeth was expected to re-embody and live up to both her father and her brother.

JOHN FOXE AND *THE ACTS AND MONUMENTS* OF 1570

If we needed further proof that the young Josiah was in the news in 1570, we have only to look again at the 1570 edition of Foxe's Book of Martyrs (above p. 33). This huge new two-volume edition which probably came out towards the end of 1570, was a vastly enlarged and improved version of the 1563 book, and it took account of recent events. A sense of outrage at the papacy marked the new work conspicuously in several places.

Foxe added a third preface to his remodelled introductory addresses in the new edition. This posed four questions to 'all the professed frendes and folowers of the Popes procedynges'. The martyrologist here taxed the papists, after twelve years of tolerant treatment, for rising up against a lenient governor, and disrupting the peace of realm and church. The same theme was presented pictorially at the end of volume I. 'The proud primacie of Popes paynted out in Tables' displayed the various humiliations inflicted by medieval popes on emperors and kings in a series of twelve woodcuts with accompanying text. This section resembles the survey with which Bullinger closed his *Confutation*, but naturally with an English slant. King John offering up his crown to one papal legate, and Henry III kissing the knee of another, featured alongside the surrenders of the German emperors Henry IV and Frederick Barbarossa (fig. 101).

The illustrated antipapal diatribe was added to the *Acts and Monuments* as a last-minute topical appendix. This is evident from the page numbers of volume I, which finish (at page 922) immediately before the 'Primacie of Popes', to which a new sequence of separately numbered signatures is allotted. (This defect was remedied in later editions, which kept the appendix in the same place at the end of the first volume).[199]

Volume II in Foxe's new text opens his seventh book, on the reign of Henry VIII. An old metal-cut by Jacob Faber, showing the king in council (borrowed from Halle's *Chronicle* of 1548 – fig. 65 above), illustrated the beginning of this volume, but when the reader reaches the climax of the reign, the Act of Supremacy in 1534, he finds a quite different, much more exciting picture. An imposing new

*101. Foxe's picture of the popes'
treatment of German emperors:
'some they subdued and brought
to the kissing of their feet'.
Woodcut from section added to
end of vol. I of 1570 Book of
Martyrs. (Compare figs.
103–5).*

woodcut, which became the title-page to this section in the 1583 and subsequent editions of the Book of Martyrs, picks up the anti-papal theme in a mode related to that of our painting.

'The Pope suppressed by K. Henry the eight' (fig. 102) shows the broad-beamed Tudor monarch in a grand imperial pose. Henry VIII, magisterially enthroned on a central dais beneath the royal arms, holds the sword of state erect in his right hand while with his left he passes the book of law (the Bible) to Cranmer who, attended by Cromwell, has both hands ready to receive it (cf. figs. 106–8). Pope Clement VII, who has already lost his tiara and his papal cross, is crushed like a cushion beneath the royal feet. It was the supreme humiliation. 'To be a footstole' (as Walter Lynne's text put it), 'is over all the world a vyle and abiecte thinge'.[200]

While the upper part of this scene shows the calm dominance of the godly régime, the lower is given over to the unseemly flurry of the papal collapse. Bishop Fisher and Cardinal Pole (the latter remonstrating with the king) protect the pope's body, while a posse of corpulent tonsured religious rush to the pontiff's defence, readying his horse for his imminent departure. At the bottom right hand corner a group of papal supporters are reacting hysterically, one rushing in from the right with arms raised, like the Garter knight next the pope in our painting. A marginal note explains: 'The oftétymes mocioned to be sworne: but the Byshop and Syr Thom. More excused them by their writynges, in whiche they sayd, that they had written before the sayd Lady Katherine to be Quéene, and therfore could not well go from that whiche they had written. Likewise the Doctor excused, that he in preachyng had called her Quéene, & therfore now could not withsay it againe: Howbeit at length he was well contented to dissemble the matter, and so escaped : but the other two stode a-gaynst all the realme in their opinion.

From the moneth of Marche this Parlament far-thermore was proroged to the iij. day of Nouember a-bouesayd . At what tyme, amongest other diuers sta-tutes, most graciously, and by the blessed will of God it was enacted, that the Pope, and all his colledge of Car-dinals, with his pardons and Indulgences, whiche so long had clogged this realme of England, to the mise-rable slaughter of so many good men, and which neuer coulde be remoued away before, was now abolished e-radicate, & exploded out of this land, & sent home agayn to their owne countrey of Rome , from whence thei came, God be euerlastingly praysed therfore. Amen.

The Pope suppressed by K. Henry the eight.

The lamentable weepyng & howling of all the religiouse route for the fall of their god the Pope.

102. *New woodcut by unknown artist in 1570 Book of Martyrs, showing Pope Clement VII under the feet of Henry VIII in 1534: above him, king and Archbishop Cranmer both hold the Bible.*

*103. Alexander III 'setting his
foot upon the . . . neck' of the
Emperor Frederick Barbarossa,
in Foxe's 1563* Acts and
Monuments.

lamentable wepyng and howling of all the religious route for the fall
of their god the Pope'. Opposite another note reads: 'The Pope
unhorsed, but his chaplenes ready to hold the stirrup for him to get
up agayne'.[201]

This image deserved to be monumental, for it described a
monumental event. The king's arrogation of authority over the
church as part of his 'imperial crown', his banishment of papal
usurpation, represented the just reversal of many former injustices.
One of the ancient wrongs it put right was the great humiliation of
imperial power by Pope Alexander III, in exacting the complete
submission of Frederick Barbarossa at Venice in 1177. This may
seem a far cry from the manoeuvres of Henry VIII and Edward VI.
But we only need to glance back to an earlier passage and picture in
Foxe's work to see how the fall of the pope was set in the context of
the ancient contest between papacy and empire.

Henry VIII's right foot, set on the neck of Pope Clement, was the
countermove to Pope Alexander 'treading on the neck of Fredericke
the Emperoure' (fig. 103), itself an event with scriptural dimensions,
already vividly portrayed in a woodcut of the 1563 *Acts and
Monuments*, as it had been earlier in a book sponsored by Luther.
The title-page of *Bapsttrew Hadriani* (1545, fig. 104), was based on
Holbein's woodcut of *The Pope and Death* (fig. 105), to which the

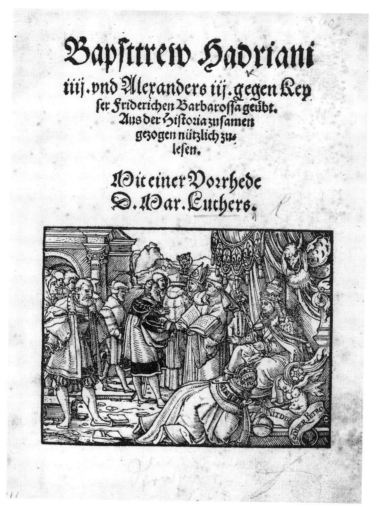

weak and simplified design in Foxe may also have made reference (for example for the figure of the standing cardinal, fig. 103).[202] As we shall see shortly, the new picture of Henry VIII in 1570, though appearing under the year 1534, in a sense took the place of some of Foxe's remarks prefacing the reign of Edward VI in the edition of 1563.

The new illustration could also be seen as a contribution to the huge flood of controversial writings that had been making waves over the foundations of the English Church in the decade since Elizabeth's accession. Jewel's 'challenge' sermon of November 1559 and his *Apology* for the Church of England formed the eye of this

105. *Holbein's 1526 woodcut of*
The Pope and Death (in the
Dance of Death series, first
published in 1538), was
influenced by Cranach's
Passional Christi und
Antichristi (1521).

Der Bapſt.

literary storm, but Foxe's *Acts and Monuments* had come in for its
share of invective. Naturally papal claims to authority featured
conspicuously in these writings. 'What if Popes have suffered great
Princes and Monarkes to kisse their feete, to holde their stiroppes, to
lead their horses by the bridle?' asked Thomas Harding in 1568,
detecting an assortment of 'foule errours, lies, sclaunders, corruptions' in the *Defence of the Apology of the Church of England* that
Jewel had published the previous year. To Harding the book seemed
a fair match for Foxe's 'huge booke of his false Martyrs', and the
detection of its untruths included a survey of the alleged ill-treatment
of kings by popes.[203]

There are some obvious points of resemblance between our
picture and Foxe's cut of the pope being suppressed by Henry VIII.
Though the pope's pose is quite different, in both cases he collapses
beneath Tudor feet, and in both depictions there is a horizontal
divide – less clear in print than painting – between the godly,
scripture-serving faithful in the upper half of the scene, and the
condemned papal affiliates below. We might even detect some
similarity between the beak-nosed profile of Bishop Fisher in the
woodcut and one of the two friars heading out of the scene in our
painting.[204]

In both depictions it is the authority of king and scripture that
vanquishes the false god of the papacy. In the painting of Edward VI
the book of scriptural law has descended from the king's hand to rest

against the pope's head. But the iconography of the Church's Supreme Head bestowing the Bible on his grateful people, which lay behind both these images, became as familiar as the vernacular scriptural text itself, thanks to the title-pages delineating this scene. Coverdale's Bible in 1535 (fig. 106) and the Great Bible in 1539 (fig. 107) both showed Henry VIII in his divinely ordained role, handing out the word of God. The former woodcut, by Hans Holbein, shows the king enthroned in state (on a cushioned dais), handing the Bible to three kneeling mitred bishops. In the Great Bible this scene is moved to the top of the title-page and now the book, explicitly labelled VERBUM DEI multiplies as it is passed down the page from the hands of Cranmer and Cromwell towards the acclaiming people. Self-evidently both these images lie behind Foxe's new woodcut of Henry VIII suppressing the pope.

Edward VI was likewise presented in this guise. Cranmer's *Catechism* of 1548 included a cut of the young king by an unknown artist which is based on Holbein's title-page of 1535 (fig. 108). Edward, in the same posture and garb as his father (note the cushion!) passes the book (now marked BIBLIA) to the mitred prelates on his right; and as before lay lords in coronets kneel on the king's left. In Edward's reign, however, this image was apparently not deemed suitable to grace the pages of scripture itself. There seem to be no illustrated title-pages comparable to those in Henrician Great Bibles, showing the young king as dispenser of the word. (See above p. 132, fig. 88.) Had the rigid iconoclasts succeeded in imposing a severer divorce between scriptural word and image?

The association of king and Book, the divine authority of the highest law that descended to the people through the Church's Supreme Head, was a visual commonplace long before the painting of Edward VI and the pope. The enduring 'Worde of the Lord' shown there was an essential link in the triangular chain of command that held the gesturing figure of the old king and his pale-faced son and heir together in the viewer's eyes. There was an inevitable centrality to the Book. The word of God has an independent power unrelated to the agency of human hands; it becomes missile, as well as divine missive.

Among the many changes that were made to Foxe's enormous work in the 1570 edition, those relating to his treatment of Edward VI are of direct interest to our theme. In 1563 Edward's reign occupied the fourth part of the martyrologist's history, and was prefaced by remarks comparing his 'mild and halcyon days' with the

106. *Holbein's title-page for Coverdale's Bible, 1535, with the king in the bottom panel, delivering the Bible to the lords spiritual, while the temporal lords kneel on his left. David and St Paul occupy the niches behind them.*

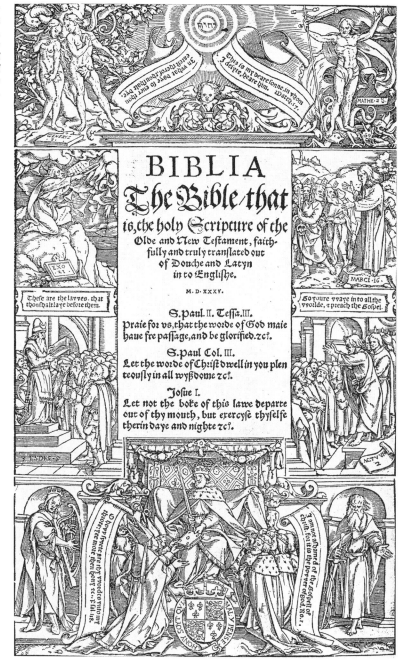

156

107. In the title-page of the Great Bible, 1539, Henry VIII (more realistically portrayed than in 1535) now dominates the scene. His large figure is placed at the top of the page, under a diminutive God the Father (represented by the tetragrammaton in 1535), from whom verbum dei emanates before starting its earthly descent. It is heard, not read, by the acclaiming crowds at the bottom.

108. Edward VI, seated on a renaissance throne, hands the Bible to the mitred bishops. Woodcut frontispiece in Cranmer's 1548 Catechism, based on Holbein.

dangerous tempests of Henry VIII. The noble father deserved due praise, but had left to his son the perfect completion of what he had begun. Henry had 'only cracked the pope's crown', not completely dispossessed him, or – using words that had been preached before the king – he 'unhorsed the pope, and put him out of the saddle', without removing the stirrups and harness which prelates could use to remount him.[205] The woodcut that accompanied this text was an unpretentious initial E (fig. 109), showing the young king enthroned among a group of lords, sword of state in his right hand while with his left he appears to be receiving a piece of paper from a humble layman dressed in boots and jerkin. This was not a new initial. It had

109. 'Emong other roughe stormes ...' Foxe's 1563 account of Edward VI opened with a capital letter used for the dedication of John Day's 1551 Bible, showing Edmund Becke (editor of the text) presenting the book to the king.

already done service twelve years earlier in a Bible printed by John Day.[206]

A lot of work went into the reshaping of this passage by 1570. Edward VI's reign now formed Book IX, and Foxe completely rewrote his introductory paragraphs on this king. He had been hunting for new materials, and in a letter to William Cecil expressed regret that none of those who had held office under Edward had thought fit to describe his life.[207] This new introduction was accompanied by a new large (nearly full-page) illustration (fig. 110). The invidious comparison with Henry VIII disappeared, and the uncompleted unhosing of the pope was featured instead (as we have seen) in pictorial form. Foxe now devoted himself to a single-minded eulogy of King Edward's 'rare commendations and virtues', stressing (as the 1563 edition did not) his role as Josiah in purging the church.

The martyrologist spent three paragraphs (from which I have quoted above, p. 34) extolling the young king as England's 'evangelical Josias' who, coming to the throne at the same age as his Old Testament exemplar, imitated that earlier 'mild' destroyer of 'all monuments of idolatry in the temple' by abolishing idolatrous masses and false invocation, bringing religion back to 'a right sincerity'. Old Josiah and New Josiah alike repaired and restored the book of God's holy word.

These themes are the topic of the new woodcut that illustrates the

110. New woodcut designed for the opening page of Foxe's Ninth Book on the reign of Edward VI in the enlarged Acts and Monuments *of 1570.*

K. Ed-
vvard. 6.
An.
1547.

1483.

¶ **The ninth booke containyng the**
Actes and thynges done in the reigne of kyng
Edvvard the 6.
(*ₓ*)

The ship of the Romish Church.

The burning of Images.

Shippe ouer your trinkets and be packing ye Papistes.

The Temple well purged.

The Papistes packyng away their paltrye.

Euery plante which my heauenly father hath not planted shalbe plucked vp. Sp. Mat. 15.

The Communion Table.

King Edward deliuering the Bible to the Prelates.

↬ *King Edward the vj.*

An.
1547.

The reigne and time of k. Edward.

After the death of kyng Henry succeded kyng Edward his sōne, beyng of the age of ir. yeares. He began hys reigne, the 28. day of January, and reigned vj.yeres, viij.moneths, and viij. dayes, and deceased. an. 1553. the 6. day of July. Of whose excellent vertues, ¢ singular graces wrought in him by the gift of God, although nothing can be said enough to his commendation: yet because the renowmed fame of such a worthy Prince shall not vtterly passe our story without some gratefull remembraunce, I thought in fewe wordes to touch some little portion of his prayse, taken out of great heapes of matter, which might bee inferred. For to stand vppon all that might be sayd of him, it would be to long: and yet to say nothing, it were to much vnkynd. If kynges and Princes which haue wisely and vertuously gouerned, haue found in all ages writers to solemnise and celebrate their Actes and memory, such as neuer knew them nor were subiect vnto them, how much then are we Englishe men bound, not to forget our duetie to kyng Edward, a Prince although but tender in yeares, yet for hys sage and mature rypenes in wytte and all princely ornamentes, as I see but few to whom he may not bee equall, so agayne I see not many, to whom he may not iustly be preferred.

And here to vse the example of Plutarch in comparyng kynges and rulers, the Latines with the Grekes together: if I should seeke with whom to match this noble Edward, I finde not with whom to make my match

Commendation of kyng Edward.

AAAa.j.

new opening of Book IX. The top half shows the purging of the temple in progress. On the left a group of men burdened with mass-books and a hamper of discarded objects (including image, cross and candlestick) is leaving a church, following a procession of others likewise engaged. Laden with huge service-books, a pastoral staff, censer and tiara, they are led by a boy carrying aspergillum and sacring bell, who is about to enter a vessel waiting with furled sails on the far side of a hill – 'The ship of the Romish Church'. In the background a man with a rope is pulling a statue of a bishop down from the niche in the church façade, while in the centre several figures tend a bonfire of assorted images and crosses.

Beneath this rather neat combination of proper purging (by burning and destruction) and condign preservation (papists packing away their 'paltry'), we see the reformed order of the reforming Josiah. On the right, the purged temple is displayed in its cleansed purity. A church denuded of all ornament is furnished for the two sacraments of baptism and the lord's supper, and an evangelical audience, duly bearing books and attentive ears, is squashed together in rapt attention to the preacher in his pulpit. On the left the young king is enthroned as restorer of scriptural law. Seated on a dais (the letters E 6 R behind him), with lay lords standing respectfully on his left, he is shown 'delivering the Bible to the Prelates' who kneel (unmitred) on his right. This image is an updated version of the woodcut (based on Holbein) we have just looked at, from Cranmer's *Catechism* (fig. 108).

Foxe and his printer John Day put a tremendous amount of time, energy and funds into the enlargement of the *Acts and Monuments* of 1570. They worked closely together on this vast enterprise, which strained the resources of the printer, three of whose presses were committed to the work. The martyrologist was a familiar figure in Day's house, sometimes staying there (as he was in January 1567) and at other times being close by in the duke of Norfolk's house at Christ Church, Aldgate. The printer's son later described how the famous author 'travailed' weekly, every Monday, from the Norfolk residence over to the Day printing-house.[208]

Prominent among the matters that had to be hammered out was the layout of the new edition, which was a substantial improvement on that of 1563. The large amount of new material which Foxe had collected since the first edition, swelling the book into two bulky volumes, necessitated much rewriting, and the publisher (who 'set a Fox to wright how Martyrs runne', as his epitaph put it)[209]

111. Two 'enemies of God's word' pull a preacher out of the pulpit, with threats of burning. Illustration of Envy in Stephen Bateman's A christall glasse *(1569).*

112. Thomas Bilney was accused of having preached at Ipswich in 1527 against false belief in the spiritual value of being buried in a Franciscan habit. This woodcut in the 1563 Book of Martyrs shows him being dragged from the pulpit by two friars.

contributed substantially to the new work (see fig. 100). He too helped to track down new information, and he gave thought to its presentation. The improvements included, besides some innovatory printing, in the shape of Anglo-Saxon type and the new fashion for bracketed tables, more and better illustrations. These were more than doubled in number,[210] and though the practice of repeating some of the smaller cuts continued, there was plenty of new illustrative material, which included both ornaments and scenes. Some of the

113. *Wrath. 'The pope is oppression' – treading on a victim while Cruelty kills before him. In the background three faithful to the gospel kneel in prayer. Woodcut in Bateman's* A christall glasse.

114. *The vain climbing of pope and cardinal, while Lucifer falls headlong towards Death, who is stationed at hell's mouth, holding up the world. Illustration 'Of Veritie' in* A christall glasse.

163

new woodcuts (like that of Henry VIII, fig. 102 above) were in quite a grandiose style, and a great improvement on those of 1563.

It is very probable that Day was able to call on the skills of foreign workmen for this new work. It was a time when there was an influx of skilled labour coming into England as Protestant refugees fled from the duke of Alva's 'slaughter and bloud' in the Low Countries.[211] These immigrants included a number of artists — of varying degrees of fame. One man, for instance, who failed to make much mark, though he could claim linguistic as well as pictorial skills (knowing Italian as well as Spanish, which he had learnt when imprisoned by the inquisition), was Derick Everwyn, painter, of Holland. He arrived in England in 1568, and the following January was recommended to the bishop of London (Edmund Grindal) by the minister of the Italian church.[212] In July 1568 or 1569 Foxe interceded with Cecil on behalf of his printer for a relaxation of the law forbidding printers to have more than four foreigners in their employment. Was John Day about to take on some of the Dutch émigrés who could help with the expanding Book of Martyrs and its illustrations?[213]

There are a few clues that seem to point towards this, supporting the impression given by some of the new cuts, that continental hands were at work. Some of the books that were coming from Day's press while Foxe's new edition was in the making are of interest to us here. In 1569 John Day published a book entitled *A christall glasse of christian reformation, wherein the godly maye beholde the coloured abuses used in this our present tyme.* This work, which expounded the vices and virtues as a source of reflection 'wherein we may learn godly reformation', was one of the first publications of Stephen Bateman (or Batman), a Cambridge man who became chaplain to Archbishop Parker, and one of his book-collectors.[214] Bateman's book, with its indications of the anti-papalism of the moment and its reforming bias, was not out of tune with Foxe's great work, to which, in a rather curious way, it was related.

Bateman's passage on Envy starts (as do his sections on the other vices) with an ornamental capital. This E is, wholly inappropriately, none other than the capital encircling the young Edward VI that had graced the opening of Foxe's Part IV in the 1563 *Acts and Monuments* (fig. 109). Clearly, if Day was ready to discard this block and cannibalize it so unsuitably in another of his publications, about a year before the appearance of Foxe's second edition, planning for the new illustrations must already have been in full swing.[215] The

Christall glasse was also an illustrated book and some of its woodcuts are linked with themes of the Book of Martyrs.

We may begin with the picture 'Of Envie' (fig. 111). It is an illustration of the preaching of the gospel, which shows a reformer of 'godly zeale' being pulled from his pulpit by two 'enemies of Gods word' – one being a friar whose left hand grasps the preacher's beard while his right points towards the fire which is ready to consume this faithful evangelist. As a reader of the Cambridge University Library copy of Bateman's book noticed, this is a version of the picture in Foxe (fig. 112) which showed Thomas Bilney (who was burned in 1531) being dragged from the pulpit in Ipswich by two friars who furiously lay hands on the preacher.[216]

Several of the pictures of Bateman's book are as vivid in their denigration of the papacy as those that were added to Foxe's first volume of 1570. The illustration for wrath portrays 'The Popes superbius crueltie' (fig. 113): the pope, wielding a sword, stands for ruthless oppression and pins his victim to the ground with his right foot. Words cited from Ambrose explain that 'There is not so much joye in climing upward, as there is sorrow in falling hard downward'. This same theme of climb and fall, again related to papal

165

misdemeanour, is represented in the illustration 'Of Veritie' (fig. 114). Here, while Christ sits above, enthroned on a rainbow, Lucifer falls between imperilled figures of pope and cardinal, each striving to climb higher.[217] The falling pope was a topical theme as England experienced the failure of a new rebellion to put back the ecclesiastical clock.

The woodcut that accompanies Bateman's passage on Wisdom (fig. 115) illustrates the lesson in the Sermon on the Mount (Matthew, 7: 24–27) describing the houses of wise and foolish men – one on a rock withstanding rain, winds and floods, the other on sand being destroyed. Not surprisingly, given the author's 'didactic Protestantism', this lesson became anti-papal. 'The signification' was given as follows. 'The house which standeth on the rocke, signifieth the stedfast beliefe of the faythfull: The other which standeth in the valy and on sandy ground, is the church of Antichrist and all popishe preaching ...' Bateman's words were taken up by the illustrator, who faithfully shows the condemned house sporting a banner with the papal keys and with a cross on its gable, while its distraught occupants – including pope, cardinal and friar, gesticulate wildly out of its windows.[218]

Who was this illustrator?

MARCUS GHEERAERTS THE ELDER

Some years ago, Edward Hodnett, gathering together all that could be gathered on the career and graphic works of Marcus Gheeraerts the elder, proposed him (mainly on stylistic grounds) as the designer of the woodcuts in the *Christall glasse*.[219] Gheeraerts, a committed Protestant in his late forties, fled to England from Bruges with his young son and namesake in March 1568 (fig. 116). He had left behind his wife (who did not share his religious allegiance) but in December the door was shut against his return when he was banned from Flanders and his property confiscated. Gheeraerts, who remarried in 1571 (his new wife being the sister of another immigrant painter) was to spend the best part of a decade in England, where his son became more famous. Arriving as he did in England, an established artist who already had experience in book-illustration, just at the time when John Day was on the lookout for skilled foreign workers, what more natural than for the printer to take Gheeraerts into his service?[220]

Gheeraerts, together with Lucas de Heere (who had come to England a year earlier), may have had a hand in the illustrations to the two editions (one in Dutch, the other French) of Jan van der Noot's *Het Theatre*, that were both published by Day in the autumn of 1568. These are the earliest etchings known to have been made in England, and the first to illustrate an English book. Appropriately, this book carried a dedication to Roger Martin, mayor of London, who had played a large part in assisting the immigrants from the Low Countries.[221]

The text of this book was bitingly topical for those who participated in its production. Fierce in its anti-papalism, it also dealt with a subject that bore directly on the lives and livelihoods of its illustrators: iconoclasm. The pope was a very Antichrist; his servitors, busy putting back, polishing up and painting the recently demoted idols of Rome, no better than priests of Baal.

Oh how many are at this instant in Brabant, Flanders, and the low countrey, and else where, whiche agaynst their belefe, conscience, and the holy ghost, maintain, allowe, and permit the manifest Babylonicall abhomination, communicating the venemous dregges of the barbarous cup of these Baals priestes?

116. Iconoclasts in action and on the gibbet. 'Heretics broke up churches: Catholics did nothing to stop them: therefore all must hang': words attributed to the president of the repressive Council of Troubles, inscribed on 1568 Netherlands medal.

Such was the view given to English readers of the work of the Spanish authorities, trying to reverse the effects of the 1566 iconoclasts, as Mary Tudor in England had tried to undo the destruction of her brother. The *Theatre for Worldlings* (which was published in 1569, with some of Edmund Spenser's earliest verse) continued:

They have amended, botched, and renued agayne their idols, to some they have made a newe nose, hand, arme or legge, other some are paynted up or coloured, vernysshed and made a new, so that they now (more like mad men) do carrie them rounde aboute the citie in procession, honouryng the same images (which they have so newly arayed and decked wyth silke, velvet, golde, pearles and precious stones, beades, gyrdles, purses, flowers, greene bowes, and all manner of sweete herbes) with song and sundry musicall instrumentes, torches, candles, offerings, and all other kynde of service, and kneelyng before them bare headed, they worship, serve, and holde up theyr handes to them.[222]

English purifiers, who had dealt with such popish trash ten years earlier, could afford to feel superior.

Marcus Gheeraerts the elder has left us his own commentary on the iconoclastic process. His etching, now known as an *Allegory of Iconoclasm* is one of the most striking and strange contemporary representations of image-breaking (fig. 117). It survives in a unique copy in England (in the British Museum), and is conjecturally dated 1566 — for clearly it is based on the events of that year in the Low Countries. Swarms of figures, diminishing in size from the fore-ground upwards, fill what seems to be an anarchic picture space, until one grasps that vermin-like they populate a giant human head. It rises, complete with trees and a hedge of writhing serpents

117. Marcus Gheeraerts the elder, Allegory of Iconoclasm, c. 1566: a monstrous head with blocked eyes, ears and mouth — like a heathen idol.

(marking the tonsure of a barren terraced crown), as a grossly over-populated hill, towering over what seems to be indicated as a reforming plateau below. Perhaps it is right to see associations between this mount of corruption, and the doomed ziggurat of the Tower of Babel.[223] Though we lack the lettered key that originally accompanied the print,[224] it does not take long to discern the virulent satire of pope, monks, and catholic clergy that impugns all seven Catholic sacraments, several being lodged in the various orifices of this monstrous head. The administration of the sacrament of the altar blocks up the mouth (central instrument of the reformers' preached salvation); an ear (where God's word should enter) is stopped up by a confessor administering penance; and the eye sockets are filled by the sacraments of marriage and orders.

Gheeraerts' seething head is a literal transcript of the idols of the heathen in the Psalms: 'They have mouths, but they speak not: eyes have they, but they see not: they have ears, but they hear not . . .' – a text often cited in arguments against church images. ('O Image makers, howe lyke bee yee unto your images, . . . havyng eares to heare, and heare not, eyes to see and see not, noses to smell and smell not,' Dr. John Bridges rebuked 'brutishe Papistes' at Paul's Cross in June 1571).[225] On the spreading nose a woman and child kneel before a wayside crucifix that is hung with an assortment of votive offerings and set with a lighted candle, while below, seemingly oblivious of the fate that awaits them under the gross curvature of the territorial chin they walk on, a procession of clergy bearing crucifix, monstrance and image of the Virgin, is heading straight towards the quagmire of destruction. On the other side behatted image-breakers wield their pole-axes, and cast wheelbarrows of rejected objects into their flaming bonfire. The papal master of this corrupt Leviathan sits enthroned on the crown of the head, under a canopy that is hung with all the tinselled trappings of his trade, like a tinker's stall at a fair. His takings are being poured into a coffer, and his tonsured servitors circle subserviently round him, themselves forming a veritable human tonsure.

To the right, placed below the pope at the centre of the forehead, is a small dilapidated thatched house with belfry (marked C), and crosses on every corner. Beside this building a fat priest (E) is trumpeting to the world below with a trumpet bearing the emblem of the papal keys. This part of Gheeraerts' etching – which presumably stands for the crumbling house of the Roman Church – forms a link in my chain of evidence, because it has certain

similarities to the picture illustrating Wisdom in Stephen Bateman's *Christall glasse*. Both small houses (more like hovels) are topped with crosses and sport papal banners, and there is an overall resemblance in their appearance.

About twelve years later Gheeraerts dealt again – more obliquely – with the same topic. One of the known successes of his career was a series of illustrations to Aesop's Fables, which first appeared at Bruges in 1567 (the year before Gheeraerts fled to England), and then was printed again in 1578 at Antwerp for Philip Galle (now enlarged and with a French text). The *Esbatement Moral, des Animaux* had 125 instead of 107 etchings, and among the new ones was a version of Aesop's fable of the man selling a wooden statue of Hermes (fig. 118). The depiction 'Of a man and his God of wood' has become an allegory of both idolatry and iconoclasm. 'En Calicut estoit un Bouvier idolatre / Qui prioit sans cesser un Image de bois / Du luy faire du bien . . .' The ox-herd who prayed constantly to his wooden image lost patience and knocked it down, with the result that a pile of gold previously concealed in it cascaded to his feet. The beneficiary abused this wooden god for only being able to serve him when cut to pieces. 'Don't expect to do good by force'. Beheading ill-doers would not produce the same result, and the moral for true faith was 'if we deny him he will also deny us'.[226]

Gheeraerts the elder was seemingly no stranger in John Day's office. Nor was John Foxe, who was so hard at work there at the

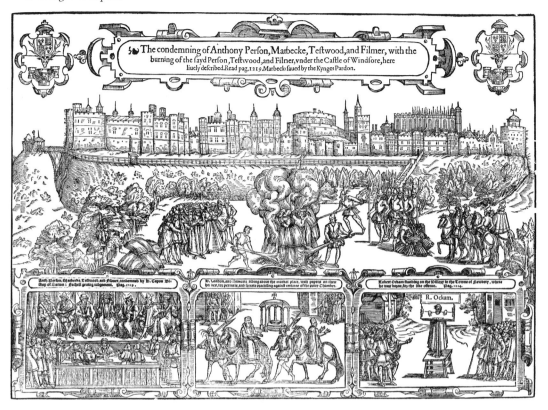

✠ The condemning of Anthony Perſon, Marbecke, Teſtwood, and Filmer, with the
burning of the ſayd Perſon, Teſtwood, and Filmer, vnder the Caſtle of Windſore, here
liuely deſcribed. Read pag. 1219. Marbeck ſaued by the Kynges Pardon.

119. 'The Description of Windsor Castle'. Woodcut illustrating the burning of the three Windsor martyrs of 1543, from the 1583 edition of Foxe's Acts and Monuments.

time, any stranger himself to the cause of iconoclasm. There must have been plenty of stories to swap against the clatter of the presses as work went ahead producing the anti-papal books of 1569–70. Did Gheeraerts, if he played some part in the illustrations for Bateman's text, have any hand in the much more important work of the Book of Martyrs? This possibility may be seen by comparing one of the new illustrations added to Foxe's 1570 edition with an acknowledged work of Gheeraerts.

One of the sections of Foxe's history that was much expanded in the 1570 *Acts and Monuments* was the story of four men of Windsor who were condemned in 1543. In 1563 this had taken up only a few pages, and was not illustrated. But in 1570 'The trouble and persecution of four Wyndsore men' (Robert Testwood, Henry Filmer, Anthony Person, and John Marbeck), had expanded to fill fourteen folio pages and was now accompanied by a large double-page inset illustration (fig. 119). This imposing woodcut was a panorama, which depicted the full story of the Windsor men, with

an inset showing their judgement and condemnation (below), and (in the centre) the burning of the three of them (Marbeck was pardoned) in a field below Windsor Castle, the line of whose various buildings is detailed across the top of the picture. In fact in Foxe's next two editions (1576 and 1583) this woodcut is headed 'THE DESCRIPSION OF WINDSORE CASTLE', with a subheading on the martyrs, and it remained an unpaginated inset (in 1576 bearing the printer's name) suggesting that perhaps it was also sold as an independent print.[227]

What is of interest to us is that the long line of Windsor Castle, with its chapel, round tower, gothic gateway, keep, and the terraced walkway ending in a kind of gazebo to the left, bears a very close resemblance to the view that appears in Gheeraerts' *Procession of the Knights of the Garter* of 1576 (fig. 120).[228] The building at the extreme right is topped in both cases by a curious feature that might be a weather-vane. The detail of the Garter Procession is finer, and

120. Procession of the Knights of the Garter: 1576 etching by Marcus Gheeraerts the Elder. Part of the first sheet, showing the queen in Garter robes, holding an ostrich-feather fan, with Windsor Castle and its recently reconstructed eastern terrace behind.

(with deer browsing where Foxe's martyrs burned) the bosky slope and palisaded field under the castle are of a different and more delicate order. But the viewpoint is exactly the same, and so are the essential features of the castle — even allowing for the column of the arcade in the Garter print, which though it cuts across the panorama has not been allowed to eliminate any significant part of it.

There is, however, one important difference, which tells us that Gheeraerts' view was an up-to-date rendering of the Windsor scene. He shows (seemingly accurately) the eastern half of the terrace as it had been rebuilt between 1572 and November 1575, when the previous timber structure which sustained the Queen's walk was replaced by masonry. The new terrace, which included a bridge of two arches over the ditch (see fig. 120), and an ornamental balustrade set with pedestals and beasts, cost the huge sum of £1,200, and (as Gheeraerts shows) the western section still had to be finished. Elizabeth herself took considerable interest in this work (the new structure had twice to be rebuilt to improve its ornamentation), which became one of Windsor's prides: in 1598 Paul Hentzner admired the 'incredible loveliness' of this walkway. Understandably Gheeraerts made sure that the Windsor Castle behind the queen in the Garter Procession incorporated this improvement. Yet, years later, the panorama of Windsor illustrating Berkshire in John Speed's *Theatre of the Empire of Great Britain* (1611), still showed the old wooden terrace, as it was in Foxe's print.[229]

Apart from this there is another complication. For in 1575 was published the second volume of George Braun and Franciscus Hogenberg's *Civitates Orbis Terrarum*. This work includes a print of Windsor Castle seen from exactly the same northern viewpoint delineating — with more space for detail — the same long line of its buildings, set in a more open and undulating landscape, and with a group of figures in the foreground. Here too the eastern terrace appears (rather sketchily) in its unaltered state. This scene is given as the work of George (Joris) Hoefnagel, who is thought to have drawn the scene about 1569, when he was visiting England.[230]

What was the relationship between these various Windsor panoramas? Did some unknown draughtsman, Hoefnagel, and the elder Gheeraerts all make trips to Windsor and draw almost identical panoramas of the castle? The *Civitates* view was published before the Garter procession, but Foxe's antedated both, and there are some details common to the Windsor Castle depicted in both the *Acts and Monuments* and the Garter procession that could not have been derived from Hoefnagel's drawing – at least as published. Possibly Gheeraerts (who had already produced a panoramic view of Bruges before he came to England) had a hand in the original Windsor panorama, or at least possessed a version of it that remained in England after Hoefnagel's departure. Maybe he updated an earlier drawing for the 1576 production.

The Windsor print leaves some unanswered questions about the artists who moved in and out of Foxe's orbit. As well as Marcus Gheeraerts we should not forget that a role might have been played by Franciscus Hogenberg, co-producer of the *Civitates*, who left England in 1570, perhaps causing problems for Archbishop Parker and his folio Bible.[231] There is at least one connection between the Windsor illustration and that Bible. For the Book of Martyrs panorama bears two sets of initials which maybe one day will tell us more about the cutters of Foxe's blocks, if not the designers they worked for. Underneath the person halfway up the tree on the left in figure 119 stands 'MD', while in the strapwork of the lower right margin is 'RB' – already encountered above in the 1572 Bishops' Bible (fig. 33).

With this new visual evidence in mind, it is worth looking again at Foxe's 1570 woodcut of 'The Pope suppressed by King Henry VIII' (fig. 102). If we set this beside Gheeraerts' *Allegory of Iconoclasm* (fig. 117), one can see (for all the obvious differences of artistic quality) some family likeness – for instance between the full-figured religious with their wide tonsures and bushy rings of hair. Without trying to push the point too far, we may keep open the hypothesis that Gheeraerts and his work were on hand when the new illustrations for the revised *Acts and Monuments* were being designed.

We have not strayed as far as it might seem from *Edward VI and the Pope*. For the theme of that picture is (I have argued) closely related to Foxe's theme of 1570. It was based on sources that came (as did Gheeraerts and Hogenberg and others) from the Low Countries. It was concerned (as were both Hogenberg and Gheeraerts) with iconoclasm. Our picture cannot have been painted by Marcus Gheeraerts the elder; it is far too incompetent for his hand. But it can be related obliquely to his work.

HADRIANUS JUNIUS

There is one person encountered more than once above whom we need to consider more fully. Hadrianus Junius, or Adriaen de Jonghe (1511–75), the celebrated Haarlem humanist, has entered these pages as the friend of Philip Galle, who engraved both the Heemskerck prints used in our painting, and also as the author of the text inscribed on one of them (above, pp. 56, 67). We know too that Junius, physician, poet and scholar, the most learned Netherlander since Erasmus, had readers in England of other works beside his popular emblem book (above, p. 87).

In addition to this there are other circumstances that make Junius of interest to us. For the Dutchman himself had a career in England which takes us straight back to the group of councillors in our painting, where Edward and Thomas Seymour are placed in such confident proximity to Edward VI, with their ally Mr Secretary Paget seated nearby at the end of the council table (colour pl. I and above pp. 15–21). Through his service to the Howards, whose downfall in 1547 was brought about by the Seymour brothers and their following, Junius was directly affected by the web of intrigue that surrounded the death of Henry VIII. The execution of the earl of Surrey and the attainder of the duke of Norfolk ruined some of Junius's prospects in England. He managed to reconstruct his career, and in due course returned to the Continent, where he might well have been content to remain. But then in the 1560s, just at the time which concerns us, Junius revisited England, seemingly with ideas of re-entering the Howard circle. He had not lost touch with his English acquaintances, and his reappearance at this juncture is suggestive.[232] For these reasons, the career of a Dutch humanist who has not made much of a mark in English history books, may be significant for this enquiry.

Junius's first visit to England took place in the later years of Henry VIII. Then in his early thirties, he was appointed physician in the Norfolk household, being salaried by Henry Howard, poet and earl of Surrey, the son of Thomas Howard, third duke of Norfolk. Surrey, who was six years younger than Junius, was a generous patron who during his short life made his mark in architecture as

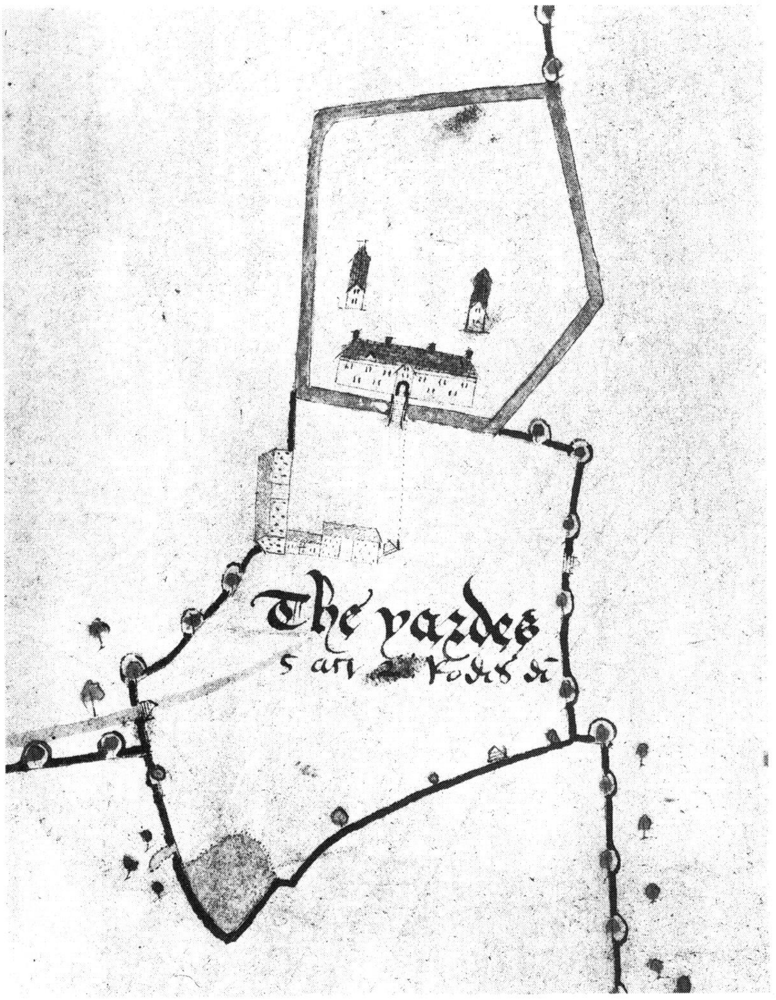

121. 'A true discription of Shelfanger Hall', Norfolk: detail from parchment map 'platted and calculated' by Thomas Waterman in 1618. The house in which Junius may have lodged is surrounded by a pentagonal moat – almost complete to this day.

well as letters. This Maecenas, who was currently engaged in building himself a grand renaissance house, Mount Surrey, near Norwich, gave the Dutch humanist the large annual stipend of fifty angels a year, in addition to his keep. Junius had lodgings on the Howard family estate near Kenninghall in Norfolk – itself a veritable palace (see below p. 211, fig. 126) – where the various generations of the dynasty clustered. There was no lack of cultivated company. Thomas Churchyard (future Elizabethan poet) was another member of Surrey's household, and the rooms in the lower storey of 'Shelfehangres Lodging' at Kenninghall (fig. 121) included, next 'Mr Adryan's Chamber' (furnished with three feather-beds, three pairs of blankets, four bolsters, two quilts and a tester), 'Mr Godsalve's Chamber'. The Godsalves were a Norfolk family, and it is possible that the occupant of this room was John Godsalve, who had been painted with his father by Holbein in 1528, and was knighted by Edward VI in 1547 after service under Henry VIII at Boulogne, where Surrey was also active, in 1544.[233]

The earl of Surrey's quarters at Kenninghall also housed 'The Master of the Children' (his chamber was on the floor above Junius's), but it seems certain that the physician's duties included tutoring the earl's children. There were five of them: Jane (b. 1537), Thomas (b. 1538), Catherine (b. 1539), Henry (b. 1540), and Margaret (b. 1543). Junius penned a stilted Latin letter on behalf of the young Howards and the rest of the household at Kenninghall, to Surrey in 1544, congratulating him on his success in France. He remained long enough with these pupils to graft some humanist tastes on to the minds of the elder children, though events were to separate him from them abruptly, before the death of Henry VIII.[234]

Junius was on terms of intimate friendship with his patron, the earl of Surrey (fig. 122). He must have had first-hand accounts of the roistering and riotous glass-breaking in the city of London that had resulted in Surrey's arrest and imprisonment in April 1543, the year before the Dutchman first came to England. Junius's command of English later — if not then — would have encompassed the lines that his patron addressed rebukingly to the city that had accused him.

> Thy wyndowes had don me no spight;
> But prowd people that drede no fall,
> Clothed with falshed and unright
> Bred in the closures of thy wall.

The poet set himself in the mantle of righteous reformer 'wrested to wrathe in fervent zeale', on a course that had to await the following reign for full implementation. London with its 'wicked walles' was presented in biblical terms, held captive just as Jerusalem was captive to 'false Babylon' in the second book of Kings, while Surrey, recklessly waking 'sluggardes with my bowe' as a divine 'scourge for synn' — breaking windows with pebbles in a nocturnal escapade — was acting like the 'archers against Babylon' in Jeremiah, 50. The city's fall was foreseen in apocalyptic terms — stricken like Babylon by the blaze of God's wrath. We know the impact of 'the fearfull thonder clapp' and 'soddayne flame at hand' in that event from the

122. *Holbein's drawing of Henry Howard, Earl of Surrey (wrongly inscribed 'Thomas'), made between about 1532, when he married Frances de Vere, and 1535, when they started living together.*

later depictions of both Cornelis Anthonisz. and Maarten van Heemskerck (figs. 53, 57).

> Thy prowd towers and turretes hye,
>   Enmyes to God, beat stone from stone;
>   Thyne idolles burnt, that wrought iniquitie;
> When none thy ruyne shall bemone,
>   But render unto the right wise Lord,
>   That so hath judged Babylon,
> Imortall praise with one accord.[235]

By the narrowest of margins Surrey missed seeing the window-breaking and idol-burning started by Henry VIII carried forward in

179

earnest by Edward VI. The revels for the young king's first Christmas included expenses for the 'makyng of a Towre Recemling the Tower of babylon with all thinges belonging to the same' – a structure that was taken (together with the 'maskyng garmentes') all the way from Blackfriars in London to Hampton Court and back. And the accounts for the coronation, which took place on 20 February 1547, included payments for making gilded 'Crownes and Crosse for the Poope in playe'.[236]

Henry Howard had died a month earlier. He was executed for treason on 19 January 1547, nine days before Henry VIII's death. The charges against the earl of Surrey, pressed forward as the king's end visibly approached and the Seymour brothers manipulated their affinity against the house of Howard, centred on his use of the arms of Edward the Confessor, but also included questioning about reported planning by the Howards to gain control over the young king during the forthcoming minority. Clearly the matter of who was going to pull the strings of power at Edward VI's accession was important to these moves against the family. Surrey's father, the duke of Norfolk, who in 1546 had been scheming to hitch the Howards to the rising star of the Seymours by a series of marriage alliances, was also convicted – perhaps trapped by the very faction he had sought to join. He was only spared because the king died the night before his execution, and he was to spend the whole of Edward's reign in custody.[237]

Junius's career was temporarily interrupted by the catastrophe that overtook the Howard family. The tremors were already to be felt at Kenninghall at the end of 1546, when royal commissioners arrived to question the duke of Norfolk's mistress (Elizabeth Holland) and his daughter (the duchess of Richmond). Junius, who was in London some weeks before Surrey's execution, bothered by the loss of a large part of his library (which had been housed with the Howards in distant Norfolk) as well as by his loss of earnings, busily cultivated new connections.[238] Lamenting the calumnies that took the life of his friend and patron, bringing ruin on the entire family, the Dutchman tried to make a fresh start in London. He seems to have landed on his feet. Lodged in Bridewell (sometime royal palace, on lease to an ambassador), Junius found another post as physician, and devoted his literary energies to winning favour with the young king.[239]

Though probably earning his bread and butter through his medical skills, Junius worked strenuously at gaining the patronage of

Edward VI and the government through his writings. On 25 March 1550 he received a substantial grant of £25, on the orders of the Privy Council, 'for making and dedycating certain bookes to the Kinges Majestie'. One of these books was an enlarged edition of a dictionary that was published at Basel in August 1548. Junius had been at work on this great tome for some time, and originally planned to dedicate it to both Henry VIII and Prince Edward. This was not to be, but he made up for it by the lavish eulogies bestowed on both monarchs in the 1548 preface.[240]

The *Lexicon Graecolatinum per Hadrianum Junium novissime auctum* opens with a long preface by the author to Edward VI, new Defender of the Faith and Supreme Head of the English Church. Junius, having described the great labours involved in compiling this monumental work (intended to overcome the shortcomings of earlier dictionaries), explained that no one could be so appropriate a recipient as Edward VI. The young king, so worthy a successor to Henry VIII 'of blessed memory' – whose fame and virtues were known to all the world – was lauded for his erudition. Nor was Protector Somerset left out of this verbose accolade. Junius, showing himself fully posted on contemporary affairs of state, poured a torrent of praise over the duke for the success of his Scottish expedition.[241]

At the beginning of March 1550 Junius addressed another book to King Edward. *De Anno et Mensibus Commentarius* was a short (though learned) work which explained the calendar and different divisions of time in a manner designed to interest the royal adolescent. Junius, who presented the king with a copy of this 'little gift' written in his own fair hand, had done his homework efficiently. Besides the preface, rich in adulation of the king's wisdom and love of learning (and the skills of his tutor, John Cheke), Junius's text shows that he had put himself out to collect material pleasing to his royal reader. The calendar has its fill of English kings – accessions and deaths of Edwards I to IV – as well as the dates of the reigning Edward's birthday and coronation.[242]

At this time Junius was becoming rather well equipped to carve out a successful career in England. His friends and acquaintances (as revealed by his letters) came to include leading lights in the circle that educated and served the young king. Among them were Walter Haddon (friend of Cheke and Roger Ascham) and Nicholas Wotton, diplomat and privy councillor. He also knew William Cecil, who succeeded Wotton as principal secretary in September 1550.[243] If he was wary about committing his religious convictions to paper, Junius evinced every sign of commitment to a government that was following the most radical course of reform known at the time.

In 1548, when that radicalism was declared to the world by the wholesale clearance of church imagery (following the iconoclastic pattern set long since by Zurich), Junius was living near London. There was an outbreak of plague in the capital that summer,[244] but in August, staying in a country house eleven miles away, the doctor was still close to the hub of events. He described the condition of the Church in England in a letter to Nicholas Palemburg. 'Images of saints and votive panels are being removed from churches: walls and altars speak the word of God: God alone is renewing men's hearts …' He itemized knowledgeably the recent changes in ceremonial: increased preaching, the use of English in the communion, the abolition of devotional lights (except for two on the high altar); a state of reversal such that 'previously discredited divine service is now back in place'. Junius related the official changes that so delighted reforming radicals with a certain detachment – and without shock.[245]

The shock came from the other side. Junius's writings came under the ban of Rome, and his open cultivation of Edward VI counted against him. The *Lexicon Graecolatinum* played its share in this, and its author had cause to regret having placed himself so unreservedly behind the advanced protestant government of the young Josiah. It put both his career and his scholarship in jeopardy. According to Junius himself (writing to some highly placed cleric in an effort to undo this damage) it was Paul III – who died in 1549 – who placed a ban on his books, on account of the terms in which he had addressed Edward VI in the *Lexicon*. The author, in exculpation, protested that to have deprived the king of the title of Supreme Head would have laid him open to the penalties of the law, and had nothing to do with his own opinions. One surviving copy of the *Lexicon* (which seems to have become rather a rare book) entirely lacks the author's damaging preface – probably thanks to its having been removed by a Catholic owner. Junius's writings continued to be placed under a wholesale proscription in the lists of prohibited books issued by Paul IV in 1559 and Pius IV in 1564.[246]

Junius was nothing if not a survivor. Fate struck his English aspirations a second time when Edward VI died, to be succeeded by Mary. But it did not take the indefatigable doctor long to muster his energies for a new literary bid for favour. He now tuned his song to suit the Catholic sensibilities of Mary and her husband, and managed to scramble into print a 'carmen heroicum' effusively celebrating the royal wedding of 25 July 1554. Junius's verse, grandly entitled *Philippeis, seu, in Nuptias Divi Philippi . . . et Heroinae Mariae* was published (in more than one edition) in London within weeks of that event, and was unsparing in the sugary flattery it spread on the actors and circumstances of the occasion.[247]

Junius also thought it worth while to put his calendrical text back on the drawing board. Updating it for Queen Mary necessitated quite a lot of work, for besides rewriting his prefatory address (not without allusion to his recent *Philippeida*!), he was at pains to remodel his calendar of notable events to suit the new monarch. Naturally this involved discreet allusions to both Philip and Mary (19 July happily combined proclamation of the queen in 1553 and arrival of her husband-to-be in England a year later), and at the same time Junius took the opportunity to fill up dates that had lacked events in his earlier edition. Here too circumstances dictated the choice of material. Besides matters relating to the history of the empire and of Rome, Junius added notices of the deaths of Thomas More and Erasmus, and the burning of John Hus 'Bohemian heretic'.[248]

By the time this book appeared, its author's restless place-seeking had taken him away from England. The revised *De Anno et Mensibus Commentarius* was printed in Basel in March 1556, and Junius himself was back in Haarlem when he prefaced the book at the beginning of that month. From there (where he had married) he moved to Copenhagen, to serve as physician to the Danish king, Frederick II. Was this departure from England connected with his religious views – or official attitudes towards them? Though the doctor was clearly ready enough to serve Catholic monarchs, he left England about the time that the Marian heresy burnings started, and his own publications were certainly seen as aligning him with Protestants. A few years later, when his thoughts turned back to England, it was through a Protestant exile that his lines of communication were kept vibrating. In 1558 either Junius or his publisher persuaded Laurence Humphrey, who spent part of his Marian exile in Basel (where he, like John Foxe, worked as a proof-corrector for Froben), to write the preface to the edition of Eustathius's commentary on Homer, which was printed by Froben. It was an opportunity for Humphrey to remind his college (Magdalen College, Oxford) of his existence, as well as to jolt memories of Junius's contributions to English learning.[249]

As it turned out, Junius's English days were not over — nor were his seemingly unending hopes of patronage. In the 1560s (and this is where he properly re-enters our story), Junius was again residing in Haarlem, as town physician and rector of the Latin school, and collaborating with Philip Galle in various editions of Maarten van Heemskerck's prints. During this period he once again crossed the Channel to England.

JUNIUS, HEEMSKERCK, AND ELIZABETH

During the 1560s many of the prints of Heemskerck's work were accompanied by verses written by Junius. In a few cases the lines are signed, and in others their authorship is proclaimed by their having been reprinted, many years after Junius's death, in the collection of his verse – *Poëmatum Liber Primus* – which Albert Verlaan, his grandson, brought out in 1598. Clearly Heemskerck and Junius were close associates, and the print series on which they collaborated included a range of topics – allegorical and mythological themes, as well as biblical subjects. The majority of these prints were the work of Philip Galle. The extent to which the painter may himself have drawn inspiration and ideas from Junius and his other learned friends remains an open question. The form of Junius's verses indicates that they were descriptive, rather than schematic; they read as captions composed to accompany an existing picture, not as lines of libretto to be developed by the artist. It is reasonable to suppose that Junius had Heemskerck's drawings in front of him as he composed his verses.[250]

In the section on painting in his *Batavia* (another posthumous work, published in 1588), Junius was generous in his praise of Heemskerck, describing the excellence of his 'subtle invention' and variety of delineation.

Maarten, versatile in every kind of subject matter, second to none in the subtlety of his invention, is wonderfully fertile in depicting so attractively the lie of valleys and farms, the course of rivers and narrows, vessels under sail, people going to town by mule or carts, or walking about in broad-brimmed hats against the sun.[251]

This tribute reflects Junius's appreciation of painting and drawing. He undoubtedly had first-hand knowledge of the artist's working methods, and took full account of the wide range of his graphic output. Heemskerck, he relates (adapting the motto *nulla dies sine linea*), was so sparing of his time that he would not let a day pass without exercising his art 'in drawing a line or in some multitude of works, nearly infinite in variety, both in painting and drawing, to be made into printed plates'. A few pages later Junius also praised the mastery of Philip Galle, for the skill of his engravings of histories and other matters.[252]

Another celebration of Heemskerck penned by Junius appeared in his *Poëmata*. This took the form of a poem describing Opportunity 'the inconstant goddess' and her companion, Regret, as represented by the famous painter. No such depiction by Heemskerck is known, but the subject was an appropriate one for Junius's pen, given the way he had (as he put it in 1559) 'wrestled with fickle fortune in England'. We might postulate that Heemskerck was in fact associated with one of the humanist doctor's repeated attempts to grasp the forelock of the all too elusive goddess.[253]

If, as seems likely, Heemskerck himself was responsible for initially commissioning Hadrianus Junius to write lines for his prints, there was also a close connection between the humanist and the engraver/author Philip Galle. In 1572 Junius described Galle as 'my friend and companion', and ten years before this Galle had engraved a portrait of Junius for which the subject wrote the accompanying chronogram (fig. 123). The drawing from which the print was made had been executed – perhaps by Heemskerck – on Junius's fortieth birthday, in 1551.[254] The three men, themselves with an age differential of nearly forty years, formed a group of friends.

This triangular relationship between Junius, Heemskerck and Galle is of direct interest to our investigation. The story of Esther, engraved by Galle in 1564, was one of the prints that bore Junius's accompanying text. It was from this series that the painter of our picture borrowed the figure of Henry VIII and his bed. It is certainly true that there was no shortage of links between England and the artists of the Low Countries in 1567–9. Hadrianus Junius, however, presents us with a direct line of communication between Heemskerck, one of the works which was a source for our painting, and potential English patrons. This link, moreover, was revitalized at the precise moment that we are concerned with.

In 1568 Junius returned to England. He might well have felt that the goddess *Occasio* had deserted him, more than once, in this country, but he remained her suppliant. Junius, now in his late fifties (an age at which many contemporaries would have preferred to stay put), is found once more cultivating English connections. It is a move that seems to call for some explanation. Though he had felt himself quite an habitué in English affairs Junius had not been expecting to revive his old connections in person. In the early years

of Elizabeth's reign he was writing as if his English experience was a thing of the past. What made him change his mind?[255]

If his timing was affected by current events, doubtless Hadrianus Junius, like so many others, had plenty to worry about as the duke of Alva drove on his ruthless repression. But in fact Junius's own city of Haarlem was one of the towns of Holland that came unscathed through the iconoclasm of 1566–7. Thanks to the personal efforts of Dirck Volckertsz. Coornhert – the learned town clerk of Haarlem, and one of Heemskerck's engravers – all the town's churches had been barred against the iconoclasts for four months after 23 August

1566, and Haarlem was not severely affected by disturbances until its siege in 1572–3 (above p. 57). Perhaps we should also consider the possibility that events in England might themselves have had something to do with the ageing humanist's decision to risk crossing the Channel once again.

On 1 March 1568 Junius dedicated his Latin version of Eunapius (which was printed in Antwerp that year) to Queen Elizabeth, with a reminder of his long residence in England. He also included a complimentary acrostic verse, using the letters of the queen's name and title. A month later, when he was making himself known in the highest quarters, Junius may already have reached this country. On 12 April he sent a complimentary acrostic verse to Sir William Cecil, asking him to 'commend our gifts to the goddess'. He had come carrying a copy of his new work, according to the English translation of his Eunapius which appeared eleven years later (naturalizing the book, after its author's death, in his adopted homeland). Two days before this Junius had written a letter to the son of his long-lost Maecenas, the old pupil of Kenninghall days, Thomas Howard, duke of Norfolk. The doctor described the stormy sea-crossing he had had, and expressed the hope of seeing his Howard patron again. This was not a mere courtesy. Junius was also firing off missives to other members of the Howard household. In July (then in London) he wrote to Gregory Martin, the brilliant academic associate of Edmund Campion (and like him to become a Catholic émigré in the 1570s), who the previous Easter had been appointed tutor to Norfolk's heir, the ten-year-old Philip Howard. Another, adulatory letter was sent to Philip himself, praising a Latin epistle he had written, and offering to serve once more as a Howard teacher.[256] We do not know that anything came of this, but Junius pursued his English interests with determination. Several addresses written in his firm italic hand survive in the Public Records, reflecting his hopes in that summer of 1568.

Queen Elizabeth, in recompense for the labours of the Eunapius edition, was requested on 9 July, four months after its appearance, to grant the editor licence to export sixty dickers of ox-hides. At the same time (to ease the passage of this petition) Junius sent off that July no less than five complimentary verses to the Cecils – three addressed to William and two to his wife Mildred – which, though cast in the graceful indirectness of the humanist's complimentary phrases, amounted to begging letters. Was this 'most devoted',

'Hadrianus Junius medicus' — as he signed himself — in some genuine difficulty after the stormy events of recent years?[257]

There were obviously any number of ways by which the Heemskerck prints utilized by the painter of *Edward VI and the Pope* could have reached England.[258] But the reappearance in England in 1568 of someone who was so closely connected with Maarten van Heemskerck and the prints made from his drawings by Philip Galle is intriguing. Maybe Hadrianus Junius followed the example of Charles Utenhove of Ghent who, besides addressing poems and letters to both the Cecils, had in 1567 sent the queen's secretary a copy of an emblematic engraving foretelling the destruction of Flanders in 1568. Such pictorial presents might be intended to serve public or private ends. If Utenhove (who had had a hand in designing the 1565 medal of Elizabeth) had hopes of persuading the English queen to send aid to Flanders,[259] Junius might have used similar means with the object of resuming his interrupted English career. Maybe he knew about the help that his old pupil, the duke of Norfolk, had recently given to the community of Dutch immigrants in Norwich.[260] Perhaps too, the attention bestowed again on his old Howard patrons in the summer of 1568 was significant in its timing.

JUNIUS, FOXE, AND THE HOWARDS

At the time when Hadrianus Junius, after an absence of about thirteen years, made his return to England, the Howard family was moving towards a new crisis. The duke of Norfolk (fig. 124), who had just reached the age at which his father was executed (he celebrated his thirtieth birthday on 10 March 1568), was contemplating the marriage with Mary Queen of Scots which was to be his downfall, and to take him also to the block on 2 June 1572.

It is impossible to know the exact date at which Thomas Howard recklessly set his sights on this projected fourth marriage. It was not a new idea in 1568, and had been mooted several years earlier by Queen Elizabeth herself. But at this moment it was an idea with very different dimensions, thanks to the circumstances surrounding Darnley's death and the arrival of the Scottish queen in England. Some time between that event (in the spring of 1568) and the beginning of 1569, the duke took the fateful decision. The first eight months of Mary's captivity in England were spent in the custody of Henry, Lord Scrope of Bolton, the Warden of the Western Marches, first at Carlisle Castle, and then at Bolton Castle in Wensleydale. Norfolk's sister Margaret, Lady Scrope, who was thus involved in the reception of the Scottish queen and was sympathetic to her plight, may have encouraged the match.[261]

In the middle of May 1568, when Mary crossed the border into England, Elizabeth's councillors gathered in a state of concern. The duke of Norfolk (ill and depressed since the death of his third wife and her baby in childbirth the previous autumn) was not present, but he remained in London – most unusually – throughout July and August, awaiting the outcome of the discussions. On 6 July (three days before Junius addressed his letter to the queen), the duke entertained Elizabeth to dinner at Howard House, and it was soon public knowledge that he was to play an important role in the proceedings concerning the Scottish queen. In September he was appointed one of the commissioners to consider the charges against Mary, and by October he was in York. Rumours about his projected royal marriage began to circulate in the capital and court gossips took advantage of his absence.[262]

Junius did not move on to the stage of these events, but his presence in England at this time is intriguing. Could he have known what was in the wind? Was he at that dinner party at Howard House? How might he have viewed his ex-pupil's Scottish match? Given his past record, it seems unlikely that such a royal connection would have been taken amiss by the humanist physician who was apparently still ready to bid for a post in the Howard household. If Junius was sufficiently closely in touch to know about Gregory Martin's appointment as Philip Howard's tutor (which was arranged when the duke of Norfolk visited his brother Henry Howard in Oxford at Easter 1568), maybe he had not lost all contact with two other ex-pupils who were deeply involved in the events of 1568–9: Margaret, Lady Scrope, and Jane, countess of Westmorland.[263]

These grown-up members of the Kenninghall schoolroom were all caught up in a venture which seemed to place them and their brother Thomas Howard in a very different religious camp from that of their father, with his challenge to Lent and London pride. But the earl of Surrey's children had had plenty of opportunity to become schooled in the 'fervent zeal' of reform after they had left Junius's hands. For their next tutor — whose charge lasted longer than Junius's — was John Foxe. He was appointed by Mary Fitzroy, the widowed duchess of Richmond,[264] who became guardian of her nephews and nieces when their father was executed and their grandfather imprisoned. It was thanks to her reforming interests that the Howard schoolroom, now located on the duke of Norfolk's estate at Reigate in Surrey, was entrusted to the future martyrologist. He took his duties seriously, trying to implant the true faith in the parish, as well as in the minds of his pupils.

The group tutored at Reigate Castle included, besides the children to whom Junius had imparted the skills of humanist script (something that Foxe did not emulate), a Howard cousin. Charles Howard (born 1536), the elder son of Lord William Howard, was only a year older than Jane, the oldest of his cousins, though belonging to an earlier generation of the family. He became famous as Lord Howard of Effingham, the admiral in command of the English fleet at the time of the Spanish Armada, and when he died at a ripe old age in 1624 was to be buried at Reigate.[265]

In 1607 the preface to a posthumous edition of one of John Foxe's works was addressed to the admiral's son, William Howard, and recalled an event that had taken place at Reigate half a century earlier when the martyrologist (who was ordained deacon in 1550) had taken an initiative in the Edwardian battle against idolatry. The book, *Christ Jesus Triumphant*, was an English version of the apocalyptic Antichrist 'comedy', *Christus Triumphans*, which Foxe had written during his days at Magdalen College, Oxford, in the 1540s. The 1607 translation was the work of Richard Day (son of Foxe's printer and close associate John Day), who might have seen the play since it was produced at Trinity College, Cambridge, in 1572, when he was a student at King's.

Richard Day, fulsome as he was in praising the man his father had helped to make famous, knew what he was talking about, even though it was so long after the event. As vicar of Reigate from 1583 to 1584 he had followed closely in Foxe's footsteps, acting as tutor to William Howard (who was born at Reigate in 1577). Day now reminded his old pupil of the time when his father had joined the group of Howard cousins to be taught by that 'most excellent man' of learning and integrity, John Foxe. It was as one Reigate man and Howard servant, praising another, that Richard Day described how the great martyrologist, the first English preacher in the place – though not the incumbent – had made his mark in downing an idol.

He was the first man that ever preached the Gospell in that place: even when Idolatry was yet in great strength: exceedingly did his free and voluntary labors fructifie among them; for many were there converted from darkness to the light, and from the power of Sathan, unto God: Witnesse hereof the olde superstitious and Idolatrous Lady of Ouldsworth, an Image, or Idoll Saint, who was worshipped there at Reigate, in place of God for hir miraculous power of saving health . . . but this olde Saint lost hir name, hir place, hir power, and frierly [*sic*] false miracles there, through the ministries of this good man . . .[266]

What with his fiery preaching, and some transactions with a pirate on the Dorset coast, Foxe gave the young Howards an exciting time.[267]

How did the two ex-tutors react, respectively, to the dilemma of their sometime pupils in 1568–9? Junius and Foxe were no strangers, but their relations may not have been cordial. Junius had lost to Foxe his post as tutor to the Howard children, thanks to the duchess of Richmond's reforming sympathies. Foxe, in his turn, is unlikely to have looked kindly on one who was ready to offer such effusive compliments to Mary and Philip – not to mention Junius's view of John Hus (above p. 183).[268] The apparent lack of any evidence of communication between them in their quite voluminous literary remains could indicate some mutual lack of sympathy between two men of such utterly different backgrounds and outlook.

Did the young Howards grow fond of Junius? Was the polite diction of his Latin style combined with vernacular banter? Foxe – who was younger by six years – served a longer span with pupils who were older, besides sharing their nationality. Thomas Howard was certainly fond of his second tutor. At the beginning of Elizabeth's reign, when Foxe was still in Basel at work on the enlarged Latin edition of his Book of Martyrs that was published there by Oporinus, there was an affectionate exchange of greetings.

125. John Foxe, the martyrologist (d. 1587), from Henry Holland's Herωologia Anglica *(1620). According to a note in two copies of the book this was based on a picture in 'Dr Fox his son's house' — pointing to Foxe's son Simeon.*

The martyrologist dedicated his *Rerum in Ecclesia Gestarum* to 'my Thomas' from 'your old teacher, or, if you prefer it, now from your new client' — pointing out the inspirational value of his topic. Another tract included an epilogue addressed to the duke announcing Foxe's forthcoming return. The struggling author received the warmest response from his devoted scholar, who polished up his rusty Latin to reply 'To my right loving schoolmaster' with warm offers of hospitality in London and the country. It was an offer that Foxe took up, and from 1560 to 1570 he lived in Norfolk's house at Christ Church, Aldgate, where his son Simeon was born in 1568.[269]

The martyrologist strove as best he could to prevent Thomas

Howard's plan of marrying the royal adulterer and idolater of Scotland. He was not alone. The duke's friends and relations did their uttermost to rescue him from the slope of disaster down which they saw him slipping. Could Surrey's son, at almost exactly the same age as his father, be so foolhardily risking himself and his family's fortunes all over again? Those who had lived through, and helped to rebuild Howard confidence and happiness after that earlier disaster, told Thomas Howard to think again. One who did not hesitate to speak his mind was the duke's old tutor, John Foxe.

A draft of part of a letter from Foxe to the duke of Norfolk survives among the martyrologist's papers. It was probably written in the autumn of 1569, when the duke's blunders were closing in on him. His last view of Kenninghall was on 1 October and the next week found him lodged in the Tower, where he remained for ten months. A wiser man might have reflected that an old schoolmaster's advice may be tendered with disinterest as well as affection.

May it please your Grace, [wrote Foxe] ther is a great rumor with us here in London, and soe farr spread, that it is in every mans mouth almost, of your marriage with the Scottish Queene: which rumor as I trust to bee false, soe would I bee sorry, that it should bee true, for two respects. The one for the good will I beare to you, the other for the love I beare to the common wealth, for that I see noe other, and many besides mee, doe see noe lesse, butt the day of that marriage when soever it beginneth, will end with such a catastophe as wilbee ether ruinous to your selfe, or dangerous to the tranquillity of the realme: the peace whereof standing soe long amongst us through the great mercy of God, God forbidd it should nowe beginn to break by you.

The sometime tutor penned the clearest of warnings.

Your grace knoweth [he continued] what enimies we have both within, and without, against whome wee have always trusted, and doe yet trust, next under God and the queene, to have you a sure scipio unto us: to the contrary whereof thes rumors cannot perswade mee, butt that as you have vertuously begunn, soe by the Lords grace you will constantly continue still. Howebeit since the noise and clamour of the people maketh mee somewhat to muse and bycause true love is always full of feare, I beseech you lett mee say to you what I thinke in this matter. That in case you take this way to marry with this Lady in our Queens days, it will in the end turne you to noe great good. I beseech you ther fore for Gods sake bee circumspect, and marke well what they bee, that sett you on this worke, and wherunto they shoote. Ther is noe greater cunning in these days then to knowe, whome a man may trust. Ensamples you have enough, within the compasse of your owne days, wherby you may learne, what noble men have bin cast away by them, whom they seemed most to trust. Remember I pray you the ensample of Mephibosheth, wherof I told you being yong, howe first hee was under foote, then again . . .²⁷⁰

There the letter breaks off. But we have learnt enough to guess the nature of this reminder. Foxe must have comforted the young Thomas with the story (in the second book of Samuel) of Mephibosheth, the son of Jonathan, who was lamed in an accident as his nurse fled with him, aged five, at the deaths of his father and grandfather, Saul. It was a tale with a happy ending. King David sent for Mephibosheth, wishing to show kindness for Jonathan's sake to any remaining members of the house of Saul. 'And David said unto him, Fear not: for I will surely show thee kindness for Jonathan thy father's sake, and will restore thee all the land of Saul thy father; and thou shalt eat bread at my table continually'. Yet the restored Mephibosheth still had to watch his ways. When he seemed in danger of giving offence to the king on a later occasion he replied to David; 'For all of my father's house were but dead men before my lord the king: yet didst thou set thy servant among them that did eat at thine own table. What right therefore have I yet to cry any more unto the king?' In September 1571 the inventory of the duke's possessions at Kenninghall included 'eight hangings of David and Saul'. Did these include the story of Mephibosheth?²⁷¹

'Remember the example of Mephibosheth . . . how first he was under foot, then again . . .'. Thomas Howard was two months short of nine years old at the time of his father's execution. Foxe surely knew the memories he could stir. And what about the other tutor, who had been so much more directly involved with the young Howards at that time? Did Junius too have something to add, either directly or by Old Testament analogy, to the heartfelt admonitions addressed to the duke of Norfolk? Probably we shall never know. But we might reflect that there was a special inwardness for the Howards in the two biblical prints by Heemskerck that contributed to the painting of Edward VI (whoever brought them to England). The destruction of the Tower of Babel–Babylon ('*Alta cadit Babylon* . . .') recalled the theme of Surrey's reckless exploit as the scourge of London–Babylon, immortalised in his own lines ('London, hast thow accused me / Of breche of lawes, the roote of stryfe?' – above, p. 178). The scene of Ahasuerus (*Rex, ubi non habitum virtuti discit honorem*, above, pp. 67–8) shows a king who learns about honour from the dishonourable, and whose faithless servant has had the gallows set up in readiness for the execution of the faithful – shades of 1547.

In August 1570, after the northern rising and about the time of Felton's posting of the papal bull, Norfolk was released from the Tower, having written 'ragged lines' of submission to the queen. He was not free, but the walls in which he was confined were those of his own Howard House. Nor had he learnt his lesson. In September the following year he was back in the Tower, deeply compromised by Cecil's findings about his secret correspondence with the plotter Ridolfi and his renewed contacts with the imprisoned Scottish queen. The battle to save him still went on, but it was difficult to remain hopeful.[272]

On 22 September 1571 the duke's younger brother, the learned Henry Howard, probably the most receptive of Junius's Howard pupils, wrote a long letter of appeal to William Cecil. It survives in the beautiful italic hand which is a smaller more flowing version of his tutor's. Henry Howard put all his learned resources into this urgent plea, beseeching Lord Burghley ('most noble Burghley' – as he had recently become) for help, at least for the opportunity to put his brother's case himself to the queen, while at the same time ('cautious pilot' as he was) keeping his own head well above water. Even so, the younger Howard was himself arrested when charges were brought against his brother, and had to appeal again to Burghley for his own release.[273]

Two days later, Norfolk's son and heir Philip Howard addressed his own supplication to Lord Burghley. The young earl of Surrey, who earlier this year had celebrated his fourteenth birthday and his marriage to Lady Anne Dacre, was already burdened with the cares of the world. As he wrote at Kenninghall, the royal visitors sent to inventory all Norfolk's possessions were completing their work, and plans were soon in train for moving the entire household of the duke's children and step-children from Kenninghall to Audley End. Philip's 'moste dutifull requeste' to his father's good lord and friend of times past reflected deep anxiety. 'The comminge of the commissioners ... doth make me greatly affrayde that the quene is very muche displeased with my Lord my father'. He was ready to come to court if it would help to mitigate the queen's anger and relieve his father's unhappy state.[274]

Thomas Howard continued to trust in Burghley's friendship. He appointed him as the 'adopted father' of his 'orphan children', and provided that this old friend should receive as keepsakes a ruby ring and a piece of cloth of gold.[275] But the royal minister had uncovered too many mistakes and misjudgements to allow friendship to interfere with policy. It was too late for favours, and treason set charity out of doors. Things had passed the point of no return.

During his last months and days the duke of Norfolk affirmed his scriptural faith and turned back to Foxe, his favourite tutor, for support. He was convicted on 16 January 1572, and then spent an intolerable period of waiting in strict confinement in the Tower, uncertain of his fate, thanks to the demoralizing indecision of the queen, who painfully reprieved and postponed his execution until 2 June. The two spiritual advisers who helped Thomas Howard through these last weeks were Alexander Nowell, dean of St Paul's, and John Foxe, the martyrologist.

Norfolk asked for Nowell to visit, and his gaoler, Sir Henry Skipwith, reported the day after his conviction that 'he also longethe muche for Mr Foxe his old scholemaister, to whome he muche desyres to performe that faithe whiche he first grounded him in'. At this brink of death Thomas Howard also sought permission for Edward Dering and Thomas Sampson to come to see him. Harry Skipwith endorsed this request as he forwarded it to Burghley, 'for the more good men that shall talk with him in this tyme (in my symple opinion) yt is the better'.[276] Both these men were purists with strong views on papal idolatry, who had proved their zeal by advocating or practising iconoclasm. Both were well known to the duke, and Sampson had officiated with Bishop Parkhurst in 1564 at the funeral of his second wife, Margaret, who was buried at Norwich with due attention to reforming proprieties – '*sine crux, sine lux, at non sine tinkling*'.[277] Such were the formulae (joking aside) that Thomas Howard was endorsing during his final hours. The spiritual advice he sought at this time was (like that of his schoolroom days at Reigate) consonant with the messages of *Edward VI and the Pope*.

Dean Nowell and John Foxe supported the condemned man through the agony of these days, as his health deteriorated and his personality was taxed to its limits. Nowell visited regularly. Foxe remained close to the end, and the duke's last wishes included the desire that £20 a year should 'be allowed to Mr. Foxe'. Nowell and Foxe were both with the duke to take their last farewells on the scaffold at eight o'clock in the morning of 2 June 1572.[278]

We have seen how staunch were the reformed beliefs of both men in their opposition to idolatry. They helped during these prolonged last weeks of heart-searching to keep Norfolk on the scriptural path he had seemed to be so hopelessly deserting. The duke's last long letter of advice to his children anxiously stressed his abhorrence of the papal religion which his pursuit of the Scottish marriage had appeared to endorse. 'And upon my blessing beware of blinde papistry', he told Philip, explaining his belief in faith and works. 'I write somewhat the more herein, because perchance you have heretofore heard, or perchance hereafter shall heare, false brutes that I was a papist'. Such rumours were indeed rife at this very time, reinforced by a ballad of William Elderton. 'How manie devises to do her grace wronge, / By Pope holie practise, were pact in his braines'. It was untrue, Thomas Howard wrote to his son. His faith had always been that which he died in, whatever his failures to bear witness to it. And his children should find comfort and salvation, as he had himself, in the reading of scripture.[279]

Might our painting of Edward VI have been put together by some kind of joint effort, to add pictorial persuasion to the copious flow of words that aimed to change Thomas Howard's mind – or perhaps to say through the visual medium things that were too embarrassing or hazardous to put into words? There was no shortage of effort. Friends, relations, and spiritual advisers, were doing their best to bring him to his senses. And John Foxe, the old tutor, who remained on such close terms with his sometime pupil, addressing the duke in his publications, being offered and accepting his hospitality, was not afraid to give firm advice. There were ample opportunities for the martyrologist to gain access to the pictorial sources which – whether or not they came via Hadrianus Junius – contributed to our picture. There were also artists at work on the Book of Martyrs who could have advised on, or helped with its design. Undoubtedly, too, Foxe (like his friend Nowell, who himself ventured on the risky business of picture-making for the queen), held exactly that view of the Edward–Josiah that was represented in our panel. Was this a visual warning, prepared in the hour of the duke of Norfolk's danger?

IDOLATRY AGAIN

It may be hard now to grasp the terrible spectre of England's apostasy that seemed to loom in Norfolk's match with the Scottish queen. The duke may never personally have veered towards Rome, but he had consorted heedlessly with 'filthy idolaters', as put by George Buchanan, who regarded him as 'the principal enemy of the religion of Christ in this isle', threatening the state of the Church in both England and Scotland.[280] There were many also in England who expressed similar fears and strove to avert this horror.

The proposed marriage imposed a heavy burden on those who felt themselves the guardians of the duke's conscience. One such was Edward Dering (fig. 77), who served Norfolk as chaplain in the late 1560s. In the autumn of 1569, when clouds were gathering over his lord's future, Dering joined with Edward Hansbie (another ducal chaplain) to draw up a collection of prayers for use in his household. And in March the next year Dering sought permission from Cecil for the imprisoned duke to come to the sermon whenever he preached in the Tower (where he was chaplain), as a means to help drive 'all strange fancies ... out of mie lord of Norfolkes hed'.[281]

Yet, when Thomas Howard's fate was known, Dering blamed himself for having allowed tact or deference to mute his advice. Like Foxe and Nowell, he bestowed what comfort he could, and wrote more than once to send words of consolation. The good warranty that he was among the elect should enable Thomas Howard to 'be bold to die'; 'you are but one steppe from this glorious blessing', and there was solace in the thought that 'all flesh is grasse ...'. But temptation would continue 'even to the Axe' so he must be ever watchful to 'doe the worke of a trewe gospiller'. For himself Dering had to ask forgiveness. 'You know howe in my time I have perswaded you from your wicked servants, from your Popish friendes, and from your adulterous woman. But (alas) my Lord, your high calling hath bridled my wordes, I could not speake as I should, my words were too soft to heale so olde a disease'. Writing his last letter as a brother to a fellow Christian stripped of worldly honour, Dering learnt that the end had come: 'it was toulde me your daye was appointed to morrowe'. He added a reminder to his final call to prayer. 'Remember well howe religious the state of a prince shoulde be unto us, and into what daunger you have brought your Sovereigne Lade . . .'[282]

Another reforming preacher was Thomas Lever, who, as warden of Sherburn Hospital near Durham at the time of the Scottish queen's arrival in England, had direct experience of northern dangers. On 24 February 1569 Lever wrote in urgent tones to the earl of Leicester and Sir William Cecil, pressing them to prevent England's descent into ungodliness. There was grave danger of religious subversion, and 'the moost godli and faithfull subiects be maini times worst suspected and reported'. The history of Ahasuerus showed how faithful subjects might be falsely accused as breakers of the king's laws though – thanks to Esther – they had happily been delivered. Lever addressed himself particularly to the danger described by the prophet Ezekiel (chapter 14), of those hypocritical idolaters who had the appearance of godliness while 'keping their idols in their hartes, and setting their stombling blockes afore their faces'. The preacher did not only write in veiled biblical terms. He had specific perils in mind, namely 'notable papistrie in England and Scotland', and pointed out that

the old stombling stockes be sett openli of mani thinges in mani places, and especialli of the crucifix in England, and of the masse in Scotland afore the faces of the hieghest, is daili to be seen of idolators and traitors with reioiecing and hoping of a dai . . .

'Hoping for a day': that fateful longing for a return of the old catholic order, which lay behind the rising of 1569.[283]

Cross and crucifix, the cause of repeated flurries of anxiety in Queen Elizabeth's chapel, were by 1570 seen in some quarters as ensigns of papal subterfuge and sedition. In 1569 the northern rebels who trooped under the banner of the five wounds, were led by a venerable old gentleman, Richard Norton, 'bearing a cross with a streamer before them'.[284] A contemporary ballad, *Northomberland newes*, took the northerners to task as 'Catholiques old' who 'carie dead images uppe and downe', raising cross and crucifix. And much good it did them, faithless in allegiance as they were.

> For thoughe ye spoile churches and burne up the Bible,
> And worshippe gaie crosses in every towne,
> Your idolles you asses are never possible,
> To save ye that will not be trew to the crowne.[285]

201

Lady Margaret Douglas, who at the beginning of 1568 commissioned the memorial painting of her murdered son, Lord Darnley, had no doubts about the virtues of mass and crucifix. Some notes made by Burghley on the seditious state of Lancashire and Cheshire in 1571, included the report that Lady Margaret had been giving out silver crosses to local gentlewomen to wear round their necks as relics. Lady Margaret suffered several terms of detention in the course of her headstrong career, and in the Darnley Jewel which she had made between 1571 and 1578 (a work that was rich in emblematic messages) her religious persecution was represented by a stake surrounded by small crosses in flames.[286]

Only three months before the painting of the Darnley picture (colour pl. III), the iconoclasts had for a second time showed their views of the 'idol' in the royal chapel. Leading courtiers who, as we have seen, were suspected of complicity in these acts of derring-do included Sir Francis Knollys, who escorted Norfolk to the Tower in October 1569, and the duke's arch-enemy Robert Dudley, the earl of Leicester. Affairs in the north accentuated old alarmism about the pernicious example of remaining imagery.

Among the expressions of alarm was an anonymous pamphlet, several editions of which appeared about 1569, arguing strongly against the mooted marriage as a danger to both England's queen and religion. Possible authors of this work include Francis Walsingham (who played a leading part in unravelling Ridolfi's schemes and foiling the Scottish marriage), and Thomas Sampson (whose nonconformity had lost him the deanery of Christ Church in Oxford, where in 1561 he had made a demonstrative bonfire of 'superstitious utensils').[287] The *Discourse touching the pretended match betwene the Duke of Norfolke and the Queene of Scottes* strenuously refuted the claim that the continuance of the gospel and the safety of the English sovereign would be served by Norfolk, rather than a foreigner, allying himself with Mary. She had shown herself to be dangerously disposed towards Elizabeth, and was too 'corruptible a vessell' to serve true religion, while the duke had been too trustful of papists. England's religious state was in peril, with possibly two thirds of the realm inclined to papistry and atheism. Were the country's premier peer to marry the idolatrous Scottish queen, what terrible evil might not befall?[288]

To reinforce this point the pamphlet turned to a well-known example – the idolatry of Solomon, which, as we have seen (figs. 41–2, pp. 61–3), became a topos for Reformation iconoclasts. It was cited in the Elizabethan homily, as a dread example for the modern ruler. 'Solomon also, the wisest of all men ... suffering his wanton paramours to bring their idols into his court and palace, was by carnal harlots persuaded, and brought at the last to the committing of spiritual fornication with idols', so that from being the wisest and godliest of princes, he was reduced to the 'foolishest and wickedest'. Or, as put more pithily by Armado in *Love's Labour's Lost*, 'yet was Solomon so seduced, and he had a very good wit'.[289] If the great Solomon had succumbed in this way, what hope was there (asked the *Discourse*) for the hapless English duke, were he to join himself to one who was his superior both in social degree and in subtlety of wit? Presumably there was no need – given the Scottish queen's sexual record – to embroider the parallel between her and Solomon's paramours. The danger was self-evident.

And for proofe hereof, [let] the onelye example of Salomon teach us so to thinke. Dyd not he by matchyng with an idolatresse Aegyptian, become an idolater, wherby ensued to him Gods high displeasure, to the great plague of his kin and posteritie? ... That lawe which forbad Salomon to marry with the Aegyptian idolatresse, standeth in force stil, and forbiddeth the Duke to mary with the Scottish idolatresse, least that punishment which fell upon Salomons kinne, teach the Duke to beware of like punishment.[290]

It was much the same warning as John Foxe's. The marriage with the sinner of Scotland would take not only the duke, but the entire English nation, back into the pit of idolatry.

Elizabethans lived with a relentlessly scriptural religion, so that biblical events and figures brushed constantly against the daily world. During the crisis years of 1569–70 – critical both for the Tudor régime and for the house of Howard – Old Testament parallels were on many lips. And there was more than one Solomon who could have been expected to take heed. The queen and her premier noble had both been put on alert. If Queen Elizabeth's continuing readiness to retain images seemed (to some) like dicing with idolatry, the duke of Norfolk was suspected of selling his own soul and that of England's believers, by alliance with the most egregious royal idolatress.

If we look at *Edward VI and the Pope* through the eyes of either Queen Elizabeth or the duke of Norfolk at this time of danger to them both about the year 1570, there are unavoidable personal messages to be read in it. They might have induced discomfort, or pain, if not the self-reproach which the commissioner of the painting perhaps wanted to arouse.

> Our Queene is the daughter of Henry theight,
> Who brought every altar and imagerie downe.[291]

Elizabeth was haunted (if not hounded) by the persuasions – unhistorical as they might sometimes be – of those who insisted on her inherited religious obligations.

The deathbed of Henry VIII held poignant memories for queen as well as duke. For Elizabeth it marked the beginning of a decade of uncertainty, that had included a spell in the Tower at the time of Wyatt's rebellion under Mary, and before that – when she was in her teens – the suspicions and examinations that surrounded her frolics with Thomas Seymour, culminating in his execution in March 1549.

There was little pleasure, either for Elizabeth or Norfolk, in contemplating a depiction of the 'apotheosis of the Somerset régime';[292] of Edward and Thomas Seymour, twenty years after the event. The queen, still making the most of matrimonial diplomacy as her fortieth birthday loomed closer, had rueful memories of her adolescent flirtations with the witty admiral, whose portrait hung in her collection (fig. 13). Both these royal step-uncles had gone to the block before Elizabeth was nineteen, and Catherine Parr – the most agreeable and potentially maternal of her stepmothers – had died on Elizabeth's fifteenth birthday, after giving birth to Thomas Seymour's daughter.

But there was no one – not excluding his own daughter – for whom Henry VIII's deathbed could have been more acutely painful a recollection than it was for Thomas Howard. Between 1569 and 1572 he often had cause to reflect on the terror of those days in 1546–47, when the king's commissioners had come to list all the familiar objects he had grown up with at Kenninghall, when his father and grandfather had both been swept away, one to be beheaded on Tower Hill, the other to prison in the Tower. 'When my grandfather dyed I was not much above a yeare older then you are now', the duke wrote after his conviction to his eldest son. When his own father was executed he was younger still. 'Let a gallows be made ...' (above, p. 68) 'a paire of galowes of fiftie cubites hie'[293] (figs. 48, 50).

The dying Henry VIII, pointing towards his son and heir and the erect figure of the duke of Somerset at his side, indicated the man who, in his ambitious thrust for power over the young king, had doomed the earl of Surrey. The disaster that overcame the Howards at the time of Edward VI's accession overshadowed the fourth duke's life, and in 1570 he was about to repeat it. 'For all of my

father's house were but dead men before my lord the king ...'
(above, p. 196). It was only the extraordinary providence of King
Henry VIII dying in the nick of time that saved the third duke of
Norfolk in 1547. The fourth duke, occupying in 1569–70 the
selfsame room in the Constable's lodging in the Tower that had
confined his grandfather for six years, had ample time to reflect on
the biblical words with which Foxe had sought to comfort him.[294]

The picture of the confident Seymours, placed in such advant-
ageous proximity to the young king, held odious associations for
Thomas Howard. There were so many intimate personal insults that
might have poisoned his eight-year-old mind in 1547, when the
Seymour pack fastened on the spoils of his father and grandfather,
sending officials to pry and inventory. They deliberately arrived in
the early hours of the morning ten days before Christmas 1546, to
take the household by surprise. Thomas Howard's aunt, the duchess
of Richmond, was still not dressed, and shaking like a leaf. His
mother, Frances, countess of Surrey, who was heavily pregnant at
the time, miscarried owing to the shock of these events. It was small
consolation to her that the commissioners allowed her to keep 'to put
aboute her in her charyot' an old black satin nightgown of her
father-in-law's, 'moche worne and furred with conye and lambe'.
The countess, now the wife of Thomas Steynings, was still alive in
1572, when her eldest son tried to spur her departure from London,
greatly afraid that 'if she shull happen to be in towne at the tyme of
his execution, the sodeyne newes thereof mowght happen to be the
deathe of hyr'.[295]

Was the George depicted hanging on Somerset's chest the one he
had impounded from the third duke of Norfolk? The fourth duke,
who sold most of his own valuables in the cause that was his ruin, had
seen his grandfather's jewels and rich personal possessions confiscated for the benefit of the Seymours and their allies. The Garter
collar and George (the latter set with diamonds and a ruby) were
delivered to Somerset, who kept the George, passing on the collar to
Sir William Paget. The duke of Norfolk's parliament robe was also
handed over to the protector, who took for his own use a 'vernacle'
of gold arras which had adorned the head of the duke's bed, while
clothing belonging to the duchess was allocated to the rapacious
Seymours. Items from the earl of Surrey's wardrobe, including
doublets of orange and black velvet embroidered with white satin,
went to another Seymour brother, Sir Henry Seymour. Was part of
the punishment of a traitor's family the humiliation of seeing one's

parents' (or grandparents') best clothing on the backs of the despoilers? They were insults an eight-year-old was not likely to forget, and in 1571 Somerset's heir, the earl of Hertford (another Edward Seymour), was counted by the duke among the handful of irreconcilable 'foes' to his ambitions. If the fourth duke of Norfolk looked in 1572 at this Ahasuerus—Henry with his Josiah heir, he knew what wretched humiliations would fall on his own son.[296]

'All fleshe is grasse'. Idolater or no, the words were cutting for a man whose father had died by the axe as he was to die himself, at roughly the same age, only twenty-five years later. He felt as crushed as 'a dede flye', 'a deade doge in thys worlde', as he waited helplessly for this repetition of events. If the papal minions tugging at their chains were a reminder of the insecurity of earthly crowns ('O Philip! Philip!' wrote Thomas Howard, 'Beware of high degrees!')[297] that posse of power surrounding Edward VI in 1547 represented his own position, threatened by another scheming group. What the Seymours had been to his father and grandfather, the Dudleys had become to him. They effected his overthrow, and the collapse of his house, just as the Seymours had brought about the downfall of his father and grandfather.

'Beware of blind papistry'. The pope with his satellites, depicted endeavouring to pull down the Tudor Josiah, recalled the foolish sangfroid with which the duke had allowed Ridolfi to make use of his name. Had he not effectively set his hand to a letter promising Pope Pius V 'to hazard my life for the glory of God' in an enterprise to place a Catholic monarch on the throne of England, wishing his holiness success in this plan and 'length of days to govern his church'?[298]

Neither Elizabeth—Hezekiah, nor the failed queen-consort duke would have particularly enjoyed contemplating a picture which made such an issue of the 'evangelical Josiah' purging his realm (above, p. 34), together with the treacherous undermining of the English throne by the idolatrous pope. Neither would have relished the all-too-conspicuous reminders that the path of duty lay in fidelity to particular scriptural laws which proscribed the misbeliefs of 'papistry', including retention of the cross of Christ and his image 'which neither carver nor painter can make' (above, p. 144). If there were inscribed texts which pressed home these lessons yet more unambiguously than the painted imagery, the picture would have been that much more provoking.

Even without all its texts, the queen would not have missed the picture's message. The young Josiah became an all too familiar invocation to implement a kind of reform for which she lacked enthusiasm. Reminders of the iconoclastic achievements of her brother's short reign carried inevitable implications for her own chapel furnishings and her refusal to see Cheapside Cross go the way so many church crosses had already gone. Papal flesh falling before royal feet meant something different in 1569–70 from what it had in 1547. Catholic sympathies and the primacy of Rome were now placed in a new, and for Elizabeth an unpleasantly confrontational relationship; political realities cut awkwardly across the queen's religious management.

A jewel that the earl of Leicester presented to the queen as his new year's gift in 1571 contained its own significance – witness the interest of the Spanish ambassador, who sent a description of it home to Madrid. The painting inside this jewel showed Elizabeth enthroned, with the Queen of Scots in chains at her feet, begging for mercy, while Spain and France were covered by waves of the sea, and Neptune and others bowed to England's queen.[299] The wish-fulfilment induced by the Scottish queen could take many forms.

'Feyned holines' was the accepted English proscription of the papacy, and 'idolatry' and 'supersticioun', as written about the falling pope in our painting, were the inevitable companions of the condemned Roman religion. How many lectures had the queen already heard on that subject before Pius V issued his bull of excommunication? The subject made threadbare by so many zealous preachers was a decidedly unpromising topic for verbal addresses to Elizabeth. Perhaps, since she was known to snub publicly those of ill-judged courage who hectored her on this matter, a silent speaking picture seemed a more tactful mode of delivering an urgent message. Plenty of other ways had already been tried to convince her that godliness and images did not consort together, and that the Supreme Governor of the Church could not be a law unto herself. Religion 'to her people's and her own content' must mean taking down cross and crucifix, whether in the queen's private chapel or in that most public of London thoroughfares, Cheapside.

Such readings of our picture are hypothetical, but at the end of the day, we can only read this historical painting with a historical hypothesis. I have here suggested two such interpretations. Either is possible: neither is proved. Probably neither can be.

SEQUEL

The history of the painting is obscure. It first appears in Christie's sale of 20 March 1874, where the category of 'Early English' paintings consisted of lot 9: 'Edward VI. and his Council: an allegory of the Reformation'. It was then being sold as part of the collection of pictures 'ancient and modern' that had belonged to the late Thomas Green, Esq., of Ipswich and Upper Wimpole Street, 'Formed by himself and his Family during the last Century, and early Part of the present Century'.[300]

In the 1950s *Edward VI and the Pope* was in the possession of the Colvile family (to whom it had come by bequest), and on 18 November 1959 was once again up for sale, this time at Sotheby's (as lot 111). It was then bought in for £160. The National Portrait Gallery, which had been in correspondence with Mrs Colvile about the picture in 1953, had decided against purchase in October 1958 on the grounds that 'it appears likely that the persons represented in the group are, at best, derivatives', and indeed some were questionable as 'likenesses of particular individuals'. This decision had been reached after sounding historical experts, including Professor S. T. Bindoff and Dr G. R. Elton. However, it was allowed that 'should the identities of more of the individuals be established, and the painting of the group also be established as contemporary', the Gallery might reconsider purchase. In the event, though neither of these criteria can be said to have been completely satisfied, the painting was bought from Captain R. M. Colvile for an undisclosed sum in October 1960. As we have already seen, it was in this year that Dr Roy Strong (who became Assistant Keeper at the Gallery in 1959) published his findings in the *Journal of the Warburg and Courtauld Institutes*.[301]

The Thomas Green whose picture collection came under the hammer in 1874 – some years after the death of its last owner, one in a line of Thomas Greens – is an interesting character. He was the younger of two men of this name, both of Ipswich, whose literary output, chiefly of pamphlets on political and religious issues, earned them mention in the *Dictionary of National Biography*. The second Thomas Green (1769–1825), was called to the bar but dropped out of professional practice on inheriting his father's estate in 1794, which enabled him to devote himself entirely to reading, travel and – though the evidence on this is unfortunately sparse – building up his picture collection. His visual appreciation was acute. This emerges from the *Extracts from The Diary of a Lover of Literature* that he published in 1810, which for the most part was a record of his reading ('merely Literary', he warned), but which also contained observations on scenery and paintings. Green was particularly struck by the sea view by Turner which he saw at the Royal Academy in 1797 (probably *Fishermen coming ashore at Sun Set previous to a Gale*). 'I am entirely unacquainted with the artist,' Green wrote in his journal (Turner was then twenty-two and this was one of the first oils he exhibited), 'but if he proceeds as he has begun, he cannot fail to become the first in his department.' Two years later he was again delighted by Turner's landscapes, commenting; 'he always throws some peculiar and striking *character* into the scene he represents'.[302]

Thomas Green combined what his biographer called 'an ardent admiration of paintings' with discriminating judgement. When he died in 1825 he left behind at Ipswich – where he had spent most of his life – a 'numerous collection', the acquisition of which did not, regrettably, feature much in the pages of his diary (at least as published). But his pride in his collection is evident in his record on 15 March 1824, that he had completed the making of a priced catalogue, which put a total value on his pictures (excluding those inherited from his father and Lord Chedworth) of £1,500.[303] This picture collection contributed to his local fame and was celebrated in publications relating to his native town. In 1858, articles in the *Suffolk Chronicle* on the two Thomas Greens as 'Suffolk worthies', commented on the younger:

He possessed by far the most valuable collection of paintings in Ipswich, and was not merely acquainted with the different styles of the art, but was able to point out the various excellences of the old masters in a manner which left him few superiors. This attachment to paintings seems to increase with age. Even his love of literature had to yield to love of pictures.

Only three weeks before his death he was writing delightedly about his acquisition of two Gainsboroughs.[304]

This collection was left to Thomas Green's only son, a third Thomas Green, who was a minor (not quite fourteen) at the time of his father's death. His guardians were instructed to see him packed off to Harrow, and then 'transplanted, not too early', to Trinity

College, Cambridge. Meanwhile the care of the pictures was assigned to the boy's sometime nurse, Sarah Ann Birkett, who had long been in the Greens' service and was now kept on as housekeeper, living on an annuity in the cottage next the coach-house, and (providing she remained separate from her husband) given the duty of ensuring 'that the house, pictures, furniture etc.' were kept 'in capital condition'.[305] In 1830, when Thomas Green III had two years to go to attain his majority, the picture collection remained in the house in Brook Street, Ipswich, where his father had lived, and in 1843 it was still intact in the town, though in another location, awaiting 'a fresh arrangement'.[306] What happened to it between then and the sale of 1874 is obscure. The third Thomas Green died before 1858, and I have failed to trace either his will or the manuscripts that had been left to him by his father 'as a future amusement perhaps'.[307]

Thomas Green II stipulated in his will (made in September 1812) that at his death an inventory should be made of all his household goods, pictures included. Were this to be found it might perhaps push back the documented history of our painting. The story of the Green picture collection does at least give some sort of terminus, suggesting (without proof) that the picture was in Ipswich, in the family house in Brook Street, by 1825.

Having reached this point half a century before the sale of 1874 we might end with a little speculation – adding hypothesis to hypothesis for good measure (given what has gone before)!

The geographical location has its interest. Although the 1874 sale catalogue places the late Thomas Green's property in London as well as Ipswich, the collection as a whole certainly started life in East Anglia. Thomas Green II was a traveller, and clearly added to his collection from various sources. But it is a distinct possibility that the 'Early English' item we are interested in was a local acquisition, specially in view of the inherent improbability, given Green's tastes (and those of his time), that he would have gone out of his way to get hold of this 'allegory of the Reformation'. Not that the Edward VI picture was alone of its kind on his walls. Green also owned portraits listed (by Christie's in 1874) as being of Henry VIII; Lord Burghley; 'a Nobleman' dated 1545; and 'John Bettes; Portrait of the Earl of Surrey in a Black Dress, Gold Chain, and Jewelled Cap.[308]

Green did not have to buy all his paintings. Some (many, according to the Revd James Ford in 1825) came to him by bequest from John Howe, fourth Lord Chedworth, an extremely rich man who died unmarried in 1804, ignoring his relatives in the disposition

126. West gable and north façade of Kenninghall Place, Norfolk – all that remains of the great house built by the third duke of Norfolk, which was the centre of the Howard estates. It is still owned by the duke of Norfolk.

of his huge estate. Though his title and landed property lay in Gloucestershire, Chedworth spent most of his life in Ipswich (his mother's territory), his house being in Brook Street, where the Greens lived. He was a witness to the will of Thomas Green I, and an 'intimate friend' of Thomas Green II, who was nearer to him in age. He left to the latter 'my head of Vandyck by himself', together with the choice of 'such other of my paintings and prints as he may choose to accept'.[309] It seems that the neighbouring collector made the most of this opportunity.

These East Anglian associations might, tentatively, be linked with my hypothesis that the genesis of *Edward VI and the Pope* is located in the circle and history of Thomas Howard, fourth duke of Norfolk. His execution in 1572 marked the beginning of the severance of the dukes of Norfolk from East Anglia. Thanks to Thomas Howard's first marriage to Mary Fitzalan and the failure of

211

127. Edward VI by Baron de Triqueti. The Bible is inscribed with words from 2 Kings, 22: 1–2. Purchased by Queen Victoria in 1858, the statue was apparently in part inspired by Prince Albert, who placed it in the vestibule of Windsor Castle as an example to the future Edward VII (b. 1841).

the male line of her family, Philip Howard became through his mother heir to the earldom of Arundel. Arundel Castle took the place of Kenninghall House. The estate, including Kenninghall Lodge Farm and Shelfhanger Hall Farm — where Hadrianus Junius had once been lodged — remained in the hands of the dukes of Norfolk, but the great old house was no longer of interest as a family seat. It was pulled down in the middle of the seventeenth century and (according to Francis Blomefield), the materials 'sold for a trifle'. Apart from one portion (fig. 126), all that remained of the sometime palace were bricks built into other structures, some bearing the arms of Arundel and Howard.[310]

It is possible to imagine that family possessions as well as building materials came onto the market during this shift of residence. Unloved Howard pictures could have fetched up a century or so later on the walls of Greens in Ipswich. Who knows? Perhaps no one over all those years had much time or affection for such a derivative propagandist painting.

Yet in the middle of the last century the young Josiah still lived on, and was still a royal model. Perhaps the last representation of him in this long descent, was a statue by Baron de Triqueti that was bought by Queen Victoria in 1858 and set up at Windsor as an example for the future Edward VII (fig. 127). This elegant Edward VI points with a sceptre at those words in the Book of Kings that had so often been cited to inspire English monarchs. 'Josiah . . . did that which was right in the sight of the Lord . . .'[311] It seems like the end of an era.

CONCLUSION

Edward VI and the Pope was once hailed as a unique illustration of the action of early Tudor iconoclasts, who did such enormous damage to the artistic heritage of the English Church. We now know that though the picture's inset was indeed very closely related to contemporaries' destructive mission, it portrays this obliquely. This was a borrowed scene, just as the recumbent figure of Henry VIII was a borrowed image, and both were taken from pictorial sources that seem to have reached England from the Low Countries soon after their appearance. *Edward VI* was a historical painting, composed at least twenty years after the moment depicted, probably for clearly conceived reasons, and its content can be directly linked with the momentous events that took place in England and the Netherlands in the 1560s.

This was a time of crisis in both countries. As religious refugees from the duke of Alva's persecution flooded into England, the years from 1568 to 1571 were the most dangerous so far faced by Elizabeth's protestant régime. The imprisonment of Mary Queen of Scots, followed by the northern rebellion and the papal excommunication of 1570, posed serious threats to the Elizabethan government. Reforming certainties hardened in this time of threat. Home truths were uttered more forcefully, and the need to complete (or greatly improve) the state of England's conversion was emphasized as never before since the queen's accession.

Even those wary of historical turning-points must admit that these events, and reactions to them, marked a phase. The unyielding purifiers, who had already wrecked so much of England's art and old religious ways, now swung their destroying tools over a wider arc. In the north Archbishop Grindal dealt the final death blow to the Corpus Christi plays at York and Wakefield. Religious drama, organ-playing, dancing, a whole world of behaviour, came under the ban of 'prophanation of the sacramentes and the maunteynaunce of superstition and idolatrie',[312] while – thanks to fears of Rome – cross and crucifix became suspect as symbols of sedition.

The painting of *Edward VI and the Pope* belongs to this fresh phase of reforming purification. It has not proved possible to pinpoint its date, or to name its painter, but its sources and iconography yield some wider conclusions, and relate it to central developments in Elizabethan England.

Paintings, as much as sermons and books, prints and jewels, could be addressed to individuals and particular circumstances with specific objectives in view. I have suggested that *Edward VI and the Pope* was comparable to the Darnley Memorial picture of the same period, in having a definite purpose. In this case the assembled sources were focused for a change of policy, not an act of revenge, and I have put forward two – mutually exclusive – hypotheses as to the identity of the intended recipient. One, that the picture was intended to boost Queen Elizabeth into conscientious imitation of her Josiah brother, by acting more responsibly (that is destructively) towards potential idols, whether these were of a personal or public kind – in her own chapel, or in her capital city. The other, that the deathbed depiction of Henry VIII, making his final dispositions for the inheritance of his piously Protestant heir, aimed to jolt the errant duke of Norfolk into realization that his proposed Scottish marriage threatened the entire English nation with relapse into papal idolatry, as well as the repetition of the Howards' ruin in 1547.

Either hypothesis has some plausibility, but neither can be proved. And, given the scriptural commonplaces on which the imagery is based, there are later occasions which could also suit it. That does not, however, obliterate the value of this walk around the painting, for it has told us much about the verbal and visual furniture that stocked many sixteenth-century minds. As Cranmer's Prayer Book and the *Homilies* and Foxe's Martyrs slip away from the consciousness of twentieth-century English people, we increasingly need reminders of the figures and images that Elizabeth's subjects took (or were learning to take) for granted.

Old Testament history was closely annexed to the Tudors' own. The kings of the Books of Kings were serious models for contemporary monarchs. Ordinary parishioners, as well as their rulers, knew all about the virtuous achievements of David and Solomon, Asa, Hezekiah and Josiah, and the advent of the purified Tudor Judah was something earnest teachers and preachers taught everyone devoutly to pray for. 'The worde of the Lord endureth for ever'. This text belonged to both Testaments, and the scriptural régime many desired for the English Church embraced the law of the Decalogue alongside the law of the Gospel. The Deuteronomaic law that King Josiah recovered and implemented centred on the elimination of idols and idolaters.

Fear of idolatry and direct knowledge of image-breaking became an everyday part of English experience from the beginning of the Reformation. By 1570 it would have been a rare person who had neither experienced some parish clearance nor encountered a headless statue or some tell-tale broken stone or damaged stained-glass window. In this, England was far from being alone, and this indigenous iconoclasm was interwoven in various ways with the destruction that went on abroad.

The close links between England and the Low Countries included both art and anti-art. The large influx of immigrants after 1566 brought, together with craftsmen whose skills enriched the English cloth and book trades, artists who made a great contribution to English painting. Any number of individuals might have known and brought with them graphic works from the Netherlands, and already long before this East Anglian screen painters had been borrowing directly from engravings by Lucas van Leyden.[313] But it is of special interest to find that prints of Maarten van Heemskerck apparently arrived in England very soon after they were made, and to see how they were put to such immediate use in an English painting. Since Heemskerck belonged to a learned circle that included Holland's most celebrated humanist, the known connection of Hadrianus Junius with prominent figures in England becomes the more noteworthy. Whether or not Junius's 1568 visit had any relevance to our painting, he knew all about English iconoclasm under Edward VI, as well as knowing Heemskerck. It is intriguing to reflect that Junius's accounts of image-breaking in Edwardian England (long before the Low Countries' storm of 1566) could have informed the thinking on that subject of the Dutch artist whose delineations were, in their turn, to inform the depiction of England's reforming Josiah.

Maybe there were more interactions than have been noticed between the destroyers in the Low Countries and the destroyers in England. By 1566, among the many places that could present examples to image-breakers, England offered Netherlanders near-at-hand diversity of achievements, and some of the Flemish radicals who were responsible for iconoclasm had personal knowledge of England. The Dutch community in London (which included individuals who had themselves acted against 'idols') was in a state of uproar in the summer of 1570 after Godfried van Winghen (Wingius), minister of the Dutch church, preached on his reservations about iconoclasm. Winghen expressed the view that iconoclasm had played a large part in causing the Low Countries'

disturbances, and he went so far as to say that private individuals who took it on themselves 'in this realm or elsewhere' to throw down idolatrous statues, in churches or chapels, were to be regarded as seditious and rebellious. This, presented with other opinions by his opponents in the Dutch community on 6 August 1570, was forwarded to the bishop of London.[314] Did Winghen know about the goings-on in the queen's chapel? (above, pp. 106–7) Clearly words and deeds in England and the Netherlands were of mutual interest, and different kinds of inspiration could be exchanged.

As we look again at *Edward VI and the Pope*, we can now read it (even without its texts) with more confidence about what might have been in the thoughts of contemporary readers. Men like Francis Walsingham, John Foxe, Alexander Nowell, and Edward Dering, rejoiced in contemplating the young Josiah–Edward, who had done so much to set England on the right path of reform. Their own monarch fell regrettably short of this example, and when Pius V, Mary Queen of Scots and the duke of Norfolk renewed the spectre of idolatry and superstition, they felt impelled to speak out on behalf of their biblical models. It may be harder to read the minds of the English queen and the duke. Elizabeth was certainly not prepared to be pushed by her brother's example into rejecting the use of the cross. Norfolk's suspected popish friends were his undoing, and the gold rosary beads with pendant crucifix that Mary Queen of Scots bequeathed to his daughter-in-law, Anne Dacre, became the Howard family's heirloom reminder of that fatal miscalculation (fig. 128). But at his eleventh hour the duke set himself steadfastly towards the scriptural godliness he had learnt from Foxe in the days of King Edward's reforms.

The image of the young king combined scriptural royalty with the rejection of papal claims and Roman superstitions. Neither queen nor duke would have been happy at all times with all the implications of this painting, and there were moments when either of them might have seen in it messages quite unwelcome to their own positions. But we cannot reach their inmost thoughts, nor probe the ambiguities that lodged in their minds, or those that hedged the balancing beliefs of humanists like Maarten van Heemskerck, Hadrianus Junius and their Haarlem circle.

Edward VI and the Pope may once have spoken with silent words as well as silent images. Its silence has increased over the years, but I hope this book may help it to speak again with the voice its makers first intended.

ABBREVIATIONS

BL	British Library
BM	British Museum
CSP	*Calendar of State Papers*
DNB	*Dictionary of National Biography*
Foxe, *A & M*	John Foxe, *The Actes and Monumentes*, various sixteenth-century editions by date; modern edition ed. J. Pratt, 8 vols. (London, 1853–70)
LP	*Letters and Papers of the Reign of Henry VIII*, ed. J. S. Brewer et al. (London, 1862–1932)
NPG	National Portrait Gallery
PRO	Public Record Office
STC	*Short-Title Catalogue of Books Printed . . . 1475–1640*, revised edition by W. A. Jackson, F. S. Ferguson and K. F. Pantzer (London, 1976–86)
V & A	Victoria and Albert Museum

NOTES

1 Spatial ambiguity of this kind occurs in other Tudor paintings, but here it helps to make us 'read the scene episodically and in a fragmented way'. *Sixteenth-Century Britain: The Cambridge Cultural History of Britain*, ed. Boris Ford (Cambridge, 1992), p. 226, cf. p. 223.

2 G. Constant, *The Reformation in England*, II, trans. E. I. Watkin (London, 1942), p. 5; *CSP Spanish, 1547–1549*, pp. 36–7, 54; *CSP Foreign, 1547–1553*, p. 7.

3 Roy C. Strong, 'Edward VI and the Pope: A Tudor anti-papal allegory and its setting', *Journal of the Warburg and Courtauld Institutes*, 23 (1960), 311–13; Strong, *Tudor and Jacobean Portraits* (London, HMSO, 1969), I, pp. 344–5.

4 Roy Strong, *The English Icon: Elizabethan and Jacobean Portraiture* (London and New York, 1969), pp. 71, 74 referring (p. 71) to the 'great number of versions of the type' that survive. A common feature (shared by NPG 4165) is the angle of the head which shows the left ear. Strong comments, 'In all these portraits the clumsy and inaccurate drawing of the left ear is perpetuated'. See also Strong, *Tudor and Jacobean Portraits*, I, pp. 87–94; II, plates 164–73; Oliver Millar, *The Tudor, Stuart and Early Georgian Pictures in the Collection of Her Majesty the Queen* (London, 1963), I, pp. 64–5, no. 44.

5 Strong, *Tudor and Jacobean Portraits*, I, p. 295; II, plate 576, cf. plate 575.

6 On Teerlinc see Roy Strong, *The English Renaissance Miniature* (London, 1984), chapter 4, and pp. 66–7, 111; Strong, *Artists of the Tudor Court: The Portrait Miniature Rediscovered 1520–1620*, V. & A. Exhibition Catalogue (London, 1983), pp. 52–7; Erna Auerbach, *Tudor Artists: A Study of Painters in the Royal Service and of Portraiture on Illuminated Documents from the Accession of Henry VIII to the Death of Elizabeth I* (London, 1954), pp. 51, 75–7, 91, 97, 103–6, 187–8; Mary Edmond, *Hilliard and Oliver* (London, 1983), pp. 29–30; *DNB*, s.n. Seymour, Edward, Earl of Hertford (1539?–1621).

7 NPG 535; Strong, *Tudor and Jacobean Portraits*, I, pp. 54–6; Strong, *English Icon*, p. 78. Cranmer, born 2 July 1489, was 56 (i.e. started his 57th year) in 1545, so the picture's inscription *Anno etati 57 Julii 20* places it in 1545, not – as usually stated – 1546, as was pointed out by Jasper Ridley, *Thomas Cranmer* (Oxford, 1962), frontispiece.

8 John Ingamells, *The English Episcopal Portrait 1559–1835: A Catalogue* (privately printed by Paul Mellon Centre for Studies in British Art, 1981), pp. 316–17; C. R. L. Fletcher, *Historical Portraits, 1400–1600* (Oxford, 1909), pp. 145–6; A. M. Hind, *Engraving in England in the Sixteenth and Seventeenth Centuries*, 3 vols. (Cambridge, 1952–64), I, pp. 74–5. Ingamells thinks it more likely that the painting derived from the print than the other way round.

9   Strong, 'Edward VI and the Pope', pp. 311, 312.

10 Strong, *Tudor and Jacobean Portraits*, I, pp. 344–5.

11 M. Aston, *England's Iconoclasts*, I (Oxford, 1988), pp. 254–64; cited at p. 256; Ronald Hutton, 'The Local Impact of the Tudor Reformations', in *The English Reformation Revised*, ed. C. Haigh (Cambridge, 1987), pp. 114–38.

12 There are plenty of instances of such pictorial frames used to enclose texts placed inside pictures (such as Holbein's portrait of Amerbach and Dürer's engraving of Erasmus, in 1519 and 1526). A fairly elaborate example with a long framed English text is the rare Elizabethan religious painting, *An Allegory of Man*; Strong, *English Icon*, p. 40, fig. 33. The framed picture within a picture became a useful device for enlarging the content and allusiveness of a single panel or canvas, or for oblique commentary which could make a portrait like an *impresa*: see M. Leslie, 'The Dialogue between Bodies and Souls; Pictures and Poesy in the English Renaissance', *Word and Image*, I (1985), 16–30; examples in Strong, *English Icon*, pp. 28–32, 182–3, and *The Memorial of Lord Darnley* (colour pl. III).

13 Letter of 5 July 1955 in NPG file on no. 4165. For Henry's ulcers and death see J. J. Scarisbrick, *Henry VIII* (Harmondsworth, Penguin, 1971), pp. 625 ff.

14 D. E. Hoak, *The King's Council in the Reign of Edward VI* (Cambridge, 1976), chapter 2 on council membership; more recent works which bear on the transition are David Loades, *The Tudor Court* (London, 1986), and David Starkey et al., *The English Court: From the Wars of the Roses to the Civil War* (London and New York, 1987).

15 Also observed by John N. King, *Tudor Royal Iconography* (Princeton, 1989), p. 163; see also pp. 94–5 on *Edward VI and the Pope*, accepting the date of *c.* 1548–9.

16 Charles Wriothesley, *A Chronicle of England*, ed. W. D. Hamilton (Camden Society, 1875–7), I, p. 68.

17 Strong, *Tudor and Jacobean Portraits*, I, p. 295, II, plate 575.

18 *Cranmer Primate of all England*, Catalogue of Quincentenary Exhibition (British Library, 1989), no. 87; Ridley, *Thomas Cranmer*, p. 259; A. J. Mason, *Thomas Cranmer* (London, 1898), p. 118; Strong, *Tudor and Jacobean Portraits*, I, p. 56; G. M. Bevan, *Portraits of the Archbishops of Canterbury* (London, 1908), p. 51.

19 Hoak, *King's Council*, pp. 35, 42, 47, 49 (for lists of members), 231–9.

20 The figure (5) I postulate as possibly Paget is not however wearing a George, unlike NPG 961 (fig. 11); Strong, *Tudor and Jacobean Portraits*, I, pp. 241–2; II, plate 480; Hoak, *King's Council*, pp. 47–8.

21 T. Rymer, *Foedera* (London, 1704–35), XV, pp. 116–17; *Acts of the Privy Council of England*, ed. J. R. Dasent et al. (London 1890–1964), II, pp. 15–17. William Paget became Controller of the Household in Feb. 1547, and in July Chancellor of the Duchy of Lancaster. He was left £300 in Henry VIII's will.

22 *Acts of the Privy Council*, I, p. 566; II, pp. 12, 14, 25; *The Chronicle and Political Papers of King Edward VI*, ed. W. K. Jordan (London, 1966), p. 6; Starkey, *English Court*, pp. 121–4; John Maclean, *The Life of Sir Thomas Seymour, Knight* (London, 1869), pp. 44–7, 56–7, 67. They had barely eighteen months of married life, since she died (aged 36) at Sudeley on 7 September 1548, a week after the birth of their daughter.

23 On the portraits of Lord Sudeley see Strong, *Tudor and Jacobean Portraits*, I, pp. 357–9; II, plates 683–4; John Harington, *Orlando Furioso in English Heroical Verse* (London, 1591), p. 151; for the elder John Harington's connections with Thomas Seymour see John N. King, *English Reformation Literature* (Princeton, 1982), pp. 235–6.

24 Hoak, *King's Council*, p. 43; *DNB*.

25 On the wall over the altar curtain are inscribed (almost like a title) the words (here with extensions), TRAGICA ET LAMENTABILIS INTERNECIO / SERENISSIMI HENRICI SCOTORUM REGIS.

26 Millar, *Tudor, Stuart ... Pictures*, I, pp. 75–7, no. 90. The Goodwood House version appears to be slightly later than the Holyroodhouse one. For the inscriptions erased in the Holyrood version see D. Jacques, *A Visit to Goodwood* (Chichester, 1922), pp. 101–27. The inscription on the extreme right tablet reads (abbreviations extended); 'OPERIS HUIUS CAUSA, QUOD HOC FIERI FECERUNT HONORATISSIMI COMES LENOXAE ET DOMINA MARGARETA DOWGLAS ILLIUS UXOR LONDINI MENSE IANUARII ANNO DOMINI 1567 ...'. Millar points out the literary parallel in writings of George Buchanan; in particular see *The Tyrannous Reign of Mary Stewart*, trans. and ed. W. A. Gatherer (London, 1958) – cited here at p. 194 – but does not show how closely the details of the picture (the inset and the medallions on Darnley's tomb) follow contemporary drawings in the state papers (PRO SP 52/13*), on which see *Mary Queen of Scots*, ed. J. S. Baker (Public Record Office Pamphlets, no. 12, London, 1981), and *Tyrannous Reign*, illustration facing p. 132.

27 Trinity College Cambridge, MS R.7.31, ff. 1ʳ, 13ᵛ; Aston, *England's Iconoclasts*, I, pp. 275–7.

28 King, *Tudor Royal Iconography*, pp. 35–6, 54–6, 76–88, 93, 115–16, 252–6.

29 *Certain Sermons or Homilies* (Oxford, 1844), p. 165; cf. pp. 46, 52, 225; E. G. Withycombe, *The Oxford Dictionary of English Christian Names*, 3rd edn (Oxford, 1977), pp. xxxvi–xl, 152, 181.

30 *Three Inventories of the years 1542, 1547 and 1549–50 of Pictures in the Collections of Henry VIII and Edward VI*, ed. W. A. Shaw (Courtauld Institute Texts for the Study of Art History, no. 1, 1937), p. 54, cf. p. 50; Aston, *England's Iconoclasts*, I, p. 246. See below on Hezekiah and the brazen serpent.

31 2 Kings, 21–23, (citing 21: 22, and 22: 2); 2 Chronicles, 34 (citing 3–4). In the Vulgate the books of Samuel and Kings, which are continuous, were treated as 1–4 *Regum*, so the description of Josiah in what we now know as 2 Kings appeared as 4 Kings. Both numerations were used in the sixteenth century; references to Josiah appear here in either form. The account in Chronicles is later and has no independent validity.

32 2 Kings, 23: 1–6, 14, 20; 2 Chronicles, 34: 3–7. The discovered book of the law has for long been taken to be Deuteronomy.

33 *Miscellaneous Writings and Letters of Thomas Cranmer*, ed. E. Cox (Parker Society, Cambridge, 1846), p. 127; *Original Letters relative to the English Reformation*, ed. H. Robinson (Parker Society, Cambridge, 1846–7), I, p. 321; Aston, *England's Iconoclasts*, I, pp. 246–50.

34 *Early Writings of John Hooper*, ed. S. Carr (Parker Society, Cambridge, 1843), pp. 201–3, from the *Answer to the Bishop of Winchester's Book* (1547).

35 *Original Letters*, II, pp. 707–11; letter dated Geneva [1 Jan 1551].

36 *Homilies*, pp. 173, 225, 495. The remark about Hezekiah's burning the brazen serpent to ashes is (interestingly) unscriptural, for (as the same Homily states correctly pp. 210, 225) 2 Kings, 18: 4 only says he 'brake in pieces the brasen serpent that Moses had made'. Maybe the confusion arose from Moses' treatment of the golden calf (Exodus, 32: 20), which he burnt, ground into powder, and mixed with water which the children of Israel had to drink. Or was there conflation with Josiah's reforms (2 Kings, 23: 6, 15) – above p. 27. See also below n. 166 for Jewel's statement.

37 Foxe, *A & M*, ed. Pratt, V, pp. 698–9; 1563 edn, p. 675; 1570 edn, pp. 1483–4. See below on the differences between the 1563 and 1570 versions of Foxe's book, which are not easy to discern in the nineteenth-century editions.

38 *DNB*: John Frewen, *Certaine Sermons upon the … eleventh Chapter of S. Paule his Epistle to the Romanes* (London, 1612), sigs. D 1^r, D 5^v–6^v, L 6$^{r–v}$, L 8^v–M 2^r, M 4^r (including words on the text Accepted preached to Prince Charles); A. L. Frewen, *A History of Brickwall in Sussex and of the Parishes of Northiam and Brede* (London, 1909), pp. 25–6, 49–50, 70–81; Roger B. Manning, *Religion and Society in Elizabethan Sussex* (Leicester, 1969), pp. 172, 176, 201, 209, 210, 211, 216; John Ingamells, *Catalogue of Portraits at Bishopthorpe Palace* (York, 1972), pp. 13–14; M. A. Lower, *The Worthies of Sussex* (Lewes, 1865), pp. 45–52 states that John Frewen holds a Geneva Bible. But it seems clear from the format that it is in fact an Authorized Version, though it is not easy to identify the edition. Examples of the 1620s might fit the bill if one assumes that the painter has – to achieve legibility – shortened both the running-heads ('Iosiah his zeale, and reformation: He is slaine, Iehoiakim is subdued') and the page (chapter 23 has 37 verses, whereas only about 28 are painted, though the number of 34 is visible; verses 7–11 are also numbered, though in the original this column goes on to verse 19 and is much longer). For citation of Josiah in a Sussex petition to James I in 1603 in which John Frewen had a hand, see K. C. Fincham, 'Ramifications of the Hampton Court Conference', *Journal of Ecclesiastical History*, 36 (1985), p. 208.

39 For examples of mid-sixteenth-century reliefs closely related to Dutch Bible illustrations, and with a new exemplary iconography, see H. Miedema, 'De Bijbelse Ikonografie van twee Monumenten: De "Kraak" te Oosterend (Fr.), en het Grafmonument van Edo Wiemken te Jever', *Bulletin van de Koninklijke Nederlandse Oudheidkundige Bond*, 77 (1978), 61–88, a reference I owe to David Freedberg, who comments on these findings in his contribution to the 1986 Amsterdam exhibition catalogue, *Kunst voor de Beeldenstorm: Noordnederlandse Kunst, 1525–1580*, ed. W. Th. Kloek et al., II, pp. 39–84, 'Art and Iconoclasm; the Case of the Northern Netherlands', at pp. 78–9.

40 *Biblia Vulgare Istoriata* (Venice, 1490), sigs. h iiii^r, q vi^v. The Malermi Bible, the first printed Italian Bible, initially appeared without illustrations in 1471. On the 1490 illustrations (a sizable proportion of which were based on earlier Bibles), and those in di Giunta's 1511 Vulgate, which may be related to the Great Bible illustrations, see James Strachan, *Early Bible Illustrations* (Cambridge, 1957), pp. 27–32, 36, 83–5.

41 *Biblia: the bible* ([Cologne ?], 1535), pt. 2, ff. 61^r, 77^v. The Josiah cut appears

twice after this in Coverdale's Bible, in the Apocrypha title-page and at the beginning of Esdras III. *Biblia Altes und Newen Testament* (Frankfurt, Christian Egenolff, 1534), f. lxxvii^v. On Egenolff's Lutheran Bibles and Beham's illustrations see Philipp Schmidt, *Die Illustration der Lutherbibel 1522–1700* (Basel, 1962), pp. 175–8; Gustav Pauli, *Hans Sebald Beham* (Strasbourg, 1901), pp. 482–8, 492.

42 *The Byble in Englyshe* (London, 1541), BL, C 18 d 7, f. xli^r (*recte* f. lxi^r). Cap. 23 (f. lxiii) is headed: 'Josia readeth Deuteronomy before the people. He putteth downe ye Idolles after he had kylled the prestes therof'. For the misplacing of this cut see Strachan, *Bible Illustrations*, pp. 2, 81, 154, and fig. 118. It is the reading of the law that reveals this error.

43 J. Y. Batley, *On a Reformer's Latin Bible, Being an Essay on the Adversaria in the Vulgate of Thomas Bilney* (Cambridge, 1940); Aston, *England's Iconoclasts*, I, pp. 164–8; D. S. Dunnan, 'The Preaching of Hugh Latimer', unpublished D. Phil. thesis, Oxford, 1991, pp. 45–7.

44 This is Dr Susan Foister's point, and is explored in a chapter on 'Holbein and the English Reformation' in her forthcoming book on Holbein, which I am grateful to have read in typescript. It is worth noticing that whereas God the Father is represented traditionally at the top of the Great Bible title-page, in the Coverdale Bible he is shown by the tetragrammaton, specially interesting at this phase of English protestantism. See A. Krücke, 'Der Protestantismus und die bildliche Darstellung Gottes', *Zeitschrift für Kunstwissenschaft*, 13 (1959), 59–90 (my thanks to Sergiusz Michalski for this reference).

45 *Die gantze Bibel* (Zurich, 1531), facs. edn *Die Froschauer Bibel*, ed. H. R. Lavater (Zurich, 1983), f. cxci^v; Manfred Kästner, *Die Icones Hans Holbeins des Jüngeren* (Heidelberg, 1985), I, pp. 1–2, 263; II, pp. 652, 869–70; Strachan, *Bible Illustrations*, pp. 3, 56–7, 85; *The Images of the Old Testament* (Lyons, 1549), sig. H 2^r. The French lines included the statement that in his purging Josiah 'fait brusler les idoles par tout'. In some versions the image is reversed, as in the *Icones* printed in Paris, 1544, in which Holbein's woodcut has been considerably reworked. The 1565 Dutch Bible of H. de Laet (Antwerp) used Holbein's designs, including that of Josiah.

46 Michael von Aitsinger (Eytzinger), *De Leone Belgico* (Cologne, 1583), pp. 43, 520. The same is true of the paragraph on Hezekiah.

47 *Biblia Das ist: die gantze heilige Schrifft Deudsch* (Wittenberg, 1572), ff. 232^v, 260^v. On this Bible see Heimo Reinitzer, *Biblia deutsch: Luthers Bibelübersetzung und ihre Tradition* (Wolfenbüttel, 1983), pp. 259–61; Schmidt, *Lutherbibel*, pp. 274–96, emphasizing the unambiguous directness of the illustrations ('Der Künstler bringt sie immer wieder mit seiner Zeit in Verbindung: mit dem Widerstand gegen die wachsende Gegenreformation, seiner Treue zu Luther und der noch nicht fernen Zeit der Reformation': p. 277). I am very grateful to Sergiusz Michalski for directing me to these sources. See below on Hezekiah.

48 *The holie Bible* (London, [1568]), pt. 2, f. cix^r. Some copies of the Bible lack the Josiah scene; I. e. 2 in the British Library uses instead at f. cix^r the cut illustrating Habakkuk.

49 On the complicated history of this Bible's illustrations see Colin Clair, 'The Bishops' Bible', *Gutenberg Jahrbuch* (1962), 287–91; M. Aston, 'The *Bishops'*

Bible Illustrations', *Studies in Church History*, 28 (1992), *The Church and the Arts*, ed. Diana Wood, pp. 267–85. Another 1568 woodcut, also with Nicolai's monogram, which has the same history as the Josiah cut, is that heading 3 Kings, chapter 1. On Nicolai (active *c.* 1549–96) see Colin Clair, *Christopher Plantin* (London, 1960), pp. 182–4. I owe much here to Elizabeth Ingram's kind help and information.

50 *The holi bible* (London, 1569), pt. 1, f. 198ʳ, note to verse 6; 'And he brought out the grove from the temple of the Lorde ... and burned it ...'; *The Bible* (Geneva, 1560), f. 176ʳ, note g to 2 Kings, 23: 6.

51 Tessa Watt, *Cheap Print and Popular Piety, 1550–1640* (Cambridge, 1991), p. 169, fig. 20. These scenes constitute about a quarter of the original block for Joshua (*The holie Bible*, 1572, pt. 2, f. cxiiiiʳ), with the illustrations of chapters 7, 10 and 11 sliced in two.

52 *The holie Bible* (London, 1572), pt. 1, f. clxxiiiʳ.

53 Hind, *Engraving in England*, 1, pp. 12–16, 64–7, plates 33, 36; *Correspondence of Matthew Parker*, ed. J. Bruce (Parker Society, Cambridge, 1853), p. 426.

54 Besides the woodcut prefacing 3 Kings, these initials appear elsewhere, for instance in the cuts before Joshua and 1 Kings. I am very grateful to Elizabeth Ingram for help here too, and for the information about Tressell, on whom see R. B. McKerrow and F. S. Ferguson, *Title-page Borders used in England and Scotland 1485–1640* (London, 1932), pp. xxxvi–xxxvii, and Strong, *Artists of the Tudor Court*, p. 66, no. 65.

55 The Bishops' Bible version; *The holie Bible* (1568), New Testament, f. 136ᵛ.

56 June Osborne, *Stained Glass in England* (London, 1981), pp. 25–6, and illustration III, 8; M. H. Caviness, *The Windows of Christ Church Cathedral, Canterbury* (London, 1981), p. 46; Christopher Woodforde, *The Stained Glass of New College, Oxford* (Oxford, 1951), pp. 102–5; *A History of York Minster*, ed. G. E. Aylmer and R. Cant (Oxford, 1977), pp. 320, 372–3.

57 Lambeth Palace has this unique copy of the 1569 work. On this book (*STC* 6428–9) see Helen C. White, *The Tudor Books of Private Devotion* (Westport, Conn., 1951), pp. 188–96; Samuel S. Chew, 'The Iconography of *A Book of Christian Prayers* (1578) Illustrated', *Huntingdon Library Quarterly*, 8 (1944–5), 293–305; C. L. Oastler, *John Day, the Elizabethan Printer* (Oxford, 1975), p. 17; King, *Tudor Royal Iconography*, pp. 110–14, 118–21, 200.

58 *Niklaus Manuel Deutsch, Maler Dichter Staatsmann*, Exhibition Catalogue, Kunstmuseum Bern (1979), ed. C. Menz and H. Wagner, pp. 33–4, 293–7, nos. 132–3, plates 72–3. This wall painting on the house of Manuel's friend Antoni Noll, recorded in early eighteenth-century watercolours, was destroyed in 1758. G. R. Potter, *Huldrych Zwingli* (London, 1978), p. 80, from the ten articles presented for discussion at Berne in January 1528. On Solomon's idolatry see below.

59 A 1530 glass panel of this scene is in the church of Jegenstorf, north of Berne. Deutsch's design gave the idols attributes of Athene, Hera, Neptune and Saturn. *Niklaus Manuel Deutsch*, pp. 38, 112, no. 295, pp. 461–2, cf. nos. 296–7, plates 166–7; C.-A. Beerli, *Le Peintre Poète Nicolas Manuel et l'Evolution Sociale de son Temps* (Geneva, 1953), pp. 275–6, 380; C. M. N. Eire, *War Against the Idols* (Cambridge, 1986), pp. 100–1, 108–11; J.

Rowlands and G. Bartrum, *The Age of Dürer and Holbein* (British Museum, London, Exhibition Catalogue, 1988), pp. 211–14.

60 See the remarks of I. M. Veldman, *Maarten van Heemskerck and Dutch Humanism in the Sixteenth Century* (Maarssen, 1977), p. 131. 'The popularity and topicality of Old Testament themes, which served as models for moral behavior, were perhaps due in part to the many plays staged by the rhetoricians. Heemskerck was one of the earliest Netherlandish artists to depict these themes so extensively – generally in series of four, six, eight and sometimes more prints – as against the one, or at the most two scenes accorded them by his predecessor Lucas van Leyden'. See also the same author's *Leerrijke Reeksen van Maarten van Heemskerck* (Haarlem, 1986), pp. 13–16. What follows owes much to the former book, and I am most grateful to Professor Veldman for sending information.

61 He was in Rome from July 1532 – when he met Vasari – to about the end of 1536. Rainald Grosshans, *Maerten van Heemskerck: Die Gemälde* (Berlin, 1980), pp. 10, 21–2, 35–41.

62 C. Hülsen and H. Egger, *Die Römischen Skizzenbücher von Marten van Heemskerck im Königlichen Küpferstichkabinett zu Berlin* (Berlin, 1913–16). See Grosshans, *Heemskerck*, pp. 47, 49, on the ruins in Heemskerck's landscapes (placed in the line of development from Scorel and Patenier), and pp. 39, 68, on his self-portrait. On the latter see also R. F. Chirico, 'A Note on Heemskerck's *Self-Portrait with the Colosseum*', *Marsyas*, 18 (1976), 21; and for a suggestive argument on the relationship between Heemskerck's views of Rome and its ruins and his depictions of iconoclasm see Horst Bredekamp, 'Maarten van Heemskercks Bildersturmzyklen als Angriffe auf Rom', in *Bilder und Bildersturm im Spätmittelalter und in der frühen Neuzeit*, ed. R. Scribner and M. Warnke (Wiesbaden, 1990), pp. 203–47; I am grateful to the author for sending me a copy of this paper before its publication; my comments on fig. 45 are based on its findings.

63 Eleanor A. Saunders, 'A Commentary on Iconoclasm in Several Print Series by Maarten van Heemskerck', *Simiolus*, 10 (1978–9), 76–7. On the office of 'kerkmeester' see A. Duke, *Reformation and Revolt in the Low Countries* (London, 1990), p. 296.

64 Carel van Mander, *Het Schilder-Boeck* (Haarlem, 1604), f. 246ᵛ; *Le Livre des Peintres de Carel van Mander*, ed. H. Hymans (Paris, 1884–5), I, p. 369; cf. below p. 185 for Hadrianus Junius on Heemskerck's graphic output. For etchings and woodcuts ascribed to Heemskerck's own hand see F. W. H. Hollstein, *Dutch and Flemish Etchings, Engravings and Woodcuts ca. 1450–1700* (Amsterdam, 1949–), VII, pp. 228–36.

65 Jeremy D. Bangs, 'Maerten van Heemskerck's *Bel and the Dragon* and Iconoclasm', *Renaissance Quarterly*, 30 (1977), 8–11 (the glass panel in question being in the author's possession. Others exist in Liège).

66 Freedberg, 'Art and Iconoclasm', p. 77; Bredekamp, 'Heemskercks Bildersturmzyklen', pp. 214–15.

67 Grosshans, *Heemskerck*, pp. 43, 51–2; Saunders, 'Commentary on Iconoclasm', p. 62. See also on this whole question the various discussions by David Freedberg, to which I owe much, including 'The Problem of Images in Northern Europe and its Repercussions in the Netherlands', *Hafnia* (1976–

7), 25–45, and see his 'Art and Iconoclasm', p. 80, for the suggestion that Heemskerck wished to emphasize the importance of purifying reforms being effected by the magistrate.

68 Freedberg, 'Art and Iconoclasm', p. 75; Saunders, 'Commentary on Iconoclasm, pp. 80–1; Duke, *Reformation and Revolt*, pp. 128, 133, 145, 147.

69 Otto Benesch described Heemskerck's design as a 'satire of contemporary religious conditions in antique guise'. Veldman, *Heemskerck*, pp. 44–8, 55, n. 6; Veldman, *Leerrijke Reeksen*, pp. 20–2. One might also compare this allegory with a Lutheran satirical print of 1545 of the pope riding a sow with a handful of steaming excrement, captioned 'Papa dat concilium in Germania'; R. W. Scribner, *For the Sake of Simple Folk* (Cambridge, 1981), pp. 81–3; Scribner, *Popular Culture and Popular Movements in Reformation Germany* (London and Ronceverte, 1987), pp. 291–2, fig. 13; BL, 562* f. 28. On Coornhert's views see chapter 4 of Veldman, *Heemskerck*, including the series of prints in which fig. 75 (below p. 105) appears, entitled by this author *Jacob's ladder*, and described (p. 62) as 'a perfect visual rendition of Coornhert's personal confession of faith'.

70 Thomas Kerrich, *A Catalogue of the Prints which have been engraved after Martin Heemskerck* (Cambridge, 1829), p. 122; Kerrich bequest, vol. 1, no. 143 in the Fitzwilliam Museum, Cambridge. 'Outlandish', the Geneva Bible's word for 'strange' (1 Kings, 11: 8).

71 Michael Camille, *The Gothic Idol: Ideology and Image-making in Medieval Art* (Cambridge, 1989), pp. 300–2; R. Pigeaud, 'Woman as Temptress. Urban Morality in the 15th century', in *Saints and she-devils. Images of women in the 15th and 16th centuries*, ed. L. Dresen-Coenders (London, 1987), p. 57, n. 57; *Lexikon der Christlichen Ikonographie*, ed. E. Kirschbaum et al. (Rome and Basel, 1968–74), IV, pp. 15–23.

72 E. S. Jacobowitz and S. L. Stepanek, *The Prints of Lucas van Leyden and His Contemporaries* (National Gallery of Art, Washington, 1983), nos. 35, 46, 64, pp. 113–14, 136–7, 178–9. On the iconography of Solomon, and Reformation examples see L. Réau, *Iconographie de L'Art Chrétien*, II, i (Paris, 1956), pp. 286–99; *Symbols in Transformation: Iconographic Themes at the Time of the Reformation* (Exhibition of Prints in Memory of Erwin Panofsky, Princeton, 1969), pp. 23–4, figs. 27–30.

73 *Biblia* (1572), f. 228^r (see above, n. 47). Sexual ambiguity was perhaps called for, given the package of Solomon's gods in 1 Kings, 11: 5–7.

74 Grosshans, *Heemskerck*, pp. 203–7, no. 78, plates 111, 222; Kerrich, *Catalogue of Prints*, pp. 106–7; F. W. H. Hollstein, *Etchings*, IV, p. 189, no. 444; VIII, p. 248, no. 593; Bangs, 'Bel and the Dragon', p. 10; John Capgrave, *Ye Solace of Pilgrimes*, ed. C. A. Mills (Oxford, 1911), pp. 34–6.

75 The verb *sculpere* was used for engraving as well as carving – hence, as Stephen Gardiner pointed out in 1547, the commandment text *Non facies tibi sculptile* logically applied to printing, as a branch of engraving. *The Letters of Stephen Gardiner*, ed. J. A. Muller (Cambridge, 1933), p. 258.

76 Hülsen and Egger, *Die Römischen Skizzenbücher*, I, pp. 42–5 and plate 81; Grosshans, *Heemskerck*, pp. 17, 34, 35, 44, 55, 68, 109–16, 195–201, figs. 19, 108, 215–16, plates II and VI. Grosshans argues against dating the later painting after Coornhert's 1553 print of the sculpture court in the Casa Sassi.

227

The iconography of St Luke is an enormous topic which obviously cannot be explored here, any more than the much-discussed complexities of Heemskerck's two paintings. For references see *Kunst voor de Beeldenstorm*, II, pp. 191–2 (no. 70), 264–6 (no. 146), and for the Coornhert print pp. 266–7 (no. 147).

77 Colin Clair, *Christopher Plantin* (London, 1960), pp. 182–3, 185, 281, 286.

78 N. Sander, *A Treatise of the Images of Christ* (Louvain, 1567), f. 78^r.

79 Kerrich, *Catalogue*, p. 29 (the Fitzwilliam collection has only seven of the series, and lacks no. 6); Hollstein, *Etchings*, VII, p. 74, VIII, p. 243, nos. 248–55; H. Junius, *Poematum liber primus continens pia et moralia carmina* (Leiden, 1598), p. 176; Veldman, *Heemskerck*, pp. 103–4; L. Preibisz, *Martin van Heemskerck: ein Beitrag zur Geschichte des Romanismus in der niederländischen Malerei des XVI Jahrhunderts* (Leipzig, 1911), pp. 89–90, nos. 68–75.

80 For aglets (metal tags or ornaments attached to gowns) see *Princely Magnificence: Court Jewels of the Renaissance, 1500–1630*, Exhibition catalogue, Victoria and Albert Museum (London, 1980), p. 71, and nos. P16 and P25. I am grateful to Susan Foister for drawing my attention to this catalogue.

81 For the drawings see *Tegninger af Maerten van Heemskerck*, Exhibition catalogue, ed. Jan Garff (Copenhagen, 1971), pl. 72–9. The question of a reversed image arises in Heemskerck's latter painting of St Luke, and the derivation of the Casa Sassi courtyard from either original drawing or print. In this case the reversed view of the print is the same as that in the painting but Grosshans points out (*Heemskerck*, p. 197) that there was no problem about such reversals, which Heemskerck often made when his composition demanded it.

82 As described in the lines that accompanied the posthumous portrait of Heemskerck in H. Hondius, *Pictorum effigies* (1610); Veldman, *Heemskerck*, p. 111; Grosshans, *Heemskerck*, p. 14.

83 Veldman, *Heemskerck*, pp. 103, 148–9 (dating the second edition to 1569); Kerrich, *Catalogue*, pp. 1–3; Hollstein, *Etchings*, VII, p. 74, nos. 12–32, VIII, p. 242, nos. 202–223. For the drawings see *Tegninger*, ed. Garff, nos. 90–101; and for the title drawing Preibisz, *Heemskerck*, p. 84, no. 12; Hülsen and Egger, *Die Römischen Skizzenbücher*, I, p. 3. The date 1569 appears on the print (no. 17 of the second edition, *Inventiones*) of Jehu adoring the golden calves. The extant drawings are all dated either 1567 or 1568. It seems likely that the first edition of Galle's print series, the *Clades*, appeared in 1568, before he had the drawing of the title-print used for the second edition.

84 *Biblicae Historiae, magno artificio depictae* (Frankfurt, 1539), sig. B ii^r, has Hans Sebald Beham's version. See André Parrot, *The Tower of Babel* (Studies in Biblical Archaeology, 2, 1955), pp. 14–17, 52–7 for the etymological and archaeological associations between Babel and Babylon, and for a brief conspectus of the Tower of Babel in art.

85 'Alta cadit Babylon multa constructa virum vi, Concutit haec terras, mortalia pectora sternit'.

86 Max J. Friedländer, *Early Netherlandish Painting*, XIII, (Leiden, 1975), plate 148, no. 297; Keith P. F. Moxey, *Pieter Aertsen, Joachim Beuckelaer, and the Rise of Secular Painting in the Context of the Reformation* (New York and London, 1977), pp. 243–50, fig. 67; Freedberg, 'Art and Iconoclasm', in

Kunst voor de Beeldenstorm, II, p. 80 and no. 214, pointing to a similarity between one of Heemskerck's Shadrach, Meshach and Abed-Nego prints and Aertsen's painting. On the additions to Genesis 10: 8–10 on Nimrod, see *Catholic Encyclopedia*, 10, p. 741; C. M. Armstrong, *The Moralizing Prints of Cornelis Anthonisz* (Princeton, 1990), pp. 105–6.

87 On this print see Armstrong, *Anthonisz*, chapter 11, which argues against reading it as a Reformation statement (though contemporaries might well have done so); *Kunst voor de Beeldenstorm*, II, p. 281, no. 157. It has been shown also to have influenced the relief of the tower of Babel in the Dutch Reformed Church at Oosterend, as described by Miedema, 'De Bijbelse Ikonografie', pp. 73–4.

88 The eight Josiah prints by Philip Galle are undated; the drawings were made in 1569; *Tegninger*, ed. Garff, nos. 102–9; Veldman, *Heemskerck*, p. 108; Hollstein, *Etchings*, VIII, p. 243, nos. 240–7; Preibisz, *Heemskerck*, pp. 88–9, nos. 55–62. The text of this print is abbreviated from the Vulgate, 4 Kings, 23: 13–14.

89 On the use of the Pantheon here and elsewhere, as part of Heemskerck's 'anti-Roman image polemic' see Bredekamp, 'Heemskercks Bildersturmzyklen', pp. 211–13.

90 *Tegninger*, ed. Garff, pl. 75, 79 (drawings of 1563); Hollstein, *Etchings*, VII, p. 74, nos. 42, 46; VIII, p. 243, nos. 251, 255; Kerrich, *Catalogue*, p. 29.

91 J. R. Rand, 'Henry VIII's Succession', *History Today*, 20 (1970), 747.

92 Auerbach, *Tudor Artists*, pp. 81–9, plates 23–7; also description in Christie's Catalogue for sale of 9 December 1983, no. 197, pp. 64–5. See above fig. 4 for the carved female caryatid behind Cranmer in Flicke's 1545 portrait.

93 Edward Hall, *The Union of the two noble and illustrate fameli es of Lancastre and Yorke* (London, 1548); John Marbeck, *A Concordance to the Bible* (London, 1550); John Bale, *Illustrium maioris Britanniae scriptorum summarium* ([Wesel], 1548); Campbell Dodgson, 'Woodcuts designed by Holbein for English Printers', *Walpole Society*, 27 (1939), 8–10; McKerrow and Ferguson, 'Title-page Borders', pp. 70–2, no. 67; King, *English Reformation Literature*, pp. 111–13.

94 Strong, *Gloriana*, pp. 56–7, suggests that this frontispiece might have been the work of Levina Teerlinc; cf. Strong, *Portraits of Queen Elizabeth I* (Oxford, 1963), p. 120 (W.6).

95 H. Junius, *Emblemata* (Antwerp, 1565), facsimile edn, introd. H. M. Black (Menston, 1972), pp. 48, 131–3. For examples of such ornament see Jacobowitz and Stepanek, *Lucas van Leyden; Kunst voor de Beeldenstorm*, II, p. 142, no. 28. 3; J. S. Byrne, *Renaissance Ornament Prints and Drawings* (New York, 1981), p. 66. Junius's *Emblemata*, published by Plantin (with further editions in 1566, 1569 and 1575, and then French and Flemish translations), was among the books Nicholas England imported from Antwerp in 1567. Another English bookseller bought six copies from Plantin in 1578. Colin Clair, 'Christopher Plantin's Trade-Connexions with England and Scotland', *The Library*, 5th ser. 14 (1959), 28–45; Clair, *Christopher Plantin*, pp. 44, 184.

96 In addition to figs. 69–71 examples include illustrations to *The Story of Tamar and Amnon*, and Ahab and Jezebel in *The Story of Ahab and Naboth*. These

prints are all in the Kerrich bequest in the Fitzwilliam Museum; vol. I, nos. 30, 68, 134–5, 147, 210; Kerrich, *Catalogue*, pp., 5, 13, 23, 25, 35.

97 This has been admirably documented by Michael Camille, in his *Gothic Idol*.

98 Mario Salmi, *Luca Signorelli* (Munich, 1955), pp. 25, 72, plate 30b.

99 D. Freedberg, 'Art and Iconoclasm', in *Kunst voor de Beeldenstorm*, II, pp. 60, 79, 84 (nn. 190–1); C. White, *The Dutch Pictures in the Collection of Her Majesty the Queen* (Cambridge, 1982), pp. 9–11. The panel was bought by Charles I from Sir James Palmer. The story depicted is in the *Golden Legend*, ed. F. S. Ellis, vol. II (1928), pp. 240–3.

100 Camille, *Gothic Idol*, pp. 126, 233–4, figs. 73, 125–6.

101 Michael Baxandall, *The Limewood Sculptors of Renaissance Germany* (New Haven and London, 1980), pp. 83–4, 207; *Luther und die Folgen für die Kunst*, ed. W. Hofmann (Munich, 1983), catalogue of Hamburg Kunsthalle Exhibition, 1983–4, pp. 132–5.

102 Shirley Bury, *Jewellery Gallery Summary Catalogue* (Victoria and Albert Museum, London, 1982), p. 71, no. 8; C. Oman, 'The Jewels of Our Lady of the Pillar at Saragossa', *Apollo*, June 1967, 400–6.

103 *Early Writings of John Hooper*, p. 320 from *A declaration of the ten holy commandments*.

104 *Catechism of Thomas Becon*, ed. J. Ayre (Parker Society, Cambridge, 1844), p. 65.

105 E. Panofsky, 'Erasmus and the Visual Arts', *Journal of the Warburg and Courtauld Institutes*, 32 (1969), 208–9.

106 Aston, *England's Iconoclasts*, I, p. 107.

107 *Homilies*, p. 202; from the third part of the Homily against idolatry, a section which was not intended for uncontrolled general consumption. See Aston, *England's Iconoclasts*, I, p. 323.

108 J. Calfhill, *An Answer to John Martiall's Treatise of the Cross*, ed. R. Gibbings (Parker Society, Cambridge, 1846), pp. 273–4.

109 R. Scot, *The Discoverie of Witchcraft*, ed. B. Nicholson (London, 1886), chapters 22–6 of the 'Discourse upon divels and spirits', cited pp. 441–2; Keith Thomas, *Religion and the Decline of Magic* (London, 1971), pp. 27–8, 54.

110 T. Buddensieg, 'Gregory the Great, the Destroyer of Pagan Idols: The History of a Medieval Legend Concerning the Decline of Ancient Art and Literature', *Journal of the Warburg and Courtauld Institutes*, 28 (1965), 44–65; E. H. Gombrich, *Symbolic Images* (London, 1975), pp. 104–8, 151–2, n. 37, p. 224; Scot, *Discoverie*, p. 445.

111 As described by Sir Thomas Smith, cited Aston, *England's Iconoclasts*, I, p. 277.

112 *CSP Venetian, 1558–1580*, p. 84, no. 71; Norman L. Jones, *Faith by Statute, Parliament and the Settlement of Religion 1559* (London, 1982), p. 42; Clifford Davidson, ' "The Devil's Guts": Allegations of Superstition and Fraud in Religious Drama and Art during the Reformation', in *Iconoclasm vs. Art and Drama*, ed. C. Davidson and A. E. Nichols (Kalamazoo, 1989), pp. 92–3.

113 *CSP Spanish, 1558–1567*, p. 105, no. 66; cf. p. 401, no. 283; W. P. Haugaard, *Elizabeth and the English Reformation* (Cambridge, 1968), p. 186.

114 *Zurich Letters*, ed. H. Robinson (Parker Society, Cambridge, 1842–5), I, Letter 27, English p. 63, Latin, p. 36.

115 Society of Antiquaries, Lemon 53; printed William Herford, London, 23 March 1559/60; *STC*, 19969.4.

116 *Correspondence of Matthew Parker*, ed. J. Bruce (Parker Society, Cambridge, 1853), pp. 79, 94; Aston, *England's Iconoclasts*, I, p. 309.

117 *Zurich Letters*, I, Letter 31, English pp. 73–4, Latin pp. 42–3; Aston, *England's Iconoclasts*, I, pp. 311–12, 397, n. 51.

118 Ben Jonson, *Bartholomew Fair*, III, i. On Elizabeth's interest in pictures (not excluding religious paintings, though commissioning such was another matter), see Lorne Campbell, *The Early Flemish Pictures in the Collection of Her Majesty the Queen* (Cambridge, 1985), pp. xxviii–xxx.

119 *The Seconde Parte of a Register*, ed. A. Peel (Cambridge, 1915), II, p. 53. On William Fuller and his access to the court see P. Collinson, *The Elizabethan Puritan Movement* (London, 1967), pp. 134, 152.

120 W. Fulke, *A Defense of the sincere and true Translations*, ed. C. H. Hartshorne (Parker Society, Cambridge, 1843), pp. 204–5.

121 John Martiall, *A Treatyse of the Cross* (Antwerp, 1564), ff. 1ᵛ, 7ᵛ.

122 James Calfhill, *An Answer to John Martiall's Treatise of the Cross*, ed. R. Gibbings (Parker Society, Cambridge, 1846), pp. 5, 7.

123 I follow here the account given by Guzman de Silva (in *CSP Spanish, 1558–1567*), p. 405, no. 286, though this was not the whole or only truth. See my *England's Iconoclasts*, I, pp. 324–5 on the incident.

124 T. Harding, *A confutation of a booke intituled An apologie of the church of England* (Antwerp, 1565), prefatory address to Elizabeth, sig. *2ᵛ.

125 J. Strype, *Annals of the Reformation* (Oxford, 1824), I, ii, pp. 198–200; PRO, SP 12/36/77; *CSP Domestic, 1547–80*, p. 251; Catharine Davies, 'A Protestant Gentleman and the English Reformation: the Career and Attitudes of Richard Tracy, ?1501–1569', in *The Sudeleys – Lords of Toddington* (Manorial Society of Great Britain, 1987), pp. 121–39.

126 *CSP Spanish, 1558–1567*, pp. 419, 425, nos. 295–6. On the Teerlinc miniature (dated to c. 1565, but surprisingly not connected with the seemingly special significance of this Maundy) see Roy Strong, *Gloriana* (London, 1987), pp. 54–5; Strong, *Artists of the Tudor Court*, p. 55; Strong, *English Renaissance Miniature*, pp. 57, 62.

127 J. A. van Dorsten, *The Radical Arts* (Leiden, 1973), pp. 42–6; van Dorsten, 'Steven van Herwyck's Elizabeth (1565) – A Franco-Flemish Political Medal', *Burlington Magazine*, 111 (1969), 143–7, sees the French ambassador as the probable sponsor, while remarking 'It may seem curious that such a frank approval of the Queen's heresies should have been issued on the French King's behalf'. The possible implications of the dispute over the cross are not considered here. In 1584 the rector of East Hanningfield in Essex, was accused of omitting the Kingdom of France from the royal style in praying for the queen. *A Series of Precedents and Proceedings in Criminal Causes*, ed. William Hale, introd. R. W. Dunning (Edinburgh, 1973), p. 182.

128 *Zurich Letters*, I, pp. 122, 129 (Latin pp. 73, 77).

129 *Parker Correspondence*, p. 379; J. Strype, *The Life and Acts of Matthew Parker* (Oxford, 1821), II, pp. 35–6.

130 *Parker Correspondence*, p. 97; Strype, *Life of Parker*, I, p. 92; Loades, *Tudor Court*, pp. 204–5; Aston, *England's Iconoclasts*, I, pp. 313–14; BL, MS Lansdowne 64, no. 14, f. 47ʳ (1590) – the context here was the use of surplice and cross in baptism.

131 *CSP Spanish, 1558–67*, p. 401, no. 283.

132 Lambeth Palace Library, MS Fairhurst 3470, f. 25ʳ. I am most grateful to Dr. Bill who made this manuscript available. Its probable date is 1578; see P. Collinson, *Archbishop Grindal 1519–1583* (London, 1979, pp. 238, 262–3. For Theodore Beza's support of this view see below on 'Elizabeth as Hezekiah'.

133 Strype, *Life of Parker*, I, p. 312, quoting Dean Whittingham of Durham, writing to his patron, the earl of Leicester in 1564 – about vestments.

134 The pageants for the occasion featured St George; S. Anglo, *Spectacle Pageantry, and Early Tudor Policy* (Oxford, 1969), p. 291. For a description of the painting of this event, published not long before its destruction, see J. Topham, 'An Historical and Descriptive Account of the Ancient Painting preserved at Cowdray in Sussex', *Archaeologia*, 8 (1787), 406–22.

135 S. Brigden, *London and the Reformation* (Oxford, 1989), pp. 6–7. What follows is a summary of a longer discussion in volume 2 of my *England's Iconoclasts* (forthcoming); see also Aston, 'Iconoclasm in England: Official and Clandestine' in *Iconoclasm vs. Art and Drama*, ed. C. Davidson and A. E. Nichols (Kalamazoo, 1989), pp. 76–80.

136 John Stow, *Annales, or, A Generall Chronicle of England* (London, 1631–32), p. 694; cf. Stow, *A Survey of London*, ed. C. L. Kingsford (Oxford, 1908), I, p. 266. This description seems to have been of a seated Virgin and Child, not like the standing figure in the Basire print, so one must assume that this was another carving in the lower tier. In the *Survey* Stow tells us that the 'lowest images' that were damaged included, besides the Virgin, Christ's resurrection and Edward the Confessor.

137 Stow, *Survey*, I, pp. 266–7; II, pp. 331–2, citing Ben Jonson (*Cynthia's Revels*, I, i); 'As also their (the City magistrates') religion in pulling down a superstitious cross and advancing a Venus or Priapus in place of it'.

138 Stow, *Survey*, I, p. 267; *Analytical Index to . . . the Remembrancia . . . of the City of London* (London, 1878), pp. 65–6; *Acts of the Privy Council*, xxxi (1600–1601), p. 44, cf. xxx (1599–1600), p. 27.

139 Stow, *Survey*, I, p. 267.

140 Aston, 'Iconoclasm in England', pp. 76–7.

141 Edward Dering, *Two Godly Sermons* (Middelburg, 1590), sigs. A 4ᵛ–5ʳ, A 8ʳ, B 7ᵛ.

142 Dering, *Sermons*, sigs. B 1ʳ⁻ᵛ, B 5ʳ; *M. Derings Workes* (London, 1614), sig. K 1ʳ, cf. sig. I 7ʳ⁻ᵛ; *Parker Correspondence*, p. 476. Dering is in the *DNB*, but the best account of him is Patrick Collinson's 1965 Dr Williams's Library Lecture, 'A Mirror of Elizabethan Puritanism: The Life and Letters of "Godly Master Dering"', reprinted in *Godly People* (London, 1983), pp. 289–324. See p. 288 for the engraved portrait of Dering in Henry Holland's *Herωologia Anglica*, two copies of which (BL, C 38 h 2, and CUL, Keynes D. 5. 19) have manuscript notes on the pictorial sources.

143 *Proceedings in the Parliaments of Elizabeth I*, I, ed. T. E. Hartley (Leicester,

1981), p. 35. *A newe enterlude of godly queene Hester* (dating probably from the 1520s) was printed in 1561; R. H. Blackburn, *Biblical Drama under the Tudors* (The Hague and Paris, 1971), pp. 70–6; the text was edited from the 1561 quarto by W. W. Greg in *Materialen zur Kunde des älteren Englischen Dramas*, ed. W. Bang, v (Louvain, 1904).

144 2 Kings, 18: 2; 2 Chronicles, 29: 1.

145 W. Leigh, *Queene Elizabeth, Paraleld in her princely vertues, with David, Iosua and Hezekia* (London, 1612), pp. 105, 133–4 (numbered twice – cited at second); see Epistle Dedicatorie, sig. A 6ᵛ for date of delivery. See *DNB* for Leigh, a popular preacher and rector of Standish (Lancashire) from 1586 till his death. Court favour in James's reign brought him tutorship of Prince Henry.

146 *Parker Correspondence*, p. 89; cf. *Homilies*, p. 173. For this unscriptural statement see above n. 36.

147 Acts, 3: 1–7; 4: 7–12, my citation at 3, verses 4 and 6; text in the painting, 4: 10–12. F. Winzinger, *Wolf Huber, Das Gesamtwerk* (Munich and Zurich, 1979), no. 296, I, pp. 59, 180–1; P. Rose, *Wolf Huber Studies* (New York and London, 1977), pp. 183–7. For what might be described as an intermediate Lutheran position in the Reformation shift of this iconography, with the brazen serpent advanced as a symbol of justification by faith (that is, an image as safe as the cross itself), see D. L. Ehresmann, 'The Brazen Serpent, a Reformation Motif in the Works of Lucas Cranach the Elder and his Workshop', *Marsyas*, 13 (1966–7), 32–47. See also David Freedberg, *The Power of Images* (Chicago and London, 1989), p. 498, n. 7.

148 Martiall, *Treatyse of the Crosse*, f. 93ʳ.

149 *The Year 1200. A Centennial Exhibition at the Metropolitan Museum of Art*, Exhibition Catalogue, ed. K. Hoffmann (1970), I, pp. 52–6; T. P. F. Hoving, 'The Bury St. Edmunds Cross', *Metropolitan Museum of Art Bulletin*, NS 22 (1963–4), pp. 317–40.

150 For Holbein's brazen serpent and related Bible illustrations, see Kästner, *Die Icones*, I, pp. 219–20; II, pp. 649–50, 841.

151 *Princely Magnificence*, no. 11, pp. 48–50; G. H. Tait, 'Historiated Tudor Jewellery', *Antiquaries Journal*, 42 (1962), 232–4; Joan Evans, *A History of Jewellery 1100–1870* (London, 1953), p. 109, pl. 64.

152 2 Kings, 18: 1–4; 2 Chronicles, 31:1.

153 *The Bible* (Geneva, 1560), f. 173ᵛ; 2 Kings, 23, note b to verse 4.

154 *Correspondance de Théodore de Bèze*, ed. H. Meylan, A. Dufour et al., VII (1973), pp. 158–9 (letter of 27 June 1566); *Puritan Manifestoes*, ed. W. H. Frere and C. E. Douglas (London, 1907), p. 50.

155 A. B. Chamberlain, *Hans Holbein the Younger* (London, 1913), I, pp. 343, 347; P. Ganz, *The Paintings of Hans Holbein the Younger* (London, 1950), pp. 6, 271–2. For what remains – not including Hezekiah – of this scheme (the biblical subjects of which postdate Holbein's first visit to England) see J. Rowlands, *Holbein, The Paintings of Hans Holbein the Younger* (Oxford, 1985), pp. 55–6, 220–1.

156 R. Simpson, 'Sir Thomas Smith and the Wall Paintings at Hill Hall, Essex: Scholarly Theory and Design in the Sixteenth Century', *Journal of the British Archaeological Association*, 130 (1977), 1–20; *16th Century Britain*, ed. Boris

Ford, pp. 65, 248–9. On Smith's Hill Hall (severely damaged by fire in 1969) see Mary Dewar, *Sir Thomas Smith* (London, 1964), pp. 191–209; J. Strype, *Life of Sir Thomas Smith* (Oxford, 1820), pp. 171–3.

157 Schmidt, *Illustration der Lutherbibel*, pp. 172–3 (no. 123) – referring to comparable depictions in many Bibles, specially of Frankfurt – 273 (no. 197), 294 (no. 214), 314 (no. 232). See above p. 43, n. 47. Here too I record thanks to Sergiusz Michalski, who kindly sent me photos and a copy of his *Protestanci a Sztuka* (Warsaw, 1989), which (pp. 118–19) includes two of these cuts. On the relevance of the brazen serpent to the image debate see also Freedberg, 'Art and Iconoclasm', p. 79 and p. 84, n. 194.

158 *The first tome or volume of the Paraphrase of Erasmus upon the newe testamente* (London, 1549), from the preface, dated 30 September 1545, addressed to Queen Catherine Parr, ff. iii^v, iiii^v. On Udall and Cromwell see *LP*, 14, ii, p. 334, no. 782.

159 2 Kings, 18–20; 2 Chronicles, 29–32; Isaiah, 36–39.

160 F. S. Boas, *University Drama in the Tudor Age* (Oxford, 1914), pp. 90–7; Blackburn, *Biblical Drama*, pp. 66–8 considers (n. 6, pp. 68–9) the possibility that the play was rewritten for the 1564 production, and, while wondering about specific contemporary implications, asks; 'What, in particular, is intended by the brazen serpent whose destruction is celebrated in the opening scenes?' Hartwell's *Regina Literata* (London, 1565) is printed in J. Nichols, *The Progresses and Public Processions of Queen Elizabeth* (London, 1788–1821), I; see pp. 12–14 on the King's College entertainment. On Hartwell's praise of the earl of Leicester who (already known as a patron of puritans) was Lord High Steward of Cambridge in 1563 and became Chancellor in 1564 see Eleanor Rosenberg, *Leicester Patron of Letters* (New York, 1955), pp. 122, 139–40. Francis Knollys was with the queen on this occasion.

161 Boas, *University Drama*, p. 97; Nichols, *Progresses*, III, pp. 177–9; cf. 55, 58, 62, 100, 127, for references to Hezekiah in these disputations, including his breaking of the brazen serpent.

162 *The Bible* (Geneva, 1560), Epistle, sig. ii^v.

163 *The holie Bible* (London, [1568]), pt. 2, f. cv^v.

164 *Homilies*, pp. 224–5.

165 *Ibid.*, pp. 225, 239.

166 John Jewel, *An Apology of the Church of England*, ed. J. E. Booty (Ithaca, N.Y., 1963), pp. 115–16. The references here to Hezekiah include the same unscriptural statement as the Homilies (n. 36 above) that he had the brazen serpent not only broken to pieces but also 'beaten to powder'.

167 J. Jewel, *A Defence of the Apologie of the Churche of Englande* (London, 1567), sig. A iiii^v. The 'mother in Israel' is a reference to Deborah (Judges, 4: 4; 5: 7).

168 *The Reformation of Religion by Josiah*, sigs. B 2^{r-v}, B 3^{r-v}, C 4^v, D 1^{r-v}. This book, a copy of which is still in the library at Lambeth, was listed among the *Libri Puritanici* in the library that Richard Bancroft bequeathed in 1610 to future archbishops of Canterbury: Lambeth Palace Library, L.R.F.1, f. 76^v (one of two copies of the 1612 catalogue of Archbishop Bancroft's books and manuscripts). On Lambeth library as a resource for theological controversy

see Geoffrey Bill, 'Lambeth Palace Library', *The Library*, 5th ser. 21 (1966), 193–6.

169 2 Kings, 22: 2; *Reformation by Josiah*, sig A 4ʳ.

170 *The Treasure Houses of Britain*, ed. G. Jackson-Stops, Exhibition Catalogue (National Gallery of Art, Washington, 1985), pp. 82–3; Strong, *English Icon*, pp. 140–1, no. 95; Strong, *Portraits of Elizabeth*, pp. 79–80, no. P. 82; Strong, *Gloriana*, pp. 70–7, and cf. no. 29, pp. 50–1 for the early (*c.* 1543–7) Tudor family group that lay behind this painting; King, *Tudor Royal Iconography*, pp. 223–5. It is worth drawing attention to Henry VIII's pose, slightly turned towards his Protestant successors, instead of facing majestically frontwards.

171 Hind, *Engraving in England*, I, pp. 270–2, plate 148; Strong, *Portraits of Elizabeth*, pp. 114–15, no. E. 28; Strong, *Gloriana*, p. 77 (dating the engraving to *c.* 1590–5). There is no reference here to Mary's zeal – only to how she 'put down truth' and brought war and discord.

172 Strong, *Portraits of Elizabeth*, p. 84, no. P. 98.

173 The plausible suggestion that the scene visible in the distance behind Philip and Mary in the *Allegory of the Tudor Succession* may be intended to depict Rome, was made by Ellen Chirelstein, *Painting in Focus*, *The Allegory of the Tudor Succession* (Yale Center for British Art, n.d.), a leaflet on the 1589–95 version of the painting by an unknown artist at the Yale Center.

174 See A. S. Herbert, *Historical Catalogue of Printed Editions of the English Bible* (London, 1968), pp. 53–4, 56–7, 59–60, 111 (nos. 95, 99–100, 105, 228), for New Testaments of 1551–3 and 1595 with portrayals of Edward VI. On portraits in Bibles see also Aston, 'The *Bishops' Bible* Illustrations'. I am most grateful to Elizabeth Ingram for listing the editions that included portraits of Edward VI. There were two versions, both signed with Arnold Nicolai's monogram (see n. 49 above), which appeared in twelve editions 1560–1600. Colin Clair, 'The Myth of "Anton Sylvius"', *Gutenberg Jahrbuch* (1963), 122–7, considers this work of Nicolai.

175 Janet Arnold, 'The "Pictur" of Elizabeth I when Princess', *Burlington Magazine*, 23 (1981), 303–4; *The Letters of Queen Elizabeth*, ed. G. B. Harrison (London, 1935), pp. 15–16, nos. x, xi; Elizabeth Jenkins, *Elizabeth and Leicester* (London, 1961), pp. 12, 126–7; John Leland, *De Rebus Britannicis Collectanea* (London, 1770), I, pt. 2 (= vol. II), p. 693.

176 H. Clifford Smith, *Jewellery* (London, 1908), pp. 274–5, pl. xxxv , 7; Joan Evans, *English Jewellery from the Fifth Century to A.D. 1800* (London, 1921), p. 83; Tait, 'Historiated Tudor Jewellery' (above, n. 151), p. 235; *Holinshed's Chronicles* (London, 1807–8), III, p. 1064; IV, p. 229; *Literary Remains of King Edward the Sixth*, ed. J. G. Nichols (Roxburghe Club, London, 1857), I, pp. cxcix, ccliv.

177 H. Bullinger, *A Confutation Of the Popes Bull* (London, 1572), ff. 15ᵛ–17ʳ, cited at 16ʳ. I have not made any progress in identifying the – probably stylized – figure of the pope. Both Paul III (1534–49) and Pius V (1566–72) are usually represented as bearded and their features bear no resemblance to the pope shown here. On the other hand (as Alexander Murray, who kindly made suggestions here, points out) the beak-nosed friar looks rather like some depictions of Savonarola.

178 Foxe, *Actes and Monumentes* (London, 1576), I, p. 771. King, *Tudor Royal Iconography*, pp. 161, 171–2, comments similarly on this point and considers the traditional iconography of the scales of justice.

179 1 Peter, 1: 24–25; Isaiah, 40: 6–8; M. Schlüter, *Münzen und Medaillen zur Reformation 16. bis 20. Jahrhundert* (Catalogue of 1983 exhibition, Kestner-Museum, Hanover), p. 2, no. 3; J. S. Davenport, *German Talers 1500–1600* (Frankfurt am Main, 1979), pp. 294, 296; cf. 73–4, 254–5, 333. I have not succeeded in identifying a Bible whose spelling corresponds with all the words in the painting.

180 *Princely Magnificence*, p. 39, citing BL, MS Stowe 559, f. 14^r.

181 *Three Inventories*, ed. Shaw, p. 35; cf. pp. 28, 30 for other anti-papal 'tables': *Calendar of the Manuscripts of the Marquis of Salisbury*, Hist. MSS. Com., pt. 1 (London, 1883), p. 130.

182 John Shearman, *The Early Italian Pictures in the Collection of Her Majesty the Queen* (Cambridge, 1983), pp. 117–18; Philip Pouncey, 'Girolamo da Treviso in the Service of Henry VIII', *Burlington Magazine*, 95 (1953), 208–11; *Three Inventories*, ed. Shaw, p. 56; Strong, 'Edward VI and the Pope', p. 313; Strong, *Holbein and Henry VIII* (London, [1967]), pp. 8–9. The Coverdale Bible woodcut illustrated here had plenty of precedents.

183 *Documents Relating to the Revels at Court in the Time of King Edward VI and Queen Mary*, ed. A. Feuillerat (Louvain, Leipzig and London, 1914), pp. 6, 12 (see below, p. 180), 22 (twenty yards of white cloth of 'silver playne', 'Cutt for a long gowne for a prest for the kinges grace to pley'.

184 W. Lynne, *The beginning and endynge of all popery* (?1548), *STC* 17115; for the text in this woodcut see below, n. 195; King, *Tudor Royal Iconography*, pp. 165–9, considers the antecedents of Lynne's cuts. R. W. Scribner, *For the Sake of Simple Folk* (Cambridge, 1981), pp. 161–2; cf. pp. 155 (for the falling pope in Cranach's *Passional Christi und Antichristi*), 129–32, 143–7.

185 *Literary Remains of King Edward the Sixth*, I, pp. 181–205.

186 On Meyerbeck's etching see Hollstein, *Etchings*, xxviii, p. 90. Cf. Scribner, *Simple Folk*, pp. 81–2, 134; Scribner, *Popular Culture*, pp. 22, 293–4, 296, for earlier images of the devil's bagpipe and parody of the papal arms, repeated here.

187 *Graftons Abridgement of the Chronicles of Englande* (London, 1570), f. 194^{r-v}; *The end and Confession of John Felton* (London, [1570]), *STC* 11843, was mainly concerned with drawing the moral ('Beware you Papists all beware, / be true unto your Queene'), but *A letter to Rome* was more explicit about Felton's offence. H. L. Collmann, *Ballads & Broadsides chiefly of the Elizabethan period* (Oxford, 1912), nos. 50, 70, pp. 144–8, 203–5; see Watt, *Cheap Print*, pp. 44, 88–9, on the boom in anti-papal ballads at this time. *State Trials*, compiled by T. B. and T. J. Howell (London, 1816–28), I, cols. 1085–88, prints J. Partridge's 1570 prose work on Felton, on whom see *DNB*. For Arthur Golding's translation of Bullinger's text, dedicated to the earl of Leicester on 2 January 1571/2, see Rosenberg, *Leicester*, pp. 211–17.

188 *Zurich Letters*, I, pp. 218, 221, 225, 229, 238–9 (cited at 238). Bullinger's preface – saying he had not seen or heard of the bull before – was dated February 1571. The title of the Latin edition of Bullinger's text, refers to the bull's having been published two years earlier (*Bullae Papisticae ante*

biennium … promulgatae), and the translated version whose title likewise stated that the bull was published 'more then two yeres agoe', encouraged belief in its antedating the 1569 rising by unambiguous remarks in the dedicatory epistle. The possibility that rumours of the pope's forthcoming action may have preceded his promulgation is another question; see Rosenberg, *Leicester*, pp. 214–15, and n. 47.

189 British Museum Print Room, Political and Personal Satires, I, no. 13; F. G. Stephens, *Catalogue of Political and Personal Satires … in the British Museum*, I (London, 1870, rep. 1978), no. 13, pp. 7–10.

190 Anthony Fletcher, *Tudor Rebellions* (London, 1973), p. 150; cf. pp. 95, 104–5, 113; *Zurich Letters*, I, pp. 214–15 (Latin p. 125), letter dated London 6 Feb. 1570; J. Foxe, *A Sermon of Christ crucified* (London, 1570), *STC* 11242.3, sig. A iiiʳ; M. MacLure, *The Paul's Cross Sermons 1534–1642* (Toronto, 1958), pp. 58–9, 206–7.

191 *Homilies*, pp. 523, 526–7, 529; Aston, *England's Iconoclasts*, I, p. 385.

192 *Homilies*, pp. 517–18.

193 H. Bullinger, *A Confutation of the Popes Bull* (London, 1572), ff. 40ᵛ, 48ʳ, 49ʳ⁻ᵛ, 64ᵛ. I have compared these passages with the Latin in *Bullae Papisticae ante biennium … promulgatae* (London, 1571).

194 Bullinger, *Confutation*, ff. 73ʳ–86ᵛ.

195 Gerard van Loon, *Histoire Métallique des XVII Provinces des Pays-Bas* (The Hague, 1732–37), I, pp. 369–70; Schlüter, *Münzen und Medaillen*, p. 37, no. 34; J. A. Dopp, *Eliza's Knights: Soldiers, Poets, and Puritans in the Netherlands 1572–1586* (Alblasserdam, [1981]), pp. 65–6; Strong, *Portraits of Elizabeth*, p. 138, med. 16. The inscription on the reverse is 'QUEM DEUS CONFICIET SPIRITU ORIS SUI' – whom the Lord will consume by the spirit of his mouth (cf. 2 Thessalonians, 2: 8; Isaiah, 11: 4).

196 BM Print Room, Political and Personal Satires, I, no. 12; Stephens, *Catalogue*, I, no. 12, pp. 6–7; the Print Room has a note of 1 Jan. 1935 by F. Saxl; see also his 'Veritas Filia Temporis', in *Philosophy and History: Essays Presented to Ernst Cassirer*, ed. R. Klibansky and H. J. Paton (Oxford, 1936), pp. 209–10; Strong, *Portraits of Elizabeth*, p. 109, no. E.14. There are two different copies of this print in the British Museum.

197 Strong, *Portraits*, pp. 156–7, Post. no. 15; Saxl, 'Veritas Filia Temporis', p. 210; Hind, *Engraving*, III, p. 33, pl. 19(a).

198 Strong, *Portraits*, pp. 5–7, 119, no. W.2; Frances Yates, *Astrea* (London, 1975), pp. 42–4; King, *Tudor Royal Iconography*, pp. 154–7 (with the suggestion that the bystanders are Day, Foxe, and Thomas Norton).

199 On the evidence of extensive cancels and inserted leaves in the 1570 edition, suggestive of the large amount of new material that Foxe added at a late stage (causing his paper to run out), see L. M. Oliver, 'Single-page Imposition in Foxe's *Acts and Monuments*, 1570', *The Library*, 5th ser. 1 (1946–7), 49–56. It is suggested here that haste was caused by Foxe and Day wishing to have the book finished before the meeting of convocation on 3 April 1571. Cf. Oastler, *John Day*, pp. 26–7 (where the convocation meeting is misdated) and W. Haller, *Foxe's Book of Martyrs and the Elect Nation* (London, 1963), pp. 128–9 ff., 172–3 ff. The exact date at which the new edition appeared is unclear, though it seems Foxe was still hard at work on it when he preached at

Paul's Cross on 24 March. The added pages at the end of volume I (sigs. 2N – 2O⁴) do not seem to be in all copies of this edition. On the woodcuts see King, *Tudor Royal Iconography*, pp. 138–52; Edward Hodnett, *Image and Text, Studies in the Illustration of English Lterature* (London, 1982), pp. 35–7.

200 Lynne, *Beginning and endynge of all popery*, sig. E 4ᵛ; King, *Iconography*, p. 168. I am grateful to Eamon Duffy for pointing out the relevance here of Psalm, 110: 1 '. . . I make thine enemies thy footstool'.

201 Foxe, *Actes and Monumentes* (1570), II, p. 1201. Pole is given a cardinal's hat, though he did not become a cardinal until December 1536. On this woodcut see E. H. Hageman, 'John Foxe's Henry VIII as *Justitia*', *Sixteenth Century Journal*, 10 (1979), 35–43; King, *Iconography*, pp. 158–60. The print, used again in the 1576 edition, became a title-page prefacing volume II in 1583.

202 Foxe's woodcut appears in the edition of 1563 (p. 41) as well as in 1570 (I, p. 263). Cf. *A & M*, ed. Pratt, V, p. 69 for 'an old Prophecy of the Fall of the Pope' (1576 edition, II, p. 1028); II, pp. 195–6 for the exchanges inscribed on the print, including words of Psalm, 91: 13. King, *Tudor Royal Iconography*, pp. 130–6, points to the derivation of this illustration from *Bapsttrew Hadriani iiii. und Alexanders iii. gegen Keyser Friderichen Barbarossa geübt*, which (with preface by Luther) was printed in both Wittenberg and Strasbourg in 1545, with different depictions of the emperor's humiliation. For the Holbein 1526 woodcut, part of the Dance of Death series published in *Les simulachres & historiées faces de la mort* (Lyon, 1538), sig. C iiiʳ, see *Luther und die Folgen für die Kunst*, pp. 180–1.

203 Thomas Harding, *A Detection of sundrie foule errours* (Louvain, 1568), Preface to the Reader and ff. 16ʳ–18ʳ; A. C. Southern, *Elizabethan Recusant Prose 1559–1582* (London, 1950), chapter 3, especially pp. 59–67; Peter Milward, *Religious Controversies of the Elizabethan Age* (London, 1978), chapter 1.

204 See n. 177.

205 Foxe, *A & M*, 1563, p. 675 (*recte* 684); 1570, II, pp. 1483–4; ed. Pratt, V, pp. 697–9.

206 This Bible was edited by Edmund Becke (London, John Day, 1551), where the cut appears sig. *iiiᵛ. Herbert, *Historical Catalogue*, p. 52; King, *English Reformation Literature*, pp. 129–30. See Hodnett, *Image and Text*, p. 32 on the 'worn capital E' used in the 1563 *A & M*; and Oastler, *John Day*, p. 45, for Day's 'most distinctive' set of initial letters, which this E resembles. This long-lived initial was still doing service in 1625, when it appears at the opening ('Excellent monarch') of the dedication of Camden's *Annales* to James I.

207 BL, MS Lansdowne 10, f. 211ʳ. For the date of this letter see n. 213.

208 John Foxe, *Christ Jesus Triumphant Englished by Richard Day* (London, 1607), sig. A 4ᵛ; Oastler, *John Day*, pp. 26, 34. BL, MS Harl. 416, ff. 122ʳ⁻ᵛ, 185ʳ, has letters addressed to Foxe at both these houses, the latter (26 Jan. 1566/7) putting him as 'abidinge at Mr daies house at Aldersgate in London'.

209 Oastler, *John Day*, frontispiece and p. 26.

210 J. F. Mozley, *John Foxe and his Book* (London, 1940), p. 140 says the number of woodcuts rises from 60 to 150; for a more detailed breakdown see Hodnett, *Image and Text*, pp. 31–2, and see also King, *Tudor Royal Iconography*,

p. 133, n. 23. See *A & M*, 1570, II, pp. 1302–3, 1304–8 for Anglo-Saxon type, pp. 1481, 1566, for new ornament, and pp. 954, 1022, 1184 etc. for bracketed tables. Another improvement was the abandonment (in general) of the earlier practice of attaching some woodcuts as folded insets.

211 William Camden, *The History of ... Princess Elizabeth*, ed. W. T. MacCaffrey (Chicago, 1970), p. 101.

212 BL, MS Lansdowne 10, f. 127ʳ; Andrew Pettegree, *Foreign Protestant Communities in Sixteenth-Century London* (Oxford, 1986), pp. 201, 233. He died in 1575. The letter of recommendation says he was of Utrecht, but he had siblings in Antwerp.

213 BL, MS Lansdowne 10, f. 211ʳ. (Foxe also asked if Cecil had any relevant material he could add to his history). A pencilled note in the manuscript dates this letter 1568. Edward Hodnett, *Marcus Gheeraerts the Elder* (Utrecht 1971), p. 45; Hodnett, *Image and Text*, p. 31. Oastler, *John Day*, p. 34, places this plea in 1569; Mozley, *John Foxe*, pp. 141–2 dated it 1570, though this seems improbably late. For names of aliens in Day's service see E. J. Worman, *Alien Members of the Book-Trade during the Tudor Period* (London, 1906), pp. 14–15, and for numbers of immigrants in London in 1568 below, n. 221.

214 *DNB* s.n. Batman; for Bateman's activity in book-collecting on Parker's behalf see M. R. James, *A Descriptive Catalogue of the Manuscripts in the Library of Corpus Christi College, Cambridge* (Cambridge, 1912), I, pp. xv–xvi, MSS. 61, 194.

215 S. Bateman, *A christall glasse* (London, 1569), sig. H iiᵛ. See Oastler, *John Day*, pp. 38, 45 (fig. 5) for comparable re-use of an initial L. This was the third (but not the last) book to be served by the E (see above, n. 206).

216 Bateman, *Christall glasse*, sig. G iiiiʳ; Foxe, *A & M* (1563), p. 474; cf. *A & M*, ed. Pratt, IV, p. 627, cf. p. 649 and appendix. Foxe's text only states that Bilney was twice pulled out of the pulpit in the diocese of Norwich; the illustration places this event in Ipswich (where Bilney preached at Christ-church). John F. Davis, *Heresy and Reformation in the South East of England 1520–1559* (London, 1983), p. 50.

217 Bateman, *Christall glasse*, sigs. D iᵛ–iiʳ, O iiᵛ.

218 *Ibid.*, sig. S iiʳ; Hodnett's phrase on Bateman, *Marcus Gheeraerts*, p. 47. For an earlier illustration of this parable, and images of the collapsing or threatened structures of the papal church see Scribner, *Simple Folk*, p. 194, cf. pp. 52–4, 112–14.

219 For Elizabeth Ingram's reservations about this attribution see King, *Tudor Royal Iconography*, p. 120, n. 6. Whatever the origin of the woodcuts, some way has to be found to explain the relationship between figs. 111 and 112 above.

220 Hodnett, *Marcus Gheeraerts*, chapter 1, and pp. 46–8, 66–7; Hodnett, *Image and Text*, p. 40. On the 1568 medal (fig. 116) see van Loon, *Histoire Métallique*, I, p. 107; M. Warnke, 'Ansichten über Bilderstürmer: zur Wertbestimmung des Bildersturms in der Neuzeit', in *Bilder und Bildersturm*, ed. Scribner and Warnke, pp. 302, 314.

221 Hodnett, *Marcus Gheeraerts*, pp. 41–2, 66, 68; J. A. van Dorsten, *The Radical Arts: First Decade of an Elizabethan Renaissance* (Leiden and

London, 1973), pp. 75–85; L. S. Friedland, 'The Illustrations in the *Theatre for Worldlings*', *Huntington Library Quarterly*, 19 (1956), 107–20; Hind, *Engraving*, I, pp. 122–3, plate 50. On Roger Martin (who was knighted in March 1568) see Leonard Forster, *Janus Gruter's English Years* (Leiden and London, 1967), p. 51; A. B. Beaven, *The Aldermen of the City of London* (London, 1908–13), I, pp. 18, 48, 115, 175, 192, 246, 337; II, pp. 35, 172. On 30 July 1568 Martin returned to Cecil a certificate of the foreigners who had arrived in London in the previous four months. There were over 400. Dutchmen far outnumbered other nationalities, and well over half of them had come 'for religion'. PRO, SP 12/47/28; *CSP Domestic, 1547–1580*, p. 313.

222 *A Theatre wherein be represented as wel the miseries & calamities that follow the voluptuous Worldlings. As also the greate ioyes and plesures which the faithfull do enioy* (London, H. Bynneman, 1569); cited ff. 36ʳ–37ᵛ. The translation is discussed by van Dorsten, *Radical Arts*, pp. 75–85. For examples of altarpieces in Antwerp replaced (sometimes more than once) after the destruction and removal of images in 1566 and 1581 see David Freedberg, 'The Representation of Martyrdoms During the Early Counter-Reformation in Antwerp', *Burlington Magazine*, 98 (1976), 128–38.

223 This was suggested by Hodnett, *Marcus Gheeraerts*, pp. 26–7.

224 For another print by Gheeraerts (*William the Silent as S. George*) which has such a lettered key still present (e.g. 'Q' on the hind hoof of St George's horse stands for 'Idololatriae fuga') see Hind, *Engraving in England*, I, pp. 106, 121–2, plate 51.

225 Psalm, 115: 4–8; Psalm, 135: 15–18; John Bridges, *A Sermon preached at Paules Crosse* (London, [1571]), p. 123.

226 Hodnett, *Marcus Gheeraerts*, pp. 31–4, 68–9; Clair, *Christopher Plantin*, pp. 195–6; *Esbatement Moral, des Animaux* (Antwerp, [1578]), sigs. F 4ᵛ – G 1ʳ (citing 1 Timothy, 2: 11–12); cf. *Fables of Aesop*, trans. S. A. Handford (Harmondsworth, 1961), p. 151.

227 Foxe, *A & M*, 1563, pp. 625–8; 1570, II, pp. 1386–99; ed. Pratt, V, pp. 464–97. The woodcut appears in volume II between pp. 1398–9 (1570), 1192–3 (1576), 1218–19 (1583). For an example of one of Foxe's fold-outs being sold as a separate print see Watt, *Cheap Print*, p. 158.

228 Hind, *Engraving in England*, I, pp. 107–21, plates 52–8.

229 *The History of the King's Works*, ed. H. M. Colvin, III, 1485–1660, pt. 1 (London, 1975), pp. 322–7, plates 24–5; Hind, *Engraving in England*, II, p. 78, plate 41.

230 G. Braun and F. Hogenberg, [*Civitates Orbis Terrarum*], *Liber secundus* (Cologne, [1575]), 2b. This view does not show the steps leading up to the terrace, and unlike the other two views shows a wide space to the west of the round 'Winchester' tower. This, as well as the appearance of the chapel, might seem to point to the independence of this drawing.

231 Aston, '*Bishops' Bible* illustrations'.

232 Junius's numerous correspondents included Walter Haddon and Nicholas Wotton, and he seems to have known the printer and translator Walter Lynne (mentioned above), who was of Dutch origin. On Junius and England see van Dorsten, *The Radical Arts*, appendix iii, pp. 131–4; D. Gordon,

' "Veritas Filia Temporis": Hadrianus Junius and Geoffrey Whitney', *Journal of the Warburg and Courtauld Institutes*, 3 (1939–40), 230–6; M. Dowling, *Humanism in the Age of Henry VIII* (London, 1986), pp. 146–7. See also the life prefixed to the 1652 edition of Junius's letters. We can deduce that Junius had arrived in England by March 1544, since he states in the preface to his *Lexicon* (discussed below), dated London 15 March 1548, that he had been in England for four years. This initial visit lasted until about 1550, and was followed by a return to Haarlem (where Junius was in 1552). He was back in England during the first part of Mary's reign, being in London in September 1554 (see n. 247 below), and the letter he wrote to Stephen Gardiner from Bridewell, London (referring to an earlier six-year stay) is datable to between 24 Aug. 1554 and 12 Nov. 1555. *Hadr. Junii Epistolae* (Dordrecht [1652]), pp. 12–18, 33–6, 339.

233 PRO, LR 2/115, ff. 54ᵛ–55ʳ; LR 2/117; *Hadr. Junii Epistolae*, pp. 13, 392. (Junius says it was thanks to Edmund Bonner – then ambassador to the emperor – at the siege of Landrecies in 1543 that he came to England). Shelfhanger is a few miles east of Kenninghall, and Shelfhanger Hall Farm, together with Kenninghall Lodge and Kenninghall Place, was still in the possession of the duke of Norfolk in the 1830s: the lordship of the manor was sold in 1872, but the Kenninghall property itself has remained continuously in the family's ownership. F. W. Steer, *Arundel Castle Archives* (Chichester, 1968–78), I, pp. 72–5; II, p. 165; J. M. Robinson, *The Dukes of Norfolk. A Quincentennial History* (Oxford, 1983), p. 67. On the Godsalves see *DNB*, and Jane Roberts, *Holbein* (London, 1988), pp. 48–9; Rowlands, *Holbein*, pp. 72–3. They were closely associated with Thomas Cromwell, who helped on John's career, so this connection may be of interest for Surrey's reforming views.

234 *Hadr. Junii Epistolae*, pp. 89–91; *LP*, 21, pt. 1, p. 64, no. 146; *The Works of Henry Howard, Earl of Surrey, and of Sir Thomas Wyatt the Elder*, ed. G. F. Nott (London, 1815–16), I, pp. xvi–xvii, lx–lxiii, 171–2; Neville Williams, *Thomas Howard Fourth Duke of Norfolk* (London, 1964), pp. 4, 6–7, 12, 21. I owe a large debt to this excellent book for all that follows on the Howards.

235 Henry Howard Earl of Surrey, *Poems*, ed. Emrys Jones (Oxford, 1964), pp. 30–1, 127, where the editor accepts the argument of H. A. Mason, *Humanism and Poetry in the Early Tudor Period* (London, 1959), pp. 243–5, that these lines reflect reforming conviction; *The Arundel Harington Manuscript of Tudor Poetry*, ed. R. Hughey (Columbus, Ohio, 1960), I, pp. 119–21; II, pp. 89–91. Compare Surrey's words with Hugh Latimer's attack on London's pride, idolatry and lack of charity (also with reference to Jeremiah) in his 1548 Sermon on the Plough; *Sermons of Hugh Latimer*, ed. G. E. Corrie (Parker Society, Cambridge, 1844), pp. 63–5. On the events in London see G. Brennan and E. P. Statham, *The House of Howard* (London, 1907), II, pp. 364–79. Surrey and his friends were alleged to have broken the windows of churches as well as houses with stonebows, and to have eaten meat in Lent.

236 *Documents Relating to the Revels*, pp. 6, 26, 269. See above, p. 138.

237 Edwin Casady, *Henry Howard, Earl of Surrey* (New York, 1938), chapter 9, specially pp. 200–2; J. J. Scarisbrick, *Henry VIII* (Harmondsworth, 1971), pp. 621–3; *LP*, 21, pt. 2, no. 555, pp. 283–9; cf. no. 546, p. 276. Chapter 11 of

Lacey Baldwin Smith, *Henry VIII: The Mask of Royalty* (London, 1971), gives a good account of the Seymours' triumph over the Howards.

238 *LP*, 21, pt. 2, pp. 355–6, no. 671; *Hadriani Junii Epistolae Selectae*, ed. P. Scheltema (Leipzig, 1839), pp. 3–4; *Hadr. Junii Epistolae*, pp. 14, 179. The commissioners who reported on 14 Dec. 1546 that Mrs Holland (Norfolk's mistress) and the duchess were about to leave for London, described a depleted household with no ladies or gentlemen remaining in attendance on Surrey's wife and children – only 'certen women in the Norsery'. PRO, SP 1/227, f. 82^v.

239 Williams, *Thomas Howard*, p. 21; *Hadr. Junii Epistolae*, pp. 14, 178–9, 392 (indicating that Junius considered going home at this moment); *Epistolae*, ed. Scheltema, pp. 4, 18 has letters dated at Bridewell (one 'in familia D. Legati Caesarei'), on which see *The London Encyclopaedia*, eds. B. Weinreb and C. Hibbert (London, 1983), p. 86.

240 *Acts of the Privy Council of England*, II, 1547–1550, ed. J. R. Dasent (HMSO, 1890), p. 418; *LP*, 21, pt. 2, p. 327, no. 646.

241 *Lexicon Graecolatinum* (Basel, 1548), Cambridge University Library, SSS. 1. 4 (which lacks the title-page), 'Epistola ad Seren. Angliae Regem'; *Hadr. Junii Epistolae*, pp. 508–21. The preface is dated London, 15 March 1548. Gordon, '"Veritas Filia Temporis"', p. 231, while regarding this as customary humanistic compliment, saw Somerset as Junius's main target, which, given Norfolk's recent fate, was 'a little distressing'.

242 *De Anno et Mensibus Commentarius* (Basel, 1553), was published by Henricus Petrus in March 1553, but its prefatory address to Edward VI is dated 1 March 1550. Junius mentions the manuscript presentation copy in prefacing his new edition to Mary: 'Quod quia olim xenioli loco, fratri tuo Eduardo regi manu propria exaraturam exhibueram . . .' (1556 ed., sig. a 2^v.)

243 J. A. van Dorsten, *The Anglo-Dutch Renaissance*, eds. J. van den Berg and A. Hamilton (Leiden, 1988), p. 29.

244 John Stow, *Annales* (1615), p. 596.

245 *Hadr. Junii Epistolae*, pp. 19–21 (letter dated 5 August).

246 *Ibid.*, pp. 390–7; *Die Indices Librorum Prohibitorum des Sechzehnten Jahrhunderts*, ed. F. H. Reusch (Tübingen, 1886), pp. 188, 264. It seems that not all copies of the *Lexicon* included the offending preface (Gordon, '"Veritas Filia Temporis"', pp. 231–2) and there may have been more than one edition in 1548. The copy in the Cambridge University Library (which lacks its title-page) only has Junius's preface. The Amsterdam University Library copy (971. c. 4) 'ex officina Hieronymi Curionis, Impensis Henrichi Petri', has as its sole preliminary a brief address by the latter (who also printed Junius's *De Anno et mensibus commentarius*). These words on the back of the title-page refer to the (absent) preface by the author. I am very grateful for all the friendly help I was given by the staff of this library. Of course being on the Index could be a recommendation in some quarters. Was it Junius's *Lexicon Graeco-Latinum* that Parker gave to his Norwich scholars in Cambridge? Strype, *Parker*, I, p. 577.

247 There are two editions of this work in the British Library (1070 b 2 (2); 807 c 21 – the latter was in the Lumley Library – and its dedication is dated London, 28 Sept. 1554). Both editions were printed by Thomas Berthelet, who helped

devise the London pageants for Philip and Mary. Anglo, *Spectacle Pageantry*, p. 332. References to this work (by an author who was never short on self-advertisement) are in *Epistolae*, ed. Scheltema, pp. 2, 11. Junius seems to have hoped that Stephen Gardiner, the restored bishop of Winchester, might be able to help him to royal favour; *Hadr. Junii Epistolae*, pp. 12–15.

248 H. Junius, *De Anno et mensibus commentarius* (Basel, H. Petri, March 1556), sig. a 2^{r-v}, pp. 94 (Philip's birthday), 103, 105–6, 108–9, 118, 126. Junius's preface is dated Haarlem 1 March 1556 in BL 1607/875; 1 August 1556 in Bodl. 8° 2. 31(3) Art. Seld.

249 H. Junius, *Copiae Cornu sive Oceanus Enarrationum Homericarum, ex Eustathii ... commentariis concinnatarum* (Basel, 1558). Humphrey's prefatory epistle, addressed to the President and Fellows of Magdalen, recalled that Junius had 'lived for a long time in England' and mentioned several of his books, including the *Lexicon* 'dedicated to our most serene Edward VI', and *De Anno et mensibus commentarius*.

250 This question was explored by Veldman, *Maarten van Heemskerck*, chapter 5, pp. 95–112, to which I am much indebted. Albert Verlaan (p. 103) inherited Hadrianus's estate from his son Petrus Junius at the latter's death in 1594.

251 H. Junius, *Batavia* (Leiden, 1588), p. 239; cited Veldman, *Heemskerck*, p. 98.

252 *Batavia*, pp. 238–9, 240. This work (written in the years 1565–70) was drawn on by Carel van Mander in his *Schilder-boeck* (Haarlem, 1604); Grosshans, *Maerten van Heemskerck*, pp. 10, 12, 41.

253 *Poëmatum Hadriani Iunii Hornani Medici Liber Primus* (Leiden, 1598), p. 160; Veldman, *Heemskerck*, p. 109; *Hadr. Junii Epistolae*, p. 178. Junius's manuscript commonplace book (which descended to his son Petrus Junius) cites Andrea Alciati and Thomas More on *Occasio*: Bodleian Library, MS Marshall 43, f. 26^v.

254 'amicum et convivem meum'; Veldman, *Heemskerck*, p. 107. The chronogram which contains the date 1562 states that the portrait was of Junius on his fortieth birthday (i.e. in 1551). Veldman postulates that the original drawing may have been the work of Heemskerck, since Galle was only fourteen in 1551 (Heemskerck being then 53).

255 See J. A. van Dorsten, *Poets, Patrons, and Professors* (Leiden and London, 1962), p. 25, n. 1; van Dorsten, *Radical Arts*, p. 132, for Junius's remark in 1572 that England was a 'regio ... notissima olim' to him, and for letters of 1559 and 1562 indicating that he had put England behind him.

256 H. Junius, *Eunapius Sardianus, De Vitis Philosophorum et Sophistarum* (Antwerp, 1568); the dedicatory Epistle (p. 11) tells the queen 'regni tui incola olim diu extitit'; PRO, SP 12/46/139; *CSP Domestic, 1547–1580*, p. 309; *Hadr. Junii Epistolae*, pp. 201–5, 210–11, and cf. *Epistolae*, ed. Scheltema, pp. 81–2 for a letter to Martin written by Junius in 1573, referring to their parting in 1568. Van Dorsten, *Radical Arts*, pp. 132–3 (misdates Junius's dedication to 15 March). For Martin's appointment see *The Ven. Philip Howard Earl of Arundel 1557–1595*, eds. J. H. Pollen and W. MacMahon (Catholic Record Society, 21, 1919), p. 20; Williams, *Thomas Howard*, pp. 133, 216. PRO, SP 12/81, f. 70^v inventoried the contents of 'Doctor Martin's chamber' in Sept. 1571.

257 PRO, SP 12/47/14–20; *CSP Domestic, 1547–1580*, p. 311. Van Dorsten,

Radical Arts, p. 133, misreading 'ante quarternos menses' in the letter to the queen for 'annos', misdates the whole batch of letters to 1572, and therefore erroneously supposes (p. 131) that Junius was in England that year. He also points out that Junius (who stressed the shortage of time) told Cecil he was returning home in three days' time. The queen's letter was dated in London on 9 July and all the Cecil addresses also belong to July 1568. Van Dorsten comments: 'These documents suggest that Junius was in some distress and found both Queen and Secretary singularly unco-operative'. Cf. van Dorsten, *Anglo–Dutch Renaissance*, p. 33.

258 On Plantin's trade in prints, and his dealings with London booksellers, see Clair, *Christopher Plantin*, pp. 200–2, 209–11, and Clair, 'Christopher Plantin's Trade-Connexions'. The latter shows that in 1578 two copies of Junius's *Eunapius* were imported into England by a London dealer.

259 Van Dorsten, *Anglo–Dutch Renaissance*, pp. 34–6; van Dorsten, *Radical Arts*, appendix II, and p. 131, n. 3; above n. 104.

260 The duke wrote to Archbishop Parker in 1565 in support of the strangers being granted a vacant church in Norwich, and seems to have received some immigrants in his town house there. W. J. C. Moens, *The Walloons and their Church at Norwich* (Lymington, 1887–8), I, pp. 18, 21; II, pp. 221, 253.

261 *CSP Foreign, 1566–68*, pp. 460–1, no. 2199; P. J. Holmes, 'Mary Stewart in England', in *Mary Stewart Queen in Three Kingdoms, The Innes Review*, 38 (1987), 195–218; P. Collinson, *The English Captivity of Mary Queen of Scots* (Sheffield, 1987), pp. 30–6 has a useful chronology and itinerary; Williams, *Thomas Howard*, pp. 90, 134, 138, 145; Robinson, *Dukes of Norfolk*, pp. 52–67. Mary was taken to Carlisle on 18 May 1568 and until her removal to Tutbury early in 1569 Sir Francis Knollys and Lord Scrope shared responsibility for her custody. At his trial Norfolk vehemently denied that his sister had been an intermediary between him and the Scottish queen. *State Trials*, I, cols. 977–8.

262 *CSP Spanish, 1568–1579*, pp. 50–2, no. 37. Elizabeth Dacre died on 4 September 1567. The duke's two former wives had also died in childbirth. Williams, *Thomas Howard*, pp. 126–8, 134–41. See Strong, *English Icon*, pp. 95, 345, for Hans Eworth's portrait of the duke's second wife, Margaret Audley (d. 1563), a companion piece to the portrait of the duke, fig. 124.

263 On Jane Neville's spirited stance in the northern rebellion, and her last years at Kenninghall (where she died and was buried in 1593) – her husband living in exile in the Spanish Netherlands until his death in 1601 – see Williams, *Thomas Howard*, pp. 171–2, 179; *DNB*, s.n. Neville, Charles. The Catholic Henry Howard, later earl of Northampton, who helped to get Mary Queen of Scots gloriously entombed at Westminster, owned at his death in 1614 two portraits of that queen and two of Jane Neville, as well as three of his favourite sister Catherine Lady Berkeley. E. P. Shirley, 'An Inventory of the Effects of Henry Howard . . . 1614', *Archaeologia*, 42 (1869), 356–8, 361, 372.

264 She was married to Henry VIII's bastard son Henry Fitzroy (friend and companion of her brother, Surrey), who had died in 1536. The duchess, who

did not remarry, died in 1557, and was mentioned in the Book of Martyrs as an informant on the charity of Anne Boleyn, having served in her household. Foxe, *A & M*, ed. Pratt, v, p. 60; *DNB*, s.n. Fitzroy, Mary; Mozley, *John Foxe*, p. 29; Williams, *Thomas Howard*, p. 24.

265 Mozley, *John Foxe*, p. 30; Robinson, *Dukes of Norfolk*, pp. 80–4 and Genealogical Table II for their cousinage.

266 John Foxe, *Christ Jesus Triumphant*, Englished by Richard Day (London, 1607), sigs. A 2ᵛ, A 4ʳ, A 5ʳ; Blackburn, *Biblical Drama*, pp. 106–17; Mozley, *John Foxe*, pp. 30–1. On Richard Day see *DNB* and Oastler, *John Day*, pp. 5, 65–8. Richard Day appears to have died the year before this book came out. On Foxe's view of idolatry, and the Reigate 'idol', see Aston, *England's Iconoclasts*, I, pp. 41–2; Foxe, *A & M*, I, pp. 25–6. I am grateful to Tom Freeman for a discussion about Foxe, in which he suggested that Foxe's pastoral activities and preaching have been underestimated, and may have been important in his London parish of St Giles, Cripplegate.

267 See Neville Williams, *Captains Outrageous* (London, 1961), pp. 54–5, for Foxe helping a pirate captain at Lulworth by looking after a valuable parcel of stolen velvet and silk.

268 Van Dorsten, *Radical Arts*, p. 131, n. 3 says Junius 'must have been in close touch' with Foxe; cf. p. 134 where he exonerates Junius from either 'religious indifference' or 'gross opportunism', despite the contradictory sequence of his dedications. Cf. Gordon, ' "Veritas Filia Temporis" ', pp. 231–2.

269 J. Foxe, *Rerum in Ecclesia Gestarum* (Basel, 1559–63), sigs. A 2ʳ–3ᵛ (dedication dated Basel, 1 Sept. 1559); Strype, *Annals*, I, i, pp. 160–1; Williams, *Thomas Howard*, pp. 47–8; Mozley, *John Foxe*, pp. 60–1, 126. In 1570 Foxe moved into a house of his own in Grub Street. It is not clear if the timing of this move was in any way related to Norfolk's affairs.

270 BL, MS Harl. 416, f. 154ʳ, printed in *Queen Elizabeth and her Times*, ed. T. Wright (London, 1838), I, pp. 324–6; Williams, *Thomas Howard*, pp. 164–5. There is no proof that the letter was sent.

271 2 Samuel, 4: 4; 9 (quoting v. 7); 19: 24–30 (citing v. 28); PRO, SP 12/81, f. 71ᵛ. These hangings were kept in the ewery court, where there were also eight hangings of Jonah: in the great chamber was a tapestry of the history of Hercules, and there were eleven pictures of kings and queens in the long gallery. The duke also owned tapestry series of the histories of Abraham and Solomon and Masinissa. See S. Foister, 'Paintings and Other Works of Art in Sixteenth-century English Inventories', *Burlington Magazine*, 123 (1981), 273–82.

272 Williams, *Thomas Howard*, pp. 195, 213.

273 BL, MS Cotton Cal. C III, ff. 98ʳ–99ʳ; Strype, *Parker*, II, p. 104; Robinson, *Dukes of Norfolk*, pp. 84–9; L. L. Peck, *Northampton: Patronage and Policy at the Court of James I* (London, 1982), pp. 8–10, 21–2; *DNB*, s.n. Howard, Henry, Earl of Northampton.

274 PRO, SP 12/81, f. 61ʳ; *Ven. Philip Howard*, eds. Pollen and MacMahon, p. 2; Williams, *Thomas Howard*, pp. 120, 215–16.

275 W. Murdin, *A Collection of State Papers, relating to Affairs in the Reign of Queen Elizabeth* (London, 1759), pp. 169, 171.

276 PRO, SP 12/85/13–14.

277 Strype, *Annals*, I, ii, pp. 44–5 – Parkhurst's jovial report to Foxe; 'There was neither torch, neither taper, candle, nor any light else, beside the light of the sun; ringing there was enough'. Williams, *Thomas Howard*, p. 87.

278 Murdin, *State Papers*, p. 171. These 'gifts to my frynds' also included the note that 'Deryng is £10 behynd'; *State Trials*, I, cols. 1032, 1034–5; Williams, *Thomas Howard*, pp. 238–9, 248–9, 252–3.

279 BM, MS Harl. 787, no. 112, printed in *Queen Elizabeth and her Times*, I, pp. 402–12 (cited at p. 406); Williams, *Thomas Howard*, pp. 242, 244; *Ven. Philip Howard*, p. 14. W. Elderton, *A Balad Intituled, the Dekaye of the Duke*, Society of Antiquaries, Lemon 61 (*STC* 7552.5), appeared between the duke's sentence and execution.

280 *The Tyrannous Reign of Mary Stewart*, trans. and ed. W. A. Gatherer (Edinburgh, 1958), p. 194.

281 Collinson, *Godly People*, pp. 300–1; BL, MSS Lansdowne 388, ff. 320^r–342^r, Lansdowne 12, f. 98^r.

282 Collinson, *Godly People*, pp. 300–1; Dering, *Workes* (1614), sigs. E 1^v, 2$^{r–v}$; BL, Add. MS 33271, ff. 40^v–41^r.

283 BL, MS Lansdowne 11, ff. 9^r–10^r; Thomas Lever, *Sermons*, ed. E. Arber (English Reprints, London, 1870), pp. 6–7. The letter was dated Sherburn House by Durham 24 Feb, and is endorsed with the year 1568/9.

284 William Camden, *The History of … Princess Elizabeth*, ed. Wallace T. MacCaffrey (Chicago and London, 1970), p. 121; cf. William Camden, *Annales* (London, 1625), p. 220.

285 Collmann, *Ballads and Broadsides*, no. 41, pp. 114–16.

286 *Calendar of the Manuscripts of the Marquis of Salisbury*, pt. 1 (1883), pp. 575–6, no. 1754; *Princely Magnificence*, pp. 57–8, no. 31. The jewel was made after the death of the countess's husband, the Regent Lennox, in 1571, and before her death in 1578. Cf. Tait, 'Historiated Tudor Jewellery', p. 241, and colour pl. III.

287 Strype, *Annals*, I, i, p. 404; *Diary of Henry Machyn*, ed. J. G. Nichols (Camden Society, 42, 1848), p. 266; Strype, *Parker*, I, pp. 367–8, 371.

288 *A discourse* (BL, C 33 a 42), sig. A 4$^{r–v}$. For the four editions of ?1569, two of which may have been printed by John Day, see *STC* 13869–13870.3; Conyers Read, *Mr. Secretary Walsingham and the Policy of Queen Elizabeth* (Oxford, 1925), I, pp. 63–4, 68–74.

289 *Homilies*, p. 224; *Love's Labour's Lost*, I, 2.

290 *A discourse*, sig. A 5$^{r–v}$.

291 Collmann, *Ballads and Broadsides*, p. 114, from no. 41, *Northomberland newes*, cited above, p. 201.

292 Strong's phrase, 'Edward VI and the Pope', p. 312.

293 *A newe enterlude of godly queene Hester*, ed. Greg, p. 39, l. 1004, cf. p. 41, l. 1049.

294 *Queen Elizabeth and her Times*, I, p. 403; Williams, *Thomas Howard*, pp. 165, 240, 251.

295 PRO, SP 1/227, f. 82^r; LR 2/115, f. 16^r; SP 12/85/36; Williams, *Thomas Howard*, pp. 22, 31, 248.

296 PRO, LR 2/115, ff. 1^v, 16^r, 17^r, 21^v, 37^v; LR 2/117; *CSP Rome*, 1558–1571, no. 762, p. 400. The earl of Hertford was himself long under a cloud, owing to his

marriage with Lady Catherine Grey, but his situation improved after her death in 1568.

297 Murdin, *State Papers*, pp. 166, 168; *Queen Elizabeth and her Times*, I, p. 404; Williams, *Thomas Howard*, pp. 240, 247.

298 *CSP Rome*, 1558–1571, pp. 393–400, 411, nos. 761–2, 777; Williams, *Thomas Howard*, p. 199.

299 *CSP Spanish*, II, 1568–1579, pp. 289–90, no. 231 (9 Jan. 1570/1).

300 *Catalogue of A Collection of Ancient and Modern Pictures. The Property of the late Thomas Green, Esq.*, Christie, Manson & Woods, 20 March 1874, p. 4. Lot 123, p. 14, was a 'View of a country house with an obelisk' by T. Green.

301 From the National Portrait Gallery's file of correspondence on NPG 4165; letter of C. K. Adams to Mrs Patricia MacGregor (sometime Mrs Colvile), 28 October 1958; above p. 6.

302 [T. Green], *Extracts from The Diary of a Lover of Literature* (Ipswich, 1810), pp. vii, 35, 137–8 (entries for 2 June 1797, 3 June 1799).

303 *The Gentleman's Magazine*, NS 19 (Jan.–June 1843), p. 248.

304 [James Ford], *A Memoir of Thomas Green, Esquire, of Ipswich* (Ipswich, 1825), p. 23; *Suffolk Chronicle*, 2 and 9 Feb. 1858. Green was buried in the church of Wilby, Suffolk (the family seat), where there are monuments to him and other Greens. The Diary which Green published in 1810 was 'only a sample ... of a more considerable Work' (*Diary*, p. vii) and he left its continuation, with other manuscripts to his son (*Memoir*, p. 57). The son handed over the manuscript volumes of the diary to his father's friend John Mitford, who published more portions of the diary in *The Gentleman's Magazine*, NS 1–19 (Jan. 1834–June 1843; see 1, p. 7, and 19, pp. 582–3 for location of the diary). I have not been able to trace any of these papers except some letters to John Mitford, which are in the Osborn Collection at the University of York.

305 PRO, Prob. 11/1708, ff. 273^r–277^v, (will of 5 Sept. 1812 with codicils of 22 Nov. 1815, 30 Dec. 1824 and 5 Jan. 1825), cited at f. 277^{r-v}.

306 *Gentleman's Magazine*, NS 19 (Jan.–June 1843), p. 248, note; G. R. Clarke, *The History and Description of the Town and Borough of Ipswich* (Ipswich, 1830), p. 466 reported of Thomas Green II: 'he had the best collection of pictures of the great masters of any person in Ipswich, which still remain entire, at the house where he lately resided, in Brook-street'. I am most grateful to David L. Jones, Assistant Curator of Ipswich Museums and Galleries, for answering my enquiry about the Greens, and to Ann Nichols for helping to locate this reference.

307 'none of my letters [?] to be published but reserved as a future amusement perhaps to my son'; will, see note 305; Ford, *Memoir*, p. 57.

308 Catalogue of sale of 20 March 1874, p. 4, Lots 15–16, 22–23.

309 PRO, Prob. 11/1250, ff. 264^v–265^r (Thomas Green, 1794); Prob. 11/1417, f. 174^r (Lord Chedworth); Ford, *Memoir*, p. 23; *DNB*, s.n. Howe, John, 4th Lord Chedworth. The Revd James Ford, author of Green's *Memoir*, also lived in Brook Street; *East Anglian Daily Times*, 3 Oct. 1931. The posthumously published instalments of the Diary reflect the close relations of Green and Chedworth.

310 Williams, *Thomas Howard*, p. 258; F. Blomefield and C. Parkin, *An Essay*

towards a Topographical History of the County of Norfolk (London, 1805–10), I, p. 215; Steer, *Arundel Castle Archives*, I, pp. 72–5; see above, n. 233.

311 L. M. N. Surry, *The Portraits of Edward VI* (Portsmouth, [1925]), p. 115.

312 Harold C. Gardiner, *Mysteries End. An Investigation of the Last Days of the Medieval Religious Stage* (New Haven and London, 1946), pp. 74–80, cited at 78; Alan H. Nelson, *The Medieval English Stage, Corpus Christi Pageants and Plays* (Chicago and London, 1974), pp. 62–3, 85; P. Collinson, *From Iconoclasm to Iconophobia: the Cultural Impact of the Second English Reformation* (Reading, 1986); P. Collinson, *Archbishop Grindal* (London, 1979), p. 203.

313 For examples of panels in early sixteenth-century Norfolk church screens that closely followed prints by Lucas van Leyden, soon after their appearance, see Andrew W. Moore, *Dutch and Flemish Painting in Norfolk* (Norwich Exhibition Catalogue, 1988), pp. 2–3, 81–3; for the Dutch in Norwich under Elizabeth, including their contributions to the cloth trade and the first printing press there (1568) see W. J. C. Moens, *The Walloons and their Church at Norwich* (Publications of Huguenot Society, London, x, 1887–8).

314 *Ecclesiae Londino–Batavae Archivum*, ed. J. H. Hessels (Cambridge, 1887–97), II, pp. 341–7 (no. 102), 352–64 (no. 104), cited at 345; cf. III, pp. 148–9 (no. 175), for the case of Hans van Billevelt and his wife, living in London, who had got into trouble in Antwerp for stealing from idols under pretence of devotion; J. Lindeboom, *Austin Friars: History of the Dutch Reformed Church in London 1550–1950* (The Hague, 1950), pp. 48–51; P. M. Crew, *Calvinist Preaching and Iconoclasm in the Netherlands 1544–1569* (Cambridge, 1978), pp. 44–8; Collinson, *Archbishop Grindal*, pp. 140–3. For a conspectus of Netherlandish iconoclasm seen in a wide context, see Freedberg, *Power of Images*, chapter 14.

ILLUSTRATIONS

Figures 23–6, 33, 63, 65, 93, 100, 102, 104, 108, 110 and 118 are reproduced by permission of the British Library; figures 36, 58, 81, 83, 86, 96–9, 116–17 and 120 are reproduced by courtesy of the Trustees of the British Museum; Colour plates I and II and figures 1, 4, 6, 11, 13 and 74 are reproduced by permission of the Trustees of the National Portrait Gallery; figures 39, 77, 107, 109, 111–15, 119 and 125 are reproduced by permission of the Syndics of the Cambridge University Library.

COLOUR PLATES

FIGURES

permission of the Trustees of the Frewen Educational Trust. Photo Paul Mellon Centre for Studies in British Art.

INDEX

Italics refer to illustrations; Roman numerals to colour plates.